THE PRO WRESTLING HALL OF FAME
THE STORYTELLERS
FROM THE TERRIBLE TURK TO TWITTER

THE STORYTELLERS

from the TERRIBLE TURK to TWITTER

GREG OLIVER and STEVEN JOHNSON

THE PRO
WRESTLING
HALL OF
FAME

Published by ECW Press
665 Gerrard Street East
Toronto, Ontario, Canada M4M 1Y2
416-694-3348 / info@ecwpress.com

Editor for the Press: Michael Holmes
Cover design: Tania Craan
Front cover photo © New Japan Pro-Wrestling
Back cover photos: Tommy Dreamer © George
Tahinos; Sheik with fire © Dave Drason Burzynski

Purchase the print edition and
receive the eBook free. For details,
go to ecwpress.com/eBook.

LIBRARY AND ARCHIVES CANADA
CATALOGUING IN PUBLICATION

Title: The Pro Wrestling Hall of Fame : The
Storytellers (from the Terrible Turk to Twitter) /
Greg Oliver and Steven Johnson.

Names: Oliver, Greg, author. | Johnson, Steven, 1957–
author.

Description: Series statement: Pro wrestling hall of fame

Identifiers: Canadiana (print) 20190112549
Canadiana (ebook) 20190112581

ISBN 9781770415027 (softcover)
ISBN 9781773054223 (PDF)
ISBN 9781773054216 (ePub)

Subjects: LCSH: Wrestling. | LCSH: Storytelling.

Classification: LCC GV1195 .O45 2019
DDC 796.812—dc23

The publication of *The Pro-Wrestling Hall of Fame: The Storytellers* is funded in part by the Government of Canada. *Ce livre
est financé en partie par le gouvernement du Canada.* We also acknowledge the contribution of the Government of Ontario
through the Ontario Book Publishing Tax Credit, and through Ontario Creates for the marketing of this book.

ONTARIO
CREATES

Canadä

PRINTED AND BOUND IN CANADA

PRINTING: FRIESENS   5 4 3 2 1

MIX
Paper from
responsible sources
FSC
www.fsc.org   FSC® C016245

This book is dedicated to Dean Silverstone and
the memory of his loving wife, Ruth

Ruth and Dean Silverstone are joined by wrestler Joyce Grable (r) at a Cauliflower Alley Club reunion in Las Vegas.

Table of Contents

When Wrestling Became Content

Foreword

When I was approached to contribute to *The Pro Wrestling Hall of Fame: The Storytellers*, I thought about writing in character as The Blue Meanie. But the more I thought about it, I figured it would be better to be myself, Brian Heffron. The truth is, there's more of myself in The Blue Meanie than there was originally supposed to be.

Scott Levy — a.k.a. Raven — is one of the best minds in the wrestling business. He's given to the wrestling business more than anyone knows: he created many characters in ECW, with the most famous being The Dudley Boyz. So when Raven asked if I wanted to be a part of his stable known as "The Flock," it was a no-brainer. Even when he pitched his idea of me becoming The Blue Meanie, I never hesitated to accept.

Raven took the concept to ECW's mad scientist/owner Paul Heyman and, at November to Remember '95, The Blue Meanie was born. It was Raven's sidekick, Dancin' Stevie Richards, who brought me out of the ECW audience and baptized me into ECW and Raven's Flock. Raven had seen me and thought everything I had done up to that point as then–Brian Rollins reminded him of a villain from The Beatles's movie, *Yellow Submarine*. And at first he wanted me to be exactly like the character in the movie but, as time went on, I poured more of myself into The Blue Meanie.

I grew up with many influences, from wrestler Bam Bam Bigelow to guitar hero Eddie Van Halen to comedy icon George Carlin. Also, as a kid, I tried to mimic the wrestlers I had seen on television. I would take a camcorder and practice wrestling interviews. When I was brushing my hair in the bathroom, I would do a quick promo in the mirror. Even to this day I often think of wrestling scenarios and play out scenes and promos in my head. They have a tendency to slip out, and my wife Tracy ("Mrs. Meanie") will turn to me and say, "You're in promo land, right?"

When it came time to start my wrestling training with my soon-to-be best friend Al Snow, promo class came easy. When Raven first had me take on The Blue Meanie character, he would have me stand in the center of his living room and cut promos on whatever topic he could throw at me to keep me off-guard and keep my promo skills sharp.

Once Raven presented the idea of Stevie Richards and I doing parodies of other known characters, that's when I started to evolve. Whether I was aping Goldust as Bluedust or rocking out like KISS or demanding a better society with my Blue World Order pals, Stevie Richards and Super Nova, I was telling a story, however wacky it might have been.

But I really got my Ph.D. in how to do a promo under the tutelage of Paul Heyman. Not only was Paul an excellent speaker himself, he was clear in what he wanted his performers to say, the message we used to capture our audience.

Many a night after an ECW television taping, Paul would hold court as the ECW locker room did promos for their matches. He would also do short snippets of promos or a skit to tag on at the end of ECW TV in a segment unofficially dubbed "Pulp Fiction," which allowed everyone to get TV time and get their characters over.

Don't laugh, but all these drills have prepared me for a lot in real life.

You are cutting a promo in a job interview, aren't you? Telling a story, tying it in to why you belong there. I can improvise with the best of them, whether it's with my friends or on a movie set.

Wrestling character development has made me mentally tough. These experiences have made me the man I am today, and I have no idea where I would be in life without them. What I do know, as you'll further learn in these pages, is that I'm not alone in taking a spark of an idea and running with it, making something happen in pro wrestling.

There's something magical about the world of pro wrestling — the storytelling. Wrestling has had me run through the gamut of emotions, from the fear of the villains to the joy of when a

PHOTO BY GEORGE TAHINOS

favorite wrestler wins a match. All of that was attained through the art of storytelling, whether it be through the brilliance of the booker or subtle nuances in the way the wrestler emotes the pain, anger, or joy of contest at hand. All parties involved have had me wipe my brow, stomp my feet, pump my fist, and lose my voice.

Now that I am on the other side of the guardrail, I've been fortunate to be on the opposite ends of said emotions. I've been booed and cheered, and received punches and high fives. All thanks to the guidance of a trainer like Al Snow, a genius like Paul Heyman, an opponent like Tracy Smothers, and the vibe I fed off from the fans. All of this was done by great storytelling and great storytellers.

"The Blue Meanie"
Brian Heffron
May 2019

Introduction

Ted Tourtas was Greek by birth, but in the not-too-particular world of professional wrestling, he was billed for a spell in the Pacific Northwest as an underhanded, bile-spitting Turk. It was all the same to Tourtas, as long as he was eking out a living. When a promoter in Seattle, Washington, determined that Tourtas' malevolent persona might affect the gate receipts, that was another matter entirely.

> The promoter took me in the office. He had boxes of mail. He said, "Ted, you see that? They're all Turks, Muslims, and so on. They say they're going to start boycotting the wrestling matches if they kept booking you because you're insulting the Turks . . . You'd better switch and be the clean guy." So we get into the ring with another kid. This guy was another pretty boy. I back him into the ropes and show him like I'm going to hit him and grab his hair and they started screaming, "Why, you dirty . . ." I said, "What did I do wrong?" So I back him in a little later. I took his hand and shook his hand and backed away. Right from then on, I was a hero. "Hey, The Turk is good." So that was the end of The Turk. See, you can play with their minds any way you want. I was a hero. Old ladies would knit socks for me. They'd bring me

Ted Tourtas was a pretty boy, a Turk, a Greek, or whatever made promoters happy.

a box of cigars. I smoked cigars then. I was their hero.

A week before, they wanted to lynch me.

It might have said "wrestling" on the marquee or in the news-paper ads, and that aspect of Tourtas' work was important. But what really got fans to cheer or jeer or darn socks was the story he was telling in the ring, a tried-and-true one in pro wrestling circles — the bad guy wasn't so bad once you got to know him. Since its inception as a carnival-type attraction, pay-for-play wrestling has navigated a tricky course, drifting between outrageous entertainment and mainstream athletic competition. The common denominator in the bounce between farce and honesty has been the storyline.

Sports such as baseball, prizefighting, and horseracing regularly develop backstories to their contests — a traded player squares off against his old team, or a past-his-prime boxer gets one last shot at a championship. But that's where the storyline ends; once on the field of battle, the tales are secondary to the competition itself. Not so in wrestling. Storytelling represents the foundation of the sport. It might be a story of teacher versus pupil — Larry Zbyszko smashing a chair over the head of his mentor Bruno Sammartino because he couldn't beat him fair and square. It might be a story of a journey. In Jerry Lawler's 1974 Quest for the Title, he had to go through ten contenders to get a shot at ten pounds of championship gold. It might be a story of rebirth — and there's no better example than Tourtas' timely persona shift, a late 1940s example of a fan-induced wrestling "turn."

Wrestling stories and plots range from the tasteless to the engrossing, but they are essential to maintaining an audience, which for the business visionary is essential to building acceptance by casual fans on a wider scale. As long-time star Johnny Powers put it, "They need to be able to say, 'Oh, I get that enough; that's interesting,' or, 'It's not interesting enough; I'm not going to go to the box office. We're not going to turn a TV on to those guys.' So you need to develop storylines that are engaging but also stretching and challenging." In pro wrestling, the story is front and center. Just a few years ago, it was unfathomable to think that a pro wrestler would win the *Sports Illustrated* Muhammad Ali Legacy Award or host the *Today* show. Yet the invitation into society's front parlor has come at a price. Wrestling stories have become more scripted and less extemporaneous than ever, and some critics rue the loss of the spontaneity and originality that drove the sport during most of the twentieth century. In many respects, fandom is no longer measured by the volume of cheers for the good guy or catcalls for the bad guy. Instead, it's a matter of engagement, sharing, liking, and following. Storylines seem to change more frequently or float along unresolved and forgotten, sometimes in the same Monday night timeframe. The result is that many fear the old art of storytelling is dead, that wrestling has achieved mainstream respectability at the expense of some of the unique flavor that drew fans to local arenas week after week. Yet others feel the digital age presents opportunities to place new styles in front of more fans, and that forward thinkers are finding ways to craft stories in a manner that opens new markets.

Wrestling Storytelling

Perhaps the most striking thing about wrestling storytelling is that even the sport's top stars have a hard time explaining it. Take WWE Hall of Famer Ricky Morton, legendary for the way he could connect with audiences through his storytelling skills. Morton recalled a lesson that his father, Paul, a referee in Tennessee, passed to him forty years ago.

> He said, "Ricky, everybody can arm drag, everybody can head scissors. Everybody can dropkick. But not everybody can work. It's something you've got to learn. I cannot teach this to you because with me trying to explain this to you, I'd be better off talking to that wall because you're not going to understand it. But one day, one day you're going to be wrestling in the ring and it's going to hit you" . . . I can make them cry. I can make them madder than hell and I can make it fun or make it sad. But that's something that took me

years to develop, to understand, because it's hard
for people to even understand what I'm saying.

If an all-time great has trouble fleshing out the art of storytelling, then it's infinitely more difficult for outsiders to describe. So
we've gone the illustrative route, selectively picking and choosing
moments, trends, and personalities that affected storytelling in and
out of the ring from the 1880s to today. By no means do we pretend
to be comprehensive. Entire volumes have been written about
events to which we devote only a few words, such as the 1997 affair
in Montreal, where WWE owner Vince McMahon double-crossed
champion Bret Hart, a pivotal moment in wrestling's Attitude Era.
Our definition of storytelling is broad — this book touches on
razor blades, court battles, bears, chicken waste, prosthetic legs,
and YouTube. We've included insights and analysis from wrestlers,
promoters, writers, and fans to trace the evolution of the art of
storytelling.

And despite what cynics might say, wrestling storytelling is
an art form. To be sure, it's a particularly convoluted art form,
and wrestlers freely admit they borrow liberally from movies, TV
shows, and music. "MTV was first starting, and I got a lot of it from
there," booker/wrestler Kevin Sullivan said of his idea factory. But
to get back to our earlier example of a baseball game or a prize-
fight, to tell a story properly, pro wrestlers must convince the
audience that winning or losing really matters even if the outcome
is predetermined. Al Snow is positioned to know that better than
just about anyone. He worked in all the major companies, trained
wrestlers around the world, and in 2018 bought the Ohio Valley
Wrestling promotion.

It's evolved, it has grown, it's more sophisticated,
the production and the presentation are more developed. But there is one thing that has not changed
about wrestling, and you can go back and watch it

over the decades. The one thing that was fake in 1938 was the finish. The one thing they were selling was the finish. The one thing that the audience paid to believe in in 1962, 1975, 1984, 1996, 2018, the one thing that you're paid to believe, is that you're trying to win, and the one thing that you are selling is that you are out there trying to win. It doesn't change. It never has, and once it does, wrestling will cease to exist.

So read on about the winners and the losers, the ring generals and the never-weres, and how they told their stories. Some of our entries are funny, some are sad, and some are inspiring, but they're all part of the tapestry that pro wrestling weaves for us.

Seventy years after his wrestling career began, Ted Tourtas spins yarns at a Cauliflower Alley Club reunion.

The Origins of Sports Entertainment

Introduction

In February 1989, Vince McMahon burst everyone's bubble by acknowledging that pro wrestling was sports entertainment, with emphasis on the word "entertainment." McMahon's World Wrestling Federation wanted to get out from under the auspices of the New Jersey Athletic Commission and its levy on sports TV revenues. The WWF told the state senate that professional wrestling was "an activity in which participants struggle hand-in-hand primarily for the purpose of providing entertainment to spectators rather than conducting a bona fide athletic contest." Wrestlers and wrestling fans who'd been defending the sport's legitimacy collectively moaned. "They've got a cartoon going there," scoffed long-time star Verne Gagne, owner of the rival American Wrestling Association. "Sure there was entertainment when we wrestled, but most of us were real wrestlers."

Actually, McMahon was only about 100 years late to the party. Pro wrestling was athletic, or sports, entertainment from the get-go. And he wasn't the first promoter/confessor. In 1886, Charles E. "Parson" Davies came under fire from a citizens' decency group that attacked his Chicago boxing and wrestling promotions as "barbarous and immoral." Davies was indignant — read this carefully — saying he presented "refined, well-conducted, athletic entertainments . . .

Wrestling, sports entertainment, or both?

Why, all the exhibitions we have here are boy-play compared to what they have in some other cities."

Northwest promoter C.L. "Steve" McPherson echoed Davies in 1949: "In serious consideration, open and above board, I arrange with Hairy the Ape and Cyril Dovewing . . . to stage a main bout exhibition . . . Often we do decide in advance who will win." Promoter John Heim of Milwaukee blew the sport's cover in 1957: "There hasn't been a legitimate wrestling contest in fifty years. We tried it once — and you could have heard a pin drop." The athleticism and the skill are for real. But wrestling and sports entertainment? They've always been joined at the hip.

I. The Parson of Chicago

Think Don King without the high hair. Charles E. "Parson" Davies was everything that the boxing impresario was, only a century earlier — promoter, ring announcer, manager of champions, time-keeper, raconteur, man about town, saloon proprietor, and publicist extraordinaire with considerable access to large stakes of money, most of which belonged to other people. An Irish immigrant, orphaned as a teen, Davies started in the sporting life in Chicago in 1877 by organizing heel-to-toe footraces, called "pedestrianism," when he was just twenty-six. Legend has it that railroad magnate William K. Vanderbilt bestowed the "Parson" nickname on him in 1879 when he saw a solemn man in a black frock coat advising champion walker George Rowell during a competition in New York. Vanderbilt told a reporter that he thought the man looked like a cleric. Davies became the Parson for the rest of his life, and his congregation was the realm of athletics from boxers to wrestlers to sword fighters. To legendary sportswriter Grantland Rice, Davies was "the greatest promoter of his day."

Modern professional wrestling lacks a single defined father, such as basketball has with James Naismith. But Davies certainly has a claim to paternity. Every tour of the same cast of wrestlers, night after night, city after city, owes him a hat tip. Every vicious killing machine is a descendant of Evan "Strangler" Lewis, Davies' greatest wrestling find. And every quest for championship glory has its roots in the 1887 match between Lewis and Joe Acton of England, when Davies engineered the first orchestrated world title change. "Professional barnstorming and athletic promotion in America traces to the fine hand of Davies," said J Michael Kenyon, the late wrestling historian and Seattle sportswriter. "His work was seminal. Professional wrestling owes a considerable debt to him for getting the catch-as-catch-can business off to a rousing start."

Born in Antrim, Ireland, on July 7, 1851, Davies built a reputation as a top promoter of pedestrianism, a national fad open to anyone capable of putting one foot in front of the other for up to six days at a time. He drummed up interest in the media, managed racers, and sponsored events for purses that ranged from $500 to $5,000, including a fifty-two-hour-long man-versus-stallion race in 1879 in Chicago. (The horse, Hesing Junior, won by fifty-two miles.) When race walking faded, Davies moved into boxing, where he made his biggest mark. For nearly two decades, just about every fight or fighter of consequence bore his imprint. He promoted John L. Sullivan when the bare-knuckles champion conducted exhibitions to skirt state and local bans on prizefighting. From his Chicago base, Davies built a stable of more than two dozen boxers, though he lost a member of his brigade when heavyweight contender Jimmy Elliott, an ex-con, bolted a Davies-led tour of Kansas, returned to Chicago, and lost a gunfight with another boxer.

Wrestling had its share of rough characters too, but it was underdeveloped as a sport and came, for the most part, without the political entanglements and payoffs that plagued boxing. In short, it was ready for Davies. Parson was in charge from booking to ring bell. A match he promoted between his charge John Rabshaw and Lew Moore in 1884 in Chicago serves as an example. First, Davies came to the ropes and read the articles of agreement for the match — in this case, each side put up $250 for a two out of three falls contest. He read the rules to the crowd. He made a final money call from backers of the wrestlers. He asked each man to settle on a referee. When they couldn't agree, a Davies associate appointed one. Then Davies loaned the referee his watch.

Davies didn't come cheap. He took one-half of the gross gate receipts, an unheard-of cut for a manager/promoter in today's

Charles "Parson" Davies (r) with Hall of Fame boxer and occasional wrestler Joe Choynski around 1894.

environment. Even so, Joe Choynski, a Hall of Fame heavyweight boxer whom Davies pressed into service as wrestler, said Parson was worth every penny. "Davies was the world's best prize-fighting press agent — very liberal in booming the game," Choynski told the *Chicago Evening Post* in 1910. "His word went a long way with the promoters. He was worth all he got from the fighters he made or kept busy."

That's what the Wisconsin backers of Evan Lewis envisioned when they solicited Davies to push their local wrestling star into the national limelight. Lewis had overwhelmed foe after foe with his signature stranglehold, a move akin to a rear naked choke in today's mixed martial arts. Davies met Lewis for the first time on April 22, 1885, when he emceed a combination boxing/wrestling show in Madison, Wisconsin. In later years, Lewis told a New York newspaper that Davies rechristened him from Evan to Strangler after assuming his management. Parson knew what he was doing. On January 28, 1886, Lewis beat Matsada Sorakichi in Chicago when the Japanese wrestler quit, claiming the stranglehold was unfair. A rematch set for February 15 carried one of the earliest stipulations in wrestling — barring use of the dreaded stranglehold. Instead, as a standing-room-only crowd of 3,500 people gasped in horror, Lewis grabbed Sorakichi by the left ankle and twisted it over his own left leg in an attempt to break it like a dead branch. The fall lasted just fifty seconds. Sorakichi fainted in the ring as outraged fans shrieked, "Coward! Brute! Devil!" at the victorious Lewis. The Chicago Times reported eight or nine spectators passed out at the dreadful sight, though the supposedly maimed Sorakichi was giving wrestling exhibitions in Milwaukee eleven days later.

In Lewis, Davies had created a wrestling version of John L. Sullivan, a brute who elicited both awe and ticket sales. Now, he needed a title to complete the package. Englishman Joe Acton was the generally recognized champion at catch-as-catch-can wrestling, similar to the freewheeling style we know today. With Davies as his manager, Lewis met Acton on February 7, 1886, in Chicago for $250 a side, plus the receipts from 4,000 fans at $1.50 a ticket. Lewis had the size advantage and the stranglehold in his arsenal, but Acton, the betting favorite, took three of four falls and the match.

Things were set up just right. When the two squared off again on April 11, the stakes were raised to $500. Given what had transpired in their first match, it would have been hard for bettors to resist doubling down on Acton. But a whiff of fix was in the Chicago air. The Chicago Tribune reported that gamblers at one gaming parlor were rushing to lay money on Lewis at any odds, causing the bookkeeper to stop accepting bets. Suspicions about an arranged title change proved to be correct. In front of 3,500 fans, Acton won the first fall, but Lewis easily took the next three in a combined total of fewer than fifteen minutes. "Davies had added another champion to his résumé," his biographer Mark T. Dunn wrote in Chicago's Greatest Sportsman.

Two months later, Tom Connors of England upset Lewis in Pittsburgh, winning a decision when Lewis ignored the referee's order to stop choking his foe. Davies petitioned for a rematch in the friendly grounds of Chicago for higher stakes — $1,000 a side — but the fight fell through. Under those circumstances, Davies wanted to make doubly certain that everyone knew Lewis was the true kingpin of the world. He imported Jack Wannop, a boxer and wrestler who laid a vague claim to the British wrestling championship, and shipped him to Wisconsin to train with John Kline, a Davies confederate. The two-month buildup for the May 7, 1888, match in Chicago was spectacular. Davies appears to have planted stories that Lewis feared the Englishman's considerable abilities, and newspapers across the country billed it as the definitive match for the world championship. Lewis whipped Wannop in straight three falls in less than fifteen minutes, with an estimated $20,000 in bets changing hands. "Lewis surprised us all by the easy way in which he threw Wannop," Davies told a Pittsburgh reporter, likely with a suppressed smile.

Original "Strangler" Lewis

The original "Strangler," Evan Lewis was the greatest wrestling find of Parson Davies.

With a championship secure, Davies hit the road with his "Company of Gladiators," a forerunner of the circuits that sprung up in later years with the same wrestlers repeating similar matches in different venues. Lewis and William Muldoon were the headliners, but Sorakichi was part of the caravan too, apparently having forgiven Lewis for allegedly crippling him. They held matinees in New York, Washington, Pittsburgh, Chicago, and New York, among other places. In researching Davies' life, Dunn was impressed by the way he navigated a minefield of fans, hoodlums, politicians, and athletes. "To be as successful as he was, people had to like him, not just in wrestling or in boxing, but in all phases of life," Dunn wrote.

Davies remained as Lewis' manager through 1895, including a tour of San Francisco in 1890 in which the Strangler and a beefier Acton reprised their title fights of 1886. By then, Davies was fully concentrating on boxing. In 1889, he acquired the contract of Peter Jackson, a skilled Black heavyweight from Australia. Davies labored long and hard to secure main event matches for Jackson, especially against Sullivan, but had little success in breaking the color barrier. So the promoter cast Jackson in a version of *Uncle Tom's Cabin* and toured the country with him. Just to spice things up, Davies had Jackson and Choynski spar three rounds as part of the show. "There is no disputing the fact that 'Parson' Davies is a shrewd manipulator of sporting matters," the *San Francisco Call* opined.

A lifelong bachelor and leader in the Elks Lodge, Davies relocated to New Orleans to run a theater, music academy, and pool hall that served as a haven for gaming interests. He never lost an opportunity to rub elbows with the high and mighty. With his friend Bat Masterson, the gunslinger turned sportsman, Davies visited President Theodore Roosevelt at the White House in 1906. Always on the lookout for publicity, he brought with him Feodor Machnow, a nine-foot-three-inch tall Russian. Roosevelt glanced at the giant, threw his arm around Davies, and whisked him into his office to gossip about sports. "Come in, Parson," he said. "It is you I want to talk with."

Davies' later years were difficult. Starting in 1908, he suffered from rheumatism, endured a series of paralyzing strokes, and was confined to a wheelchair for years. In 1912, friends established a fundraiser for him after he had gone through all his money. Davies traveled to Ireland and spent time with relatives stateside until he settled into the Elks National Home in Bedford, Virginia. He died there on June 28, 1920, a few days short of his sixty-ninth birthday. "Parson Davies was the best known sportsman in the Western

Hemisphere," Masterson mourned in the New York *Morning Telegraph*. "His word was his bond. He never repudiated an obligation or failed to keep his word. Generous to a fault and courageous as a lion, he batted his way up from a poor immigrant boy to the highest distinction in the realm of sports . . . They are not growing any more Parson Davies these days."

II. The Terrible Turk

Yousouf was a monster. When his hands, strengthened by years of dock work and one-on-one combat, were not wrapped around his opponents' throats, they became shovels in his feeding exhibitions, three sirloin steaks at a time. He never took a bath, fearful that it might sap his strength. He disregarded the few wrestling rules he understood, owed his allegiance only to a vaguely sinister sultan, and paraded through the streets of New York in baggy pants and a fez. No one could describe him accurately, A.J. Liebling wrote in the *New Yorker*, because people who saw him were too frightened to take notes. There is no definite moment when you can pinpoint the transition of wrestling from a test of skill and science rooted in the ancient Greeks to lowbrow athletic farce. But March 26, 1898, seems as good a starting point as any.

That is the night that Yousouf went nuts, chucking the respected Ernest Roeber five feet off an unroped stage seventy-five seconds into their match at Madison Square Garden. The crowd, the largest ever to witness a wrestling event in the United States, erupted in a frenzy, threatened to lynch The Turk and catcalled for twenty-five minutes as a reported fifty police guards escorted him to safety. More than anything, though, The Turk's antics demonstrated wild-eyed entertainment was the way to get the fans going and the turnstiles churning. As the *New York World* concluded, "There was not one of the 9,000 spectators who will not go to the next match arranged for The Turk."

William A. Brady could not have been more pleased. A theater and sports promoter, Brady hyped Yousouf as the sport's first barbaric foreign menace, though his man had legitimate wrestling credentials. He was born Yusuf Ismail — you'll also find it as Youssuf Ishmaelo — in 1857 in the Bulgarian village of Cherna, which then was part of the Ottoman Empire. He was said to be a third-generation wrestler, an honorable man skilled at wrestling doused in olive oil, a Turkish tradition for more than six centuries. Yousouf won at least one national title at the annual Kirkpinar event, according to several accounts. He established himself as a force in France as part of a trio of invading Turkish wrestlers starting in 1895, when he was a Marseilles dock worker by day and a man-beast by night. Historian Graham Noble uncovered one particularly savage match account from Paris in which Yousouf allegedly ripped Ibrahim Mahmout's nostrils and twisted his arms. Gendarmes had to break up the devastation.

Yusuf Ismail was the first and most infamous of many terrible Turks.

How much of that is real and how much is apocryphal has been lost to the ages. Images depict Yousouf as something less than a force of nature, pushing forty years old, slump-shouldered and doughy, about six-foot-two and 250 pounds. Wrestler/promoter/ scout Antonio Pierri, known as the "Terrible Greek," brought him to the United States in February 1898, gave him a paltry twenty-five dollars a week, and stuck him in a Bowery tenement room. When Pierri handed him over for $200 to Brady, to whom the term "farfetched" seldom occurred, myth and reality became one.

Brady put The Turk front and center in New York's London Theater, offering $100 to anyone who could stay with him for fifteen minutes. Though weighing just 125 pounds, George Bothner took up the challenge. Later famous as a wrestler and gym owner, Bothner was a mere late night snack for The Turk. "The Turk picked me up as if I was a kitten . . . Before I could give a wriggle or a squirm he dashed me down on the bare boards with terrific strength knocking all the strength and wits out of me," Bothner told author Nat Fleischer in *From Milo to Londos*. To burnish his reputation, Yousouf finished off German wrestler Ernest Ziegler on the floor of the Richelieu hotel in New York in forty-five seconds and then chugged down Ziegler's bottle of wine. That was a tiny sip of alcohol compared with the twenty-five glasses of beer his publicists said he consumed daily.

Who could stop the barbarian? Maybe Ernest Roeber, a compact 190-pound German immigrant regarded by the *National Police Gazette*, the voice of U.S. sports, as the "unquestioned, undisputed, and unbeaten champion of the world." In early March 1898, Roeber put down $250 with a West Virginia sports editor as a guarantee he'd show up against Yousouf, adding that he'd never permit a Turk to carry his championship back to the sultan's domain.

The match was set for the Garden under Greco-Roman rules — no holds below the waist — for $500 a side, with the winner taking half of the gate. "I'll make that big Turk bite the dust before I get through with him," Roeber vowed. Crowd estimates vary because the Garden had an open floor arrangement — the best guess is 9,000, though the Associated Press put it at 15,000. Regardless, there is little doubt about what the enthusiasts saw. Roeber initially retreated from The Turk, wary about locking up. He backed near the corner of the stage when Yousouf bull-rushed him and drove him to the ground. Martin Julian, Roeber's manager, claimed a foul while spectators shouted, "Kill The Turk! Kick him to pieces! Tear him limb from limb!" Yousouf's response was classic heel — he snarled at the crowd, danced a jig, and threw his arms above his head, not caring a whit that he officially lost the match.

HOMER DAVENPORT'S HUMOROUS IDEA OF ROEBER'S MATCH WITH THE TERRIBLE TURK

Cartoonist Homer Davenport's depiction of the 1898 feud between Ernest Roeber and The Terrible Turk, Yusuf Ismail.

After all, as Yousouf moaned to the *New York Journal* in a March letter (certainly authored by Brady or his copywriter), Roeber's tumble was not his fault. In a pretext that would make Ric Flair proud, Yousouf swore he was innocent. In fact, Roeber was at fault for sprinting around the mat instead of fighting like a man. "When I reached for him he was near the edge of the platform and sprang back. I touched him truly, but it was his own movement rather than contact with my hands that sent him over."

If any wrestling match in history had rematch written all over it, this one did. The second bout took place in a roped ring on April 30 at the Metropolitan Opera House in New York, the first and last time the august building would host pro wrestling. "People who believed what they read in the newspapers thought Roeber should be forcibly restrained from suicide," Liebling recalled in the New Yorker. "But the prospect of bloodshed attracted them." Three thousand fans packed the Met, including a large number of women who apparently felt an opera house was a haven of sophistication. The Turk quickly disabused them of that notion. After about eighteen minutes, a frustrated Turk grabbed Roeber by the arm and slung him into an unpadded ring post. Then he did it again. When Roeber regained his balance, The Turk poked him in the eye. That was it. Roeber bounced back with fists blazing and threw at least two punches in the general direction of Yousouf, one of which staggered referee Herman Wolff. In a flash, Brady, managers, corner men, policemen, and a Greek interpreter were in the ring. From the audience came flying chairs and chants of "Fake!" as one imaginative section struck up the song, "Get Your Money's Worth." No contest, Wolff ruled. The New York Times bequeathed pro wrestling the first of its many premature obituaries: "The result of this contest has probably put an end to the attempted revival of the sport of wrestling."

Yousouf wrestled only a few more times. He beat future American heavyweight champion Tom Jenkins in Cleveland and annihilated George Heraklides at Madison Square Garden in June, winning the first fall in forty-seven seconds and a second in little more than a minute. Supposedly, he twisted Heraklides into unconsciousness with a half-nelson. A ballyhooed match on June 20 in Chicago with Evan "Strangler" Lewis, the most important champion of the late 1800s, drew 10,000 people and ended in as much controversy as the bout at the Met. With $2,500 at stake, Lewis apparently won when the referee ruled Yousouf had illegally choked the Strangler in two straight falls. Brady and his team protested loudly, and Lewis agreed to continue with a different referee, as long as he got the winner's cash. In less than fourteen minutes, The Turk forced Lewis into submission twice, each time using his own version of Lewis' famed stranglehold. "I acknowledge the corn," Lewis said somewhat strangely. "He is too powerful for me."

And then it was over, almost as quickly as it began. With his contract expiring, Yousouf went to Brady's office on July 1 to collect money before departing the next morning for Europe in steerage class, the cheapest possible, aboard the French steamer *La Bourgogne*. Shortly before dawn on July 4, the ocean liner collided in dense fog with the *Cromartyshire*, a British sailing ship, south of the province of Nova Scotia's Sable Island, known as the "Graveyard of the North Atlantic." Yousouf was among the 549 who died when the ship sank; fewer than 180 passengers and crew members survived.

Even in death, The Turk was larger than life, thanks to Team Brady. Newspaper accounts declared he was lugging an enormous amount of money, ranging from $6,000 to $14,000, which he was going to use to buy a wine store or coffee shop. With The Turk scarcely dead for a week, T.W. Bert, Brady's business agent, penned a piece claiming pure greed had sunk Yousouf; the miserly fool had put all of his earnings into heavy gold coins sealed in a waist belt. Why, there must have been forty pounds of gold on The Turk. "I am confident," Bert wrote in the *World*, "that it was this clinging to this weight that is responsible for his feeding to-day the fishes of the Atlantic." A clearly identifiable Yousouf and his belt, divested of most of its contents, purportedly washed ashore on Sable Island more than ten weeks after the crash, according to a news report from Halifax, Nova Scotia. No matter, Pierri, who had discovered Yousouf, had a second and even more dangerous version of The Terrible Turk on U.S. mats by October.

Yousouf was no monster, of course. It was all stuff and nonsense and hyperbole. Through the lens of history, it is clear Yousouf was a tool for promoters out to make some very fast money; he likely made a pittance as the sport's first monster heel. "He was an illiterate peasant who was swindled in America," said wrestling historian William Baxter of Scotland, who has traced Yousouf's legacy in Turkey. It's a strong one too, much stronger than his American mishandlers could have imagined. A Turkish writer posthumously renamed him Koca (for "Great") Yusuf. His hometown of Cherna hosts a modern house-style museum dedicated to his accomplishments. His name was given to a forty-ton floating crane at a Turkish dockyard. And in Edirne, Turkey, famous for oil wrestling, statues of three wrestlers adorn a public square. One of them is Yusuf Ismail, The Terrible Turk.

III. That Masked Man

Seldom has a piece of knitted fabric captured the fancy of so many. On December 7, 1915, a man wearing a black hangman's mask and wrestling outfit that looked like an old-fashioned two-piece bathing suit showed up at the Manhattan Opera House, the site of an international wrestling tournament. Organizer Sam Rachmann's event was in its second month and faring so-so, perhaps because of oversaturation; he was running it with forty-odd competitors virtually every night of the week save Sunday.

The Mysterious Masked Marvel was not invited, but he and manager Ed Pollard plowed their way through the box office and brashly challenged every wrestler in the field. When he started to win matches, dogged New York City journalists jumped on the case of the Marvel's secret identity like bloodhounds sniffing for clues. Sleuths tailed his limousine in taxis. Editors sent telegrams across the country to inquire about the whereabouts of putative suspects. The New York World suggested that the Marvel was none other than Francis X. Bushman, the silent picture star who filmed a short about a masked wrestler in 1914. All the while, women swooned and flocked to see him in action, making up one-third of his audiences. Zoe Beckley of the Washington Post checked him out: "Ooooooh — it was thrilling. Not a soul knows who he is! He wears a black covering stretched tight over his neck and head, with holes cut for eyes, nose, and mouth. Wow — he looked wicked!"

The Marvel, exposed in time as veteran Mort Henderson of Altoona, Pennsylvania, became such a hot commodity that his mask made its way into fashion magazines of the day. Though he was not the first masked wrestler, he was the first one who mattered because he had the powerful New York publicity machine behind him. Most importantly, the "hood," as it became known, evolved into one of the sport's most dependable stratagems, inspiring promoters and wrestlers for decades to build intricate storylines around men of shrouded mystery, from The Destroyer to the Masked Superstar to any number of Assassins and Mr. Xs.

A masked grappler first made a big splash in France in the 1860s, though one apparently worked in the Czech Republic a few years before that. In a 1904 interview with the San Francisco *Call*, Alfred Perrier recounted his surreptitious career as "Bras de Fer," one of at least two masked sensations in Paris, not to mention his ability to hold a 300-liter (79-gallon) cask of wine by his teeth. In North America, several masked men preceded Henderson, especially "Mystery," a creation of noted Chicago promoter Ed White, who said his man donned the garb to prove wrestling was not on the level.

Henderson's version of the Mysterious Masked Marvel had a more theatrical lineage; it represented an early fusion of sports enter-tainment, chicanery, intrigue, and ballet. Yes, ballet. The M.M.M., as headline writers dubbed him, traced his heritage to the Ziegfeld Follies. Mark A. Luescher was a legendary theater man with press agent credentials so strong that he once managed to stifle newspapers reporting about a herd of escaped elephants that knocked down fire hydrants on Fifth Avenue in New York. As a producer, Luescher outfitted one Daisy Peterkin, who toe danced as "La Belle Dazie" with a red mask in 1905. She proceeded to dance as "La Domino Rouge," allegedly a Russian who spoke not a lick of English, emerging as a headline hit with the Follies before marrying Luescher in 1906.

Entertainment was entertainment, Luescher reckoned. He suggested a masked wrestler to Ben Atwood, who handled press for the international wrestling tournament. In turn, Atwell secured the blessing of tournament promoters, including Jack Curley, who controlled New York City wrestling. Henderson later said Curley picked him because he was a relative unknown to Gotham fans. But there's reason to believe Luescher was in on the selection too — he was a newspaperman in Rochester, New York, as Henderson was launching his wrestling career there as the "Rochester Butcher Boy."

THE MASKED MARVEL   MORT HENDERSON

In 1916, newspapers ran side-by-side comparisons of the Masked Marvel and Mort Henderson in an effort to divine the unknown one's true identity.

The Marvel, allegedly earning $100 a week, started off the tournament like a house afire. He won his first four matches, including a thrashing of 395-pounder Pierre Le Colosse that took just five minutes. On December 15, he impressed fans and wrestling observers by going to a tough twenty-minute draw with Wladek Zbyszko, one of the best legitimate wrestlers of his era. The next day, scarcely a week into his run, the Brooklyn Daily Eagle blew his cover with, at best, third-hand sourcing, citing "a friend of an intimate friend of one of the wrestlers in the international tournament at the Manhattan Opera House." Manager Pollard denied the report, saying his charge was "a brand new wonder." Incredibly, it didn't matter. The guessing game continued as other newspapers totally disregarded the Eagle's scoop. A day later, some accounts seemed certain Dr. Benjamin F. Roller was the Marvel. A vaudeville performer named Ajax was in the running. A week after the disclosure in the Eagle, the World decided the Marvel "might just as well have stepped from Mars, so well has he hidden his identity." And Henderson's hometown paper, the Altoona Times, kept a vow of monk-like silence even though it knew his identity. "New Yorkers read the Altoona Times, and the secret of Altoona's favorite may be divulged in the east," the paper cautioned.

As promoters suspected, the fact of the mask had become more important than the name of its bearer. On December 16, the same day that the Eagle lifted the veil, the Marvel went to a remarkable twenty-minute draw with Alex Aberg, a talented Greco-Roman champion. Before the bout, Aberg strode to the ring with interpreters and declared he would not fight a man in a mask. In an early version of matchmaking by applause, the audience sided with Pollard's proposal that his wrestler would unmask only if Aberg, Zbyszko, and Ed "Strangler" Lewis beat him. Game on. Aberg tried to twist the mask off the Marvel's head, but his opponent was too resilient. "Not only did he hold his own with Aberg, but the man of mystery made the champ look foolish all the time they were on the mat," the New-York Tribune said. Nowhere was mentioned the fact that the Marvel, as Henderson, had wrestled Aberg two weeks earlier in Altoona.

The Marvel finally stumbled when Lewis, one of wrestling's most important figures, stopped him on December 20. The loss did little to dampen the fans' enthusiasm for their new hero. Two nights later, Lewis and the Marvel went to a two-hour draw before a sellout crowd of 3,000 in a match that drew rave reviews from just about every quarter. Again, newspapers noted a surprising complement of women in the crowd. A week later, the Marvel went to a no-falls, two-hour, twenty-one minute draw against Aberg. Referee George Bothner told the *Eagle* he would have given the decision to Aberg based on aggressiveness. But that was an academic exercise; the real story was another full house. "The lobby was as thick with speculators as Democrats around a vacant postmastership," the *Eagle* quipped.

Henderson was not definitively identified until the end of December, when the Marvel went to battle with Hjalmar Johnson. During a respite between the fourth and fifth rounds, manager Pollard asked, loud enough for press row to hear, "Will you have a drink of water, Mort?" Aberg finally beat the Marvel on December 31, and the hooded one started to fade in the final weeks of the tournament, perhaps from playing his role too hard and too often. A reporter from the *Altoona Times* who tracked the hometown hero in New York found that he had lost ten pounds and was fatigued to the point of vomiting after matches. Even referee Bothner said the Marvel had slowed down by twenty-five percent. In the end, Aberg was declared the champion of the tournament, though Henderson never was unmasked. In defeat, Henderson was credited with giving the sport a badly needed shot in the arm. "It isn't a difficult matter to throw the bunk stuff on New York, but just the same Mort deserves credit for pulling off the window blind gag and stirring the mat game as it hasn't been aroused in ten years," wrote Alfred R. Cratty, who penned a syndicated fisticuffs column under the alias of Jim Jab.

Someone catches a cold and everyone sneezes, or so it seems. Soon, the mask was all the rage. In February 1916, Tacoma, Washington, was abuzz over a mystery masked boxer who had made his way into the Northwest. In Los Angeles, fans watched intently in March when a Masked Marvel revealed himself to be a Californian wrestler named Herman Stroh. The sensation was not confined to the sporting world. In the world of high fashion, a countess wore a five-cent mask with her $6,000 gown, the *Day Book* of Chicago disclosed. "Last night a bevy of girls appeared masked in a Broadway restaurant and danced until the placed closed," it said. To bring it full circle, the great humorist Will Rogers appeared in the 1916 Ziegfeld Follies dressed as a masked marvel.

Henderson continued to wrestle with and without his mask until 1924, though he never again enjoyed the acclaim he had in New York. He died in 1939 at the age of sixty in Rochester after starting a second career as a police lieutenant. He pretty much divorced himself from wrestling, saying shortly before his death that he hadn't seen a match in eleven years. But renowned columnist Westbrook Pegler recognized Henderson's contribution to culture: "Many great artists of music performed in the Manhattan opera house, but, by far the most memorable, and, I might even go so far as to say, by far the most artistic program ever produced there was discoursed by a herd of wrestlers in the fall of 1915, when the famous Masked Marvel was current."

Blood, Mud, and Smelt

Introduction

Utah sportswriter Al Warden thought he had covered everything. Now mud covered him. It happened January 11, 1938, at the American Legion chateau in Ogden, where Warden found himself bathed in a gob of goo that bad guy Hy Sharman hurled during the state's first mud wrestling match. Warden could not have been more pleased. "In the span of a quarter century I have watched the greatest mat men in the world perform, have cast my optics at Jack Dempsey in two championship fights, wore out pencils at football headliners as far west as Honolulu, covered two national scholastic basketball tournaments, and countless attractions, but never in my sports career have I unloaded such guffaws as I did last night," said Warden, sports editor of the Ogden Standard-Examiner.

Promoters were pulling out all the stops to boost attendance during the Depression — rings full of fish, mud matches, women's wrestling, women's mud wrestling, freaks galore, and the first blood-lettings. Audiences and wrestlers were willing to forego headlocks and wristlocks for something that danced between low comedy and vulgarity. It didn't matter if you were a top name or a local guy. The first mud match featured former world champion Gus Sonnenberg, the game's top draw of 1929, against Harnam Singh on June 4, 1937, in Seattle, Washington. As it turned out, the match was more like a wash. Singh won when Sonnenberg nearly knocked himself

Members of the press don raincoats to counter the splatter from the first mud wrestling bout in Los Angeles.

out trying to gain a foothold in the ring. Paul Boesch, a wrestler and future promoter, was on hand and said the ring was supposed to be mostly dirt. "Someone forgot to turn off the water!" he said years later. Singh continued with a pair of mud matches in Washington as the contrivance spread like wildfire.

I. The Milwaukee Dreamer

Late at night, as Henry Tolle lay in bed at his home a few blocks west of the Milwaukee River, he let his mind race. Tolle once explained that he reserved the minutes before sleep for imagination, for conjuring up ways to get more fans to the wrestling matches he promoted in a three-story brick hall on the north side of Milwaukee. No idea was too out of bounds; no prospect was too lowbrow.

Mud wrestling. Molasses and feathers wrestling. Raw egg wrestling. Milwaukee had a sizable blue-collar population that supported mat shows every week, but it was not a regular stop on the circuit for top names and big matches, like New York or Chicago. To keep the turnstiles clicking, Tolle had to rely on creativity, and there was no better target than Chicago, where the football Bears were fierce rivals with the Green Bay Packers, who had just started to play home games . . . in Milwaukee.

So it was that on February 18, 1935, Tolle promoted the first team match in wrestling annals, pitting three-man squads from Chicago and Milwaukee against each other in a ninety-minute contest. Tolle's brainchild was the genesis of tag team wrestling and employed rules similar to what we know as WWE Survivor Series more than fifty years before the debut of the annual pay-per-view spectacular. "I've had lots of fun in my time, especially thinking up ideas for rassling shows," Tolle told Sam Levy of the *Milwaukee Journal*.

Nowadays, wrestling stories are plotted out months in advance, usually to build to a climax at a mega-event like WrestleMania. In 1935, though, wrestling was a week-to-week proposition, with little publicity other than newspapers and word of mouth. Without gimmicks and a fair dose of goofiness, promoters in smaller markets would have had to find other work during the heart of the Depression. No one was better at creating zany bills of fare than Tolle, a son of German immigrants who went from selling sewing machines to filling a wrestling ring with two tons of smelt hauled from a nearby river.

Wisconsin promoter Henry Tolle.

Yes, smelt. The match was held in Marinette, Wisconsin, on April 14, 1939, in conjunction with a festival honoring the small, silvery fish. Tolle's local promotional associate was Jack Boyle; the show was plugged as a free-for-all among four blindfolded wrestlers in fish six inches deep. Four newsreel camera companies were on hand to document the chum scuffle, though not everyone was impressed. "They are just hastening the day when Wisconsin will regulate wrestling as it does boxing," the Fond du Lac *Commonwealth Reporter* said. Once the affair started, wrestler Max Johnson didn't last long with the catch of the day. "Weakened by the pungent odor that emanates from the fish, he was tossed from the ring and landed on his head, showering smelt among the cash customers," according to an account in the *Green Bay Press-Gazette*. Veteran "Speedy" Franks of Texas won the match, earning acclaim as the "champ of Smeltania" but lost the honor to Rowdy Pocan the following week at a Tolle promotion in Menasha when Pocan gained the upper hand by shoving handfuls of fish in Franks' trunks.

Promoter Henry Tolle had a fishy idea with this 1939 match amid a slimy pile of smelt.

Tolle, pronounced "Tollie," was born November 2, 1887, in Arkansas, though his parents returned to Germany when he was two. He came back to Wisconsin around 1904 and settled in Milwaukee, working as a collector, insurance adjuster, and manager of a sewing machine store. Always interested in sports — he did some amateur wrestling growing up in Germany — Tolle landed a side job tending to the press gate at Borchert Field, home of Milwaukee's minor league baseball team. That led in 1922 to his first wrestling presentations. "Business was slow and I asked Louie Nahm, then general manager of the Braves, if I could use the ballpark to promote rassling shows," said Tolle, whose partners included wrestler Ernie Scharpegge. He didn't make a cent on his first show, but took in $260 on the next one and was off to the races. "We drew 151,000 that first season when we held indoor and outdoor shows," he said. At one point, his Borchert Field Athletic Club, featuring mostly middleweights, ran wrestling a remarkable fifty-seven weeks straight from 1933 to 1934.

The first team match in history was on the undercard of the February 18, 1935, show. Pete Holtz, Johnny Forman, and Rudy Kay represented Chicago with John Gacek, Kid Ewert, and Andy Rockne forming the hometown group. The match was a referee's nightmare; up to four men could be in the ring at once and a wrestler could relieve a partner at any time. The winner was determined on a points basis, with each fall counting for one point. If a wrestler lost two falls, he was eliminated from the competition. In the end, the ninety-minute affair was a draw — five and a half points for each team. But it sufficiently intrigued fans that Tolle repeated it half a dozen times during the year with different rooting incarnations — an international team, and an Iowa-Illinois-Indiana team, for instance.

If you thought that was complicated, try Tolle's wrestle derby matches. Roller derby, which started in Chicago, was gaining steam as a spectator sport, and Tolle thought he could adapt it to the mat. Pay close attention because you needed to buy a program from Tolle to understand the rules of a derby at the South Side Armory in January

1941. Two teams, each consisting of three men, sent one wrestler into the ring for four rounds of forty minutes each. No more than two wrestlers could be in the ring at the same time; a wrestler had to be standing to be relieved. If someone committed a foul, they landed in the penalty box and their team fought shorthanded. You had to have an abacus to keep score; pins and submissions counted for two points, with disqualifications and countouts leading to one point. In a carefully engineered miracle, the two teams tied thirty to thirty, setting up a rematch. Tolle ran derby matches on and off through 1945, tinkering with the rules in just about every outing.

But he definitely reserved his softest spot for gunk and grime. For mud wrestling shows at Milwaukee's Riverview rink, he trucked in dirt from under the centerfield bleachers at Borchert Field. Speedy Franks, of smelt fame, captured Milwaukee's first mud match from Duke Ruppenthal on January 24, 1938. Tolle forgot to set up a splash zone; he ended up forking out $190 in dry cleaning bills to patrons whose clothes were splattered. After that, he imported his mud from nearby Waukesha. "That was different mud than I had hauled from Borchert field. Waukesha mud was warm and didn't splash," he said. After mud matches, molasses was a natural. On October 24, 1938, Joe Dorsetti won two out of three falls from Buzz Reynolds in a Riverview rink ring filled with 1,500 pounds of molasses. "I spread a layer of flour over the molasses and finally substituted feathers for the flour. That was really something. Molasses and feathers!" Tolle said. And don't forget the eggs. Tolle purchased five cases of eggs and laid them one at a time on the canvas. Wrestlers walked on them, rolled in them, scooped them up, and tossed them at each other by the dozen.

Tolle got a little less gimmicky as time went on, in part because WTMJ started televising wrestling shows from the Ron-De-Voo Ballroom in the 1940s, meaning they had to be a little tamer for a viewing audience. A more traditional show with Verne Gagne as headliner drew a record crowd of 12,439 to the Milwaukee Arena in 1952. In all, Tolle ran nearly a dozen venues in Milwaukee before passing the promotion in 1953 to his twenty-seven-year-old daughter JoAnne Czarnecki, who'd handled ring announcing, tickets, and office duties for years. Her first task: retire the outlandish on the grounds that a new generation of fans, especially women, wanted entertainment that was more appealing. "Those ideas were fine a few years ago, but they're outdated now," she told reporter Joseph Benoit. "I know I'll never go in for some of the weird performances Dad used to stage." Nicknamed "The Dragon Lady" for her embroidered blouse, Czarnecki operated the business for a few years. Her father also got back in the act with a big 1956 card headed by Gagne and Wilbur Snyder that drew 16,069 fans.

Battling health issues, Tolle died October 30, 1961, in Milwaukee. His hometown *Journal* once recounted his promotional exploits, from smelt to blindfolded matches to matches without referees. "The public, in time, tired of them all," sportswriter Cleon Walfoort said. "But the resourceful Tolle was never at a loss for a new stunt or an original character to relieve the monotony. Turbaned Russians, sunburned Hindus, Japs, Indians — Tolle 'found' them all."

II. First Blood

Wherever Sailor Watkins went, blood followed. It was an odd mix given his stellar wrestling credentials. As a middleweight, he captured the All-Navy wrestling championship in February 1929 before 7,000 screaming officers and onlookers at a stadium in the Panama Canal Zone, the second year in a row that he took the service branch honors. But the jug-eared Texan was a ham at heart, and a vicious one at that. He thought nothing of relying on the time-tested method of biting a pod of blood to produce a stream of red, grinding a knuckle into an opponent's eyebrow until it bled, or slicing his rival's forehead with a sharp instrument in some of the earliest recorded instances of "blading." Within six months of his pro debut in November 1929, he was bloodying his foes, and he

Kirby "Sailor" Watkins.

didn't stop for the next twenty years. Little wonder that a Texan sportswriter described him in 1937 as "Captain Blood, himself, the bold buccaneer of middleweight wrestling."

Blood has been a part of wrestling for more than a century. In 1910, a gang of swindlers led by John C. Maybray of Arkansas landed in federal prison in connection with a $5 million multisport scam that employed chicken blood capsules. The Maybray group would find a deep-pocketed local and convince him that a match was rigged so he could win big by betting on a sure thing. It was rigged all right; the certain victor bit into a capsule during the bout, spit up blood, and was ruled unfit to continue by a Maybray-provided doctor. During the ensuing decades, blood capsules would reemerge from time to time. The Brooklyn Daily Eagle exposed the gimmick in 1922, saying, "The loser through 'internal injuries' has even been known to carry a capsule filled with chicken blood in the mouth, which was crushed at the appropriate moment and gave the poor dear all the appearance of having a hemorrhage straining to stave off defeat." As promoters cooked up tasteless ways to combat declining attendance, Watkins and contemporaries led by "Dangerous" Danny McShain found that routine bloodlettings were just the thing to incite fans. And Watkins was certainly the first to be reprimanded publicly by an athletic commissioner for intentionally slashing his opponent's face.

Kirby Carroll Watkins was born January 28, 1905, in Moody, Texas, and raised as one of nine children in Plains, a small town of fewer than 200 people near the New Mexico border. He completed eighth grade, rode broncos for a while, and took a stab at boxing before settling into amateur wrestling. Nicknamed "Tex," Watkins joined the navy in October 1925 and won the All-Navy middle-weight title in 1928 and 1929; he also reportedly won it in 1927, though there's limited evidence of that first victory. Regardless, he turned pro immediately after his discharge in October 1929, becoming "Sailor" Watkins in a bow to his military service.

From the outset, Watkins was a wild man, biting and pulling hair, beating his chest like a gorilla, and sporting huge tattoos that would fit in nicely with modern-day rappers — a winged fairy ran from pec to pec, and a side view of a lady's face adorned his left triceps. The first of his bloody battles came against a fellow navy wrestler, Otis Clingman, on April 3, 1930, in Pampa, Texas. The first fall alone took more than an hour and was a melee as Clingman's legs bore teeth marks where Watkins tried to bite his way out of a leg scissors hold. When Watkins delivered a slicing uppercut, Clingman's face exploded in blood. Dizzy and covered in crimson, Clingman managed to finish off Watkins with an airplane spin, but in victory crumpled to the mat. Watkins was on him like a tiger on a downed deer. A score of fans rushed the ring to have at Watkins; the county sheriff shoved them out, announcing they "were a disgrace to civilized society."

It didn't take much for Watkins to see where this could lead. Red on the mat meant green in the bank. Watkins briefly took his act to Oregon, where sportswriter Sid King observed that his bag of tricks included knuckling over the eye, behind the ear, and on the temple, traditional ways of drawing "hardway" blood. "Shiver our rafters but what a tough nut that Sailor Watkins is!" King exclaimed. Back in Texas, Watkins, about 160 pounds in his prime, bloodied Tex Miller so badly during a match in Alexandria, Louisiana, that a doctor stepped in and called a halt to things. Besides blood and guts, Watkins' favorite deceits included rubbing his opponent's eyes with the metal tips of his boot strings and driving a taped thumb into a rival's windpipe, thirty years before Luke Graham and Ernie Ladd made the maneuver famous. "Tex Watkins is known to every sports fan in the state," the *Pampa Daily News* said in May 1935. "He is one of the roughest and toughest grapplers in the game." But there was more to come. Wrestling in Lubbock, Texas, that November, Watkins unloaded on popular Dory Detton, pounding at his nose while he had him in a headlock. "Detton's face was a bloody pulp when Watkins finally threw him away, the Watkins fist glowing red," sportswriter Collier Parris said. "The strutting sailor elbowed his way through the mass and to the dressing room, wiping Detton's blood from his hands as he strutted."

Outside of the ring, Watkins had a wife and two children, and maintained a small farm in Mississippi where his in-laws lived. The kids stayed with the grandparents while Watkins was on the road, and he talked more than once about hanging up the boots. "I'm old enough that I should have sense to quit," he said not long after the Detton fracas. In fact, he did, for a while. Records show that he earned $2,000 in 1940, which he pumped into a nightclub and attached residence called Sailor's Place on the north side of Jackson, Mississippi. Unfortunately, Watkins displayed the same contempt for the rules of law as he did for the rules of wrestling. He was arrested three times in five weeks — twice for beating up soldiers in bar fights and once for violating prohibition laws. Early one Sunday morning in August 1941, authorities raided the dwelling, smashing the wall with a sledgehammer to reveal a hidden cache of booze. Sheriff's deputies stripped the club of its fixtures; an unrepentant Watkins purchased another club, called Twin Oaks. That didn't turn out any better. In November 1941, he was arrested yet again for skirting blue laws and operating a mini-dice gambling machine that he could control with hidden magnets to make certain numbers turn up. Compared with those struggles, going back to the blood game was an easy choice.

Watkins and Danny McShain came up through the West Texas ranks under the tutelage of noted rowdy Dutch Mantell. Watkins beat McShain in December 1935, but McShain gained revenge in December 1938, defending the light heavyweight championship against Watkins, who was billed as "the wrestling profession's terror." Soon, McShain was making as much of a mark in blood in California as Watkins had in Texas. Women purportedly fainted at the sight of McShain and "Red" Berry drenched in claret during a 1941 match in Hollywood. At that point, capsules still appeared to be the preferred method of dripping blood. Watkins and McShain were featured bad guys in Dallas, and famed World War II submariner Tim McCoy recalled seeing the tools of their trade when he sold sodas there at Wednesday night matches through 1941. "He knew the matches were fixed (he'd seen capsules of blood in the dressing room), and yet he liked watching wrestling anyway," author Larry Colton wrote of McCoy in No Ordinary Joes.

There's no certain date when chicken blood and hardways gave way to bits of concealed razor blades and bottle caps that could turn foreheads into red rivers. The great champion Lou Thesz, whose career spanned more than half a century, said blading started after World War II. "By the late 1940s, however, we'd begun to see a handful of boys who regularly used blood in their matches, and they used it for one simple reason: they couldn't do anything else. It was the cheapest way of attracting attention, but it worked, and it was a way for them to stay employed," Thesz wrote in his autobiography *Hooker*.

Cue Sailor Watkins. After being suspended in Mississippi for spewing tobacco juice at wrestler Walter Stratton, Watkins moved to Post, Texas, and the Amarillo territory run by Karl "Doc" Sarpolis. On August 14, 1947, he whipped Billy Weidner during a tournament for the Southwest junior heavyweight title in what almost certainly was a blade job. Throughout the match, Watkins feigned reaching into his trunks to pull out a foreign object. Promoter Dory Detton, who bled at Watkins' hands in 1935, inspected the bad guy's garments between falls to no avail. In the third fall, Watkins opened a cut on Weidner's forehead, but no one reported detecting a weapon. "Blood was streaming from the forehead of Weidner at the windup. The sailor couldn't have tapped more gore with a meat cleaver," the *Amarillo Daily News* said. A week later, Watkins was at it again against Al Gelz in the tournament finale, trying to turn Municipal Auditorium "into a slaughterhouse," as *Daily News* writer Frank A. Godsoe Jr. put it. "The bulbous old brawler from Post again had his 'invisible butcher knife' and he ripped and slashed at the head of Gelz like a madman." Gelz won the match, but blood won the day. Several hundred fans were turned away at the doors.

Enough, said Roy O. Greenhill, the Amarillo boxing and wrestling commissioner. In late August, he issued a public warning that Watkins would face an indefinite suspension given any indication that he used "deliberate means to cut or slash the face of an opponent." Thus deprived of his favorite tool in a late August 1947 rematch with Weidner, Watkins tore the shirt off referee Stratton, who had apparently recovered from the Mississippi tobacco juicing, and threw roundhouses at Detton and anyone who dared to enter the ring.

By that time, Watkins was forty-two and winding down his career. He refereed some matches in Louisiana in the early 1950s and operated a combination restaurant-tavern in Midfield, Alabama, for a spell in 1953. He also owned a bar in West Hollywood, Florida, where he had another brush with the law in 1961 when police arrested him for receiving stolen property as part of a burglary ring. Watkins worked for a time as a plant engineer, a trade he picked up in the navy. Active in the Masonic Lodge, he died January 1, 1988, in Birmingham, Alabama.

It's fair to say, as Thesz did, that McShain popularized bleeding. His brow looked like a graphic relief map by the time he hung up his boots in 1967. "Danny McShain will make a chopping block for anyone he faces, if it takes that to win," Godsoe of the Amarillo paper wrote in 1946. On the other hand, Watkins was engineering blood on a regular basis three years before McShain debuted as a wrestler.

Credit is less important than the overall point, though: the early blood masters changed wrestling storylines forever. In short order, bloodbaths became more pronounced and more macabre. Matches based on "first blood" rules arose as early as 1942 and became associated with Dusty Rhodes in the 1980s. New Jack sliced seventeen-year old Erich Kulas so deeply during a November 1996 Extreme Championship Wrestling match — they'd agreed on a blade job — that he severed two arteries, leading to the cancellation of a pay-per-view. Devon "Hannibal" Nicholson won a multimillion-dollar court case against Abdullah the Butcher in 2014, saying he'd contracted hepatitis C from Abby's razor blade. No, the Sailor couldn't have imagined what he'd started. But it was no big deal anyway. In a rare interview, he talked matter-of-factly not about his thirst for blood, but about his two daughters, his farm, and how he liked to hunt doves and quail. "I guess that's about all that's interesting," he said.

III. The Trustbuster

Where to begin with Jack Pfefer? Maybe with the untrimmed nail on his right pinkie finger, which he grew and honed into a small dagger. The heel Rip Hawk flipped out the first time he saw it in action: "He'd be going along in the car with you somewhere and he'd have a jar of pickles and he'd reach down with that fingernail and drive it right down through the pickle and pick it out and eat that thing. And then he'd pick his nose! If the young guys today could ever see that guy . . . it was something else. He was a wealthy man, made a lot of money, and he was just about as kooky as they could be."

Maybe with a financial double-cross of Hungarian star Sandor Szabo. Philadelphia promoter Ray Fabiani once paid Szabo $1,350 for a match and wrote the check to Pfefer as Szabo's manager. A few months later, Internal Revenue Service agents showed up at Fabiani's door, ready to nab him for falsifying his business expenses. Fabiani had reported the full payment to the IRS, but Szabo claimed only $150 in income for the match. Fortunately, Fabiani had the canceled check to verify his story. "Szabo was dumbfounded when he heard that. He got only eleven percent of the purse while Pfefer kept eighty-nine percent for himself. Perhaps that's why Pfefer has the reputation of being the richest man in the wrestling game," Fabiani mused.

Maybe with the correspondence between Pfefer and his client Ricki Starr, who took wrestling by storm with his ballet gimmick in the late 1950s. For the most part, Pfefer's stars were uncommonly devoted to their hard-driving manager, a relationship so close and intimate that the opening line in one letter from Starr to Pfefer described one of their smutty shared loves: "Dear Pickles: Glad you sent the pussy pictures."

Though he never held a major position in the industry, Pfefer combined persistence, paranoia, resourcefulness, and resentment to take wrestling to new highs and new lows. He was a manager of novelty acts, a talent scout, occasional promoter, and, above all, a

Jack Pfefer (r) with his fearsome star Ivan Poddubny.

first-rate malcontent who blabbed to the press that wrestling was rigged after promoters cut him out of a lucrative pact in 1933. "I'm in the show business, like Ringling Brothers," he boasted. "The show must go on. The main thing what the public wants is freaks, a good laugh."

Ah, the freaks. Pfefer was to collecting curiosities what Noah was to collecting animals. The son of a rabbi, Pfefer was born December

10, 1894, in Warsaw, Poland, when it was part of Russia. He immi-grated to the United States in 1921, worked as a stagehand and spear carrier for ballerina Anna Pavlova, and started in wrestling in 1924 around the Midwest by capitalizing on post–World War I hostility toward foreigners. Alexander Garkawienko of Ukraine became his Alexander the Great, capable of eating twenty eggs at a single sitting. Sergei Kalmikoff had a life-sized eagle tattooed on his chest but Pfefer converted him into an unkempt cave man from Siberia. Ferenc Holuban of Hungary was the man with no neck. Leo Pinetzki of Poland was six-foot-eight with an eight-foot wingspan. "His disposition is pretty good, for a freak," Pfefer conceded. In July 1931, he packed up for Mongolia in search of more talent with a dossier of femmes fatales under his arm. "Those Mongolian babies are plenty tough but show 'em a picture of a raving blonde and clamp a derby on their heads, and they are yours," he told Henry McLemore of United Press International.

By 1933, Pfefer had it pretty good, coordinating foreign talent for the New York office, handling bookings for his wrestlers, and taking a five percent slice of the earnings of world champion Jim Londos. That all changed just before Christmas 1933. Feuding promoters buried the hatchet at a meeting in New York, agreeing to trade talent, share profits, and back Londos as a unified champion. They excluded Pfefer from the "trust" agreement, probably because he couldn't be trusted. Case in point: Fabiani sent Harry Fields, a young wrestler and aspiring medical student, to New York in 1933 to earn some much-needed tuition money. After the match, Fields went to Pfefer to collect his purse: five dollars. "Not even enough [to cover] the cost of his return train fare," Fabiani fumed.

Pfefer went off the deep end. "Them schemers! Them manip-ulators! Them bums! All the time they want to squeeze me out," he howled. Through Dan Parker of the *New York Daily Mirror*, he laid the sport bare, divulging under-the-table payments, and titles bought and sold. The magician was revealing trade secrets. For the remaining forty years of his life, Pfefer railed against the wrestling establishment with the fervor of an evangelical preacher. His business cards read "Trustbuster." If they wanted fake, by God, Pfefer would give them fake, and gleefully. Bronko Nagurski, the star football player from Minnesota, held the National Wrestling Association world championship in 1941. Pfefer stormed into Minneapolis with his band of wrestlers led by one Brunek Zagurski. Minneapolis promoter Tony Stecher, neutral in the promotional wars, couldn't believe it as Pfefer tattled to reporters and posted stories of wrestling double-crosses and underhanded dealings at barber shops, pool halls, and hotels. "You can't possibly gain anything by it so the only thing I can assume is that your intention is to hurt me personally, although I hope that is not the case," Stecher wrote.

Meanwhile, Pfefer added to his fantastical menagerie, touring the country with a cast straight out of the *Star Wars* cantina. When Boston promoter Paul Bowser brought Maurice Tillet, the grotesque "French Angel" to America, Pfefer countered with Olaf Swenson, the slightly less deformed "Swedish Angel." Then he outdid himself with Tor Johnson, the "Super Swedish Angel," a B-movie actor. "I have just read one of those pamphlets you have had made for Tor's advertising," Johnson's wife, Greta, wrote Pfefer in 1946. "They even frighten me. No kidding. They are nice. People can not help but notice." Zimba Parker was raised by pigmies and had a "psychic eye." Marvin "Blimp" Levy was a 525-pounder who had been wrestling on small circuits in New England. Pfefer added 100 pounds to his listed weight, turned him into the fattest gimmick in wrestling, and transported him in a trailer because "Blimp" couldn't wedge himself through a train door. "Levy is my glandular champ and doctors marvel at him. Some night he'll drop dead in a ring, God forbid. He can't wrestle a lick but nobody can knock him off his feet," Pfefer shrugged to *Collier's* writer Jack Miley. He had a steady stream of women wrestlers on hand, even a "Lady Blimp," Charlene Ward. "I got to handle these freaks like I was a father," said Pfefer, a lifelong bachelor. "One day I beat them up and yell their ears off, and next day I am gentle with them like a father."

If he liked you, there were no limits to his kindness. In the 1950s, when Pfefer found out Phil Melby's parents were also Russian Jews, he demanded that Nashville, Tennessee promoter Nick Gulas give a break to the struggling wrestler. "Boy, he went in that office and he raised hell about me," Melby remembered. "He told Nick, 'I'll build an arena that'll be right across the street from you and I'll put your ass out of business.' All of a sudden my bookings got good. Then good guys started working with me." Knowing of Pfefer's reputation for fleecing his workers, Melby passed up an invitation to join his assemblage. "But he wrote me for years in Arizona wanting to know how I was doing in my career and life," Melby said.

Manager Jack Pfefer considered Marvin "Blimp" Levy one of his great freakish attractions, even though he was afraid he might die in the ring.

If Pfefer didn't like you, and it didn't take much, there were no limits to his chicanery. In 1941, he invited Ted Tourtas, about three years into his career, to visit him at a Hollywood hotel. "What kind of name is Tourtas? I'll give you a good name," Pfefer insisted. Tourtas was okay with a new *nom de guerre*, but he wanted some financial assurance before he left his home in California for Pfefer's circuit. "Well, with that, he hit the ceiling, jumped up in the air. 'You're in the goddamn business fifteen minutes and you want guarantees?'" Tourtas recalled Pfefer yelling. "On one wall, he had the heroes, the guys that he liked and on the other wall, he had Jimmy Londos and that was his shit list. 'That's what I call it, my shit list and I'm gonna put you there on my shit list.'"

Pfefer was a walking accumulation of smells, quirks, and grudges. "Unkempt" was a kind way to describe his laundry preferences; he kept rubber bands on his wrists so he could snap them at times of anxiety, and columnist Parker dubbed him the "Halitosis Kid." He kept a silver-knobbed cane ever at his side and brandished it at any wrestler who dared to ask him for money in sums of more than two dollars. Yet promoters and wrestlers continued to do business with him. Boston promoter Bowser was in hock for at least $7,000 to pay off bills. "I hate like the devil to ask you this, but I do not want anybody else to know my business," Bowser wrote him in 1937. Pfefer sent some of his wrestlers to Sam Muchnick, who was building an opposition promotion in St. Louis in the early 1940s; Muchnick never forgot the favor, even when he became the powerful president of the National Wrestling Alliance. When Muchnick invited Pfefer as a guest to the 1957 NWA convention, Montreal promoter Eddie Quinn resigned in protest, calling the outsider a "cancer" on the business. Meanwhile, Pfefer was demonstrating that he remained one of the best talent evaluators in the game. He signed up Buddy Rogers and took him to new heights as "Nature Boy" in California at a high cost — one-quarter of Rogers' 1948 earnings of $26,349. Rogers dumped Pfefer in a money dispute in May 1951, but the manager still controlled at least parts of the careers of some of the greatest wrestlers of the mid-century — the Zebra Kid, Ricki Starr, The Fabulous Moolah, Don and Jackie Fargo, the Amazing Zuma, Bearcat Wright, and Angelo Poffo. Pfefer took a twenty percent cut for booking Starr, who sent him a mash note: "Jack I don't know how much you ever took from your top boys but if it was ten percent, fifty percent, or eighty percent I'm sure you were worth every penny of it."

Obstinacy ran deep in his blood, though. When the offices in Boston and Chicago fell on hard times in the early 1960s, Pfefer stepped in with a batch of make-believe wrestlers that mocked top stars of the era. Hobo Brazil, Pierre Carpentier, and George Valentine were rip-offs of Bobo Brazil, Edouard Carpentier, and Johnny Valentine. "I never liked him," growled long-time bad guy Hans Schmidt. "He was a rat, to me, in my book! Lousy payoff man." When those promotions started to fade, Pfefer stayed in the limelight, offering Ernie Ladd $100,000 in 1968 to abandon Kansas City Chiefs football in favor of wrestling. (Ladd did so, but not with Pfefer.) He remained in contact with his favorites almost until his death September 13, 1974, in Norwell, Massachusetts, defiant to the end. "I am too far ahead or to be yellow and just give up my struggle. There are so many bastards and morons in the game which are just waiting for the day I will retire," he wrote Dave Levin, his most beloved wrestler. "All these and any other things just gives me more strength and more courage to keep punching and get more laughs."

The Spectacles

Introduction

In May 1925, Myron Batesole, just twelve years old, achieved fame, if not fortune, as marbles champion of both Crocker Grammar School and District Five in Des Moines, Iowa. A year later, Batesole went for the fortune, working in Hollywood movies and occasionally serving as a double in the old Hal Roach "Our Gang" comedies as a teen who tipped the scales at 200 pounds. A decade passed, and he merged fame and fortune by wrestling as the 350-pound Cardiff Giant, drawing on the famous hoax of a petrified man excavated in 1869 in New York.

It seemed as though everybody was trying to outdo each other in the 1930s. "Whiskers" Savage was a country boy who turned Houston wrestling on its ear with his common folk ways, hanging out at a Salvation Army and reading the funny pages perched on a curb outside an arena. Len Stecklin brought his pet raccoon Oscar to the ring and refused to wear tights because he said they were "indecent." "Man Mountain" Dean was a 300-pound ex–traffic cop and the inspiration behind Batesole's transformation from marbles ace to hulking grappler. "He was working in Hollywood when he saw Man Mountain Dean wrestle," Batesole's hometown *Des Moines Register* wrote in 1936. "That gave him an idea that he should capitalize his size on the mat and he took to grappling." Batesole outweighed Dean by thirty pounds and was four inches taller, so

Ex-marbles champion Cardiff Giant.

he had a more legitimate physical claim to "giant" status. Whether he could defend himself was another matter. In Waterloo, Iowa, an overwrought timekeeper, angered at the Giant's tactics and apparently not clued in to the inner workings of wrestling, socked him over the head with the steel rod ordinarily used to ring the bell. Cardiff needed four stitches, proving that being a wrestling spectacle often came at a price.

I. World's Greatest Manager

It wasn't fair. Every time Charlie Wilder had Count Pietro Rossi in trouble, the dapper little butterball of a wrestler slipped out of the ring. Refused to go toe to toe. Wouldn't man up. There was only one possible solution: cage him in. So on August 24, 1936, a crew strung chicken wire around the ring at the American Legion arena in Lake Worth, Florida, to ensure Rossi would stay put. The Count, said to be a nobleman from Naples, Italy, agreed on the condition that the match proceed without an arbiter. "Keep a referee from bothering me and I'll murder him," he boasted to Al MacMillan of the *Palm Beach Post*. Which he almost did. Midway through the bout, Rossi removed one of his wrestling shoes and whacked Wilder on the head and into neverland. On the final swing, a piece of lead shaped like a sole flew out of his boot. In one evening, Rossi had ushered in the loaded boot gimmick and the first cage match in the South.

If the word "innovator" is in the wrestling dictionary, there is doubtless an image next to it of Count Pietro Rossi, a beret sitting atop curly black hair that fell to his shoulders, a Van Dyke beard, a walking stick in one hand, a monocle in one eye, and a glint of mischief in the other. Rossi doubled down on behaving badly, starting as a vicious yet comedic wrestling rogue and then becoming the first heel manager in the business. In many ways, he is the forefather of every troublemaker who has ever slipped his man a foreign object, distracted a referee, or got in a shouting match with fans at ringside. "He could control an audience," marveled his son William Rossi. "He was a born antagonist, but he was a businessman. That's why he did the villain side because he knew they were the ones who brought all the money in."

All that sprung from the fertile imagination of Pietro Rosania, born June 2, 1908, in Pennsylvania as one of six children to immigrants from Italy. His older brother Sam started boxing under the loan shark–sounding name of "Shifty" Dando in 1921, and Rossi followed him into the fight game in Ohio as Pete Dando. He was eighteen when he had his first recorded boxing match, a four-round draw against Patsy Hogan in Dayton. In 1928, billed as "Wild" Pete Dando, he added wrestling to his repertoire, earning notoriety as "The Crying Wop" because he broke into tears when things weren't going his way. Between sobs, Pete trained and conditioned boxers for manager Jimmy Dunn of Cleveland, who oversaw a well-regarded crew of pugilists.

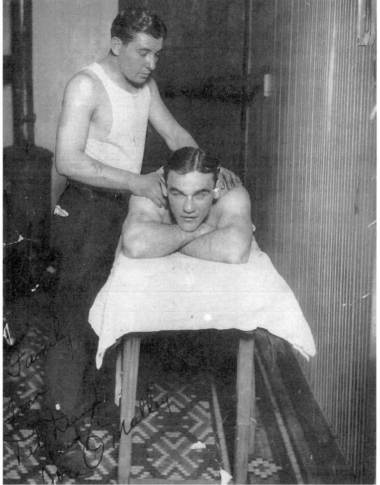

Before he was Count Rossi, he was boxing trainer Pete Dando, giving a rubdown to Joe O'Malley.

His big break came in the summer of 1932, when he got a gig in Hollywood as trainer and wrestling coach for Wallace Beery, the star of *Flesh*, a movie about a German beer garden waiter/wrestler. In 1945, after he had achieved fame and infamy as Count Rossi, he recalled his wide-eyed introduction to Tinseltown. "My job was to see that the wrestling scenes were done correctly; if not, to holler 'cut.' That made me nervous, for I didn't know anything about moving pictures. I was afraid I would stop the cameras at the wrong time." He did just fine, landing a bit part in the movie as Pete Dando, grossing $10,000 for a year's work, and hanging around to prescribe exercise routines for other actors. Most significantly, he made the acquaintance of Wladek Zbyszko, Beery's opponent in the climactic scene. Zbyszko invited Dando to South America, where he and brother Stanislaus promoted wrestling shows. As legend goes, the Zbyszko business was booming in Rio de Janeiro until one night when army officers seized the box office receipts. Dando and his colleagues decided a diversion was in order, so they touched off a riot and distracted the officers, while other wrestlers ran into the office and took what they were owed. Then everybody left town. "That's why I don't ever go back to South America," he once told his son.

The subterfuge was good practice: when he returned to North America, he started instigating riots as Count Rossi, a scoundrel in a full-length opera cape. He began in the Alabama-Tennessee territory in fall 1935, but the fun didn't really start until he moved to the South Florida circuit the following summer. In Miami, he was disqualified for trying to rearrange Chief Frank Barfoot's face with bottle caps. In Lake Worth, he reeled off twelve victories in a row before dropping a disqualification decision to Jack Ross after a ringsider, said to be brother Shifty, used The Count's cane to open a six-inch welt on Ross' head. He popularized the chicken wire match in Florida and Georgia and always produced at the gate; Rossi was getting fifty-dollar paydays, a tidy sum during the Great Depression. Bill "Pop" Rogers was the matchmaker in Lake Worth, near Palm

Beach. Just after the first cage match, Rogers scribbled a note of amazement to fellow promoter Jack Pfefer because the short, fleshy Rossi looked nothing like a typical wrestler. "This Count has gone over great here, and candidly I don't understand how he does it. I thought Morrella [Tony Morelli] the best heel I ever had in this territory. The Count in my estimation doesn't do a third [of] the things that Morrella done. Hardly ever goes to the mat and tackles, etc., are not on his life . . . But perhaps it's his contrast from extreme politeness on the opening part of the show that brings any thing he does out like a million dollars."

Rossi wrestled in the East and then returned to Florida in the winter of 1936–37, sparking a near riot in Lake Worth, where authorities had to cut the house lights to calm a crowd angry at the way he beat Joe Ferona. He lost to Jean LaBelle in an unusual stipulation match in Miami; as the loser, he had to push LaBelle in a wheelchair along Dixie Highway to the amusement of several hundred spectators. Florida promoter Al Ritchie apologized for Rossi's disruptions, though just a little, since The Count held the Southern heavyweight title. "He likes a little foolishness and horseplay, but don't overlook that not only is he the outstanding showman of the country in wrestling circles, but a master, also, of all the tricks, clean and dirty, of modern wrestling."

In wrestling's first half century, managers largely assumed a secondary function — tending to their men's needs, handling booking, publicity, and travel arrangements, and serving as personal confidants. Rossi's body was wearing down — after all, he was five-foot-five and shaped like Humpty Dumpty. So starting in January 1938 with a Masked Marvel, he redefined the role of manager as an agent provocateur who could take storylines in new and unscrupulous directions. Rossi hit the jackpot with Elmer the Great, a wild man that he claimed to have retrieved from the Ozark boondocks. Since Elmer wasn't familiar with wrestling rules, The Count brought him up to speed from ringside with nonstop instructions. "There wasn't much wrestling, but it was really funny," the *Ottawa Journal* said after Elmer beat Hal Rumberg in November 1939. "Every now and then Elmer would come to a halt just when he had managed to clamp on a hold and rush over to the corner for further signals."

Back in Florida, Rossi was in the middle of a riot in St. Petersburg in August 1940 when an irate fan grabbed his cane and monocle. His Black Panther — "Wee" Willie Davis, in this case — came to Rossi's aid and kicked away several spectators as boisterous fans stormed the ring. According to the St. Petersburg Times, "The Count, ruffled and shaking like a maple leaf in a fall breeze, led his protégé through the milling crowd as fans hurled handfuls of sand and verbal insults and followed them to the [American] Legion home." There, a band of boys ripped screens from windows so the crowd could get at Rossi and the Panther, who took refuge in a dressing room under police watch.

That scene, or something approximating it, was repeated dozens of times as Rossi piloted the careers of wrestlers with a liberal dose of the unknown — Superman, The Golden Terror, The Mysterious Ace, The Masked Cougar, The Masked Strangler, and The Masked Boom Boom. Others in his stable included include Ted "King Kong" Cox, Mayes McLain, Pancho Valdez, Lou Plummer, Frederich von Schacht, Don Evans, Tom Renesto, Don Leo Jonathan, John and Chris Tolos, and 550-pound Country Boy (Haystacks) Calhoun.

Rossi's vocation might have been hysterical, but it also was dangerous. He was stabbed twice and shot once. What motivated him? Like heel managers who followed, Rossi was convinced that everything he did was justified in the name of victory; that the real problem rested with a few bad eggs among the fans. In his booklet *The Truth About Wrestling Matches*, he wrote:

> You can take it from me, when a wrestler goes into
> the ring and tries to do the best he knows how, and
> somebody in the audience makes a nasty remark at
> the wrestler, he then feels that the people don't like
> him. The wrestler, being temperamental, as they all

are, goes wild. . . . When they are in the ring that is the way they make their livelihood. Wrestling promoters want winners, not losers, that is why they pay big money.

His knavery earned him a wife, though. Mildred Tucker got in his face one night in Fort Worth, Texas, as Rossi was returning from the ring. He did exactly what you'd expect from a heel; he picked her up and tossed her back among her friends. Fearing a lawsuit, the local promoter demanded Rossi apologize in person. He invited his critic for a cup of coffee, still in his tights, and soon Mildred became his wife and his driver — with his oversized flat feet, The Count could never quite master the gas pedal–clutch combination.

COURTESY FAMILY OF COUNT ROSSI

Brothers John (l) and Chris Tolos (r) were among Count Rossi's many charges.

Rossi managed and promoted in California for several years before butting heads with the wrestling establishment and heading to Texas. He worked the rest of his career in the Southwest, with several tricks still under his cape. In January 1953, he threw a temper tantrum in Tucson, Arizona, when referee Monte LaDue administered an overdue spanking following a match. The flustered Rossi challenged LaDue to a one-on-one the following week for a purse of twenty-five cents. But he lost his two bits when LaDue yanked on Rossi's shirt, pinned his arms to his sides, and delivered a solid smack.

Two months later in El Paso, Rossi wielded his cane to open a sizable gash on a substitute referee's forehead. An unruly mob chased them to the dressing room as Rossi and wrestlers John and Chris Tolos took cover under a shield of chairs. They barricaded the doors and turned out the lights. Security guards escorted them from the arena two hours later. An unheard-of manager-versus-promoter match versus Mike London on January 3, 1955, drew a sellout crowd of 5,000 to Albuquerque's Ice Arena. Sports editor J.D. Kailer watched as Rossi cracked his hickory cane across London's brow, bloodying his nose and triggering pandemonium. "The bell never rang starting the fight and referee Yaqui Joe never finished his pre-match instructions," Kailer wrote. "It was undoubtedly the shortest grunt 'n' groan exhibition on record. Laugh? We thought we'd pass out."

Rossi hung up his managerial boots by 1956. In retirement, he worked maintenance at a trailer park for a while and pursued his love of cooking. But Rossi's first passion was never far from his mind. "When he would talk about his wrestling days, he'd always say it was the greatest time of his life," his son said. "That was the only thing he hated about being older; he missed it so much." Battling cancer, Rossi fell and hit his head on April 25, 1979, at his home in Grand Prairie, Texas. He died two days later at the age of seventy. In the event that you are passing through Celina, Texas, an hour north of Dallas, and need any reminding about The Count, swing down Route 2478 to a cemetery more than 125 years old. A black-flecked tan tombstone marks the final resting place of Rossi and wife Mildred, who died in 2002. Under The Count's name is the inscription, "World's Greatest Manager."

II. The Red Devil

Once you saw Julius Woronick's face, you never forgot it. His eyes were deep, dark, piercing, and soulless. His face was trapezoidal, with sharp eastern European features, a cleft chin, and a slightly hooked nose. His dark hair was slicked back over his pointed, cauliflower ears. In Columbus, Ohio, where Woronick mostly lived and wrestled, street kids had a secret name for him when he walked by — *diavolul om*, or "devil man" in Romanian.

Which he was, in many ways. Among wrestling's first wave of contrived characters, Woronick brought a convincing color to a black-and-white sport as Mephisto, a fan favorite adorned head to boot in flaming red tights, shirt, and robe. "We expected any moment to see the Great Mephisto make a striking gesture toward the canvas with his pointed fingers and see arise a flash of flame and eerie smoke," Havey Boyle wrote in the *Pittsburgh Post-Gazette* in 1936. Buddy Rogers, wrestling's foremost heel, and Frankie Cain, who grew up watching Mephisto in Columbus, considered him to be the greatest worker in the history of the sport. No one before and few since have been able to use a gimmick to accentuate their in-ring skills, rather than relying on it as a diversion or a camouflage for a lack of talent. Mephisto's artifice got your attention; his artistry mesmerized you. "He was just unreal, the things he did," Cain said. "He was like a ballet dancer. He would pull moves right out of midair and you'd think, 'Where in the hell did that come from? I didn't know he could do that.' He was magic."

And yet . . . Mephisto. The name is derived from Mephistopheles, the demonic character in German literature who bestows Faust with magical powers in exchange for his soul. It fit Woronick in real life. He was as troubled outside the ring as he was gifted inside it, a chronic boozer whose abominable acts culminated in beating his aged mother and sending her to the hospital. "The fact that he drank a lot made him almost a cult figure if that makes any sense," Cain said. "I don't think anything in wrestling can be covered up for very long before the people know it. But they knew that he drank, and they would say, 'Well, I hope Mephisto is sober tonight. If he's sober tonight, he's going to kick the hell out of somebody.'"

Something possessed Woronick in the ring; something else possessed him out of it. It's hard to know which came first. As his fame grew, Woronick attributed his skill set to his carnival exploits

Though dogged by personal demons, Mephisto looks ready to cast a spell on his opponent and his audience.

as a youthful human torch, telling a news service that his German circus parents sent him up a fifty-foot-high tower in gasoline-soaked clothes and lit him ablaze as he dove into a barrel of water. (As a precaution, he added, his suit was lined with asbestos.) In reality, he was the third of five children, born April 12, 1910, to Lithuanian immigrants who lived in Meriden, Connecticut. The circus angle had some acquaintance with the truth. Woronick started his athletic career as a teenager on boxing and wrestling shows that his oldest brother, Joe, an ex-prizefighter, ran in conjunction with the local carnival circuit. Even with brotherly guidance, Woronick had a knack for finding trouble. In April 1926, when he was sixteen, a juvenile court judge sent him to reform school after he pleaded guilty to stealing a car. In January 1931, he was arrested for assaulting his mother, Mary, because she failed to have breakfast ready when he arose at 1 p.m. Eight months later, he was in court on an assault charge stemming from a fight with an out-of-town visitor to the family home on Sherman Avenue.

By then, Woronick was an established wrestler. His first recorded match was in February 1930 under his real name. He started using the Mephisto device in earnest in the fall of 1932. Credit for that is hazy but probably belongs to Jack Pfefer, a gimmick generator extraordinaire who bird-dogged for talent in the Northeast. Pfefer's promotional files at the University of Notre Dame library include a lithograph proclaiming: "The GREAT MEPHISTO / Who Is Mephisto? / Why Mephisto? / MEPHISTO'S DEADLY PILEDRIVER / You've Seen Butting Bull's Terrible Turks And Stranglers. / Now Comes His Satanic Majesty 'The Great Mephisto' to Show His Tricks."

At some point, sports stars can shine so brightly that their indiscretions are quietly swept under the rug. So it was with Woronick, who was just twenty-two when he ended the five-year reign of Steve Passas for the New England version of the world light heavyweight championship on January 10, 1933, in Boston. His cleverness was on full display for the nearly 6,000 fans who crowded Mechanics Hall; he played possum in the third and deciding fall, acting down and out from the effects of five consecutive body slams. When Passas went in for the kill, Woronick caught him by the thighs, tipped him over, and pinned him. "The championship decided, the fans gave the victor a mighty cheer, also plenty of applause, for the win was a very popular one, Mephisto having become an idol in this city," his hometown *Meriden Daily Journal* reported. "His climb up the ladder of fame was sensational."

Passas took back the championship that fall, but Mephisto regained it from Winn Robbins in Boston on October 22, 1935. By then, he was expanding his vistas to the Canadian Maritime provinces, Chicago, Detroit, and especially Columbus, where the Great Debris Battle certified the spell Mephisto had cast on fans. A crowd of 6,000 described as "intensely pro-Mephisto" filled the Columbus Auditorium in August 1935 to cheer for him against Charles "Midget" Fisher, the Midwest light heavyweight champion, even though Fischer was a regional hero. When ticket payers thought referee Ed Beardsley was favoring Fischer, they demonstrated and hurled debris into the ring. Wrestling commissioners escorted Beardsley to the back for his own safety. Cleanup crews needed another ten minutes to clear the rubbish.

Mephisto lost that bout but came back to win the Midwest title on January 1, 1936, from Walter Roxey, by day a junior college teacher. In a finish as rare then as it is commonplace today, Roxey climbed back into the ring after a nasty collision to win by countout while Mephisto was still on the floor. Ringside commissioners, perhaps with the memory of the Great Debris Battle fresh in their minds, reversed the decision and ordered the match to continue.

Mephisto won despite Roxey's protestations about the restart. "Mephisto outgrappled his rival by the proverbial mile, and easily gained the decision," the *Columbus Dispatch* wrote. "It was too bad that it had to be a tainted one, for the red-clad mystery man appears to be easily the class of the light-heavies today."

For the next fifteen years, Mephisto would be Columbus promoter Al Haft's top draw. Five times he held the region's light heavyweight championship, billed variously as a regional or world honor. After he lost a close decision in an October 1940 title match to Jules "Speedy" LaRance, he received a letter of commendation from Colonel Alfred Ballin, chairman of the Columbus boxing and wrestling commission. It was rare praise from a regulator to a wrestler. "The Commission and the public in general considers you one of the outstanding wrestlers who have ever appeared locally and feel you are a credit to the profession you so ably represent," Ballin wrote. Mephisto earned a reputation breaking out every trick in the book — kangaroo kicks, flying mares, reverse headspins, and ankle sweeps — from any position, at any time. His signature move was a piledriver; Fischer popularized it, but Mephisto took it to another dimension. Snatching his opponent's head between his thighs, he upended him in an inverted posture and held him so high that he often lost control and went crashing backward. The audience was on the edge of its seat the whole time, unsure if it would see a spectacle or debacle . . . not unlike a human torch hurtling himself into a vat of water. "The people's choice is Mephisto," the *Ohio State Journal* said in 1937, "first, last and always."

Yet there were so many odd aspects to his life. Mephisto and his wife, Ruth, lived quietly thirty miles east of Columbus in a cottage on Buckeye Lake, where he fished and grew roses. He didn't have a car and wore at most a windbreaker even in the dead of winter. He stayed put, save an occasional trip to Connecticut; Haft told inquiring promoters that Mephisto was a homebody. He barhopped all day and rarely lingered in the wrestlers' dressing room, preferring the confines of a local Greek restaurant. "I don't think anybody ever really got to know him. He was always by himself," said Cain, who watched as a kid, nose pressed against the window as Mephisto drank at nearby pubs. "I couldn't believe he was in my neighborhood. It was a bad neighborhood. It was almost like he was slumming. I'd tell my buddies, 'Mephisto's there,' and we'd all go and watch him." A decade later, Haft confided in Cain that he never knew a time when Mephisto wasn't hitting the bottle, calling his featured attraction "a waste of talent."

As his age advanced, Mephisto could still steal a show; in May 1948, the *Hartford Courant* called his undercard match with Stu Hart "the real thriller of the night" as they matched hold for hold in a forty-five-minute draw. But by 1953, Mephisto, usually trim at 180 pounds, had swelled to more than 220 during a brief swing through Kansas City, Missouri. His last recorded appearances were in Ohio in 1955 and Connecticut in 1956. Outside of wrestling, life became a struggle. For a time, Woronick worked as a landscaper in Meriden and lived for at least parts of three years at Cold Spring Home, a poorhouse run by the city. His name was on the police blotter as often as it had been in the sports section. On February 20, 1961, a patrolman arrested him at a railroad station on an intoxication charge, his forty-ninth such citation. The following August, a circuit court judge sent him to jail for thirty days for public intoxication and fined him fifteen dollars for trespassing. In April 1962, Woronick pulled his eighty-two-year-old mother, Mary, out of bed, stomped on her, and beat her around the head and neck. She was hospitalized. Woronick told authorities he remembered nothing about the incident.

The judicial system and his relatives had had enough. Speaking for the family, lawyer Joseph Noonan told a circuit court judge that Mary lived in dread fear of being battered by her son. Woronick was sentenced to a year in jail. From his cell, he wrote a letter promising the judge that he would move out of state in return for less time in jail. The court released Woronick to probation after six months and he moved to Michigan, scene of some of his greatest wrestling triumphs. At some point, he returned to Meriden, where he died after a brief illness on July 22, 1968.

Woronick was dead. Mephisto lived on. At least half a dozen wrestlers have called themselves Mephisto at some point. In Mexico, Mephisto is a champion light-heavyweight luchador whose true identity is unknown to the public. Frankie Cain borrowed his idol's name as a Middle East seer and visionary during the 1970s. But he was a heel wrestler, which caused no end of distress to one fan. Rosanne Pike complained to the Columbus *Dispatch* in 1996 that Cain had purloined Mephisto's good name. "I will always remember the original and legendary good guy, the red-garbed Great Mephisto," she wrote. Living in retirement in Florida, Buddy Rogers mailed a Christmas card to Cain one year. In his trademark pretentious fashion, the printed cards read, "Buddy Rogers was the greatest worker ever in professional wrestling." Only on this one, Rogers crossed out his own name, and scrawled in the name of the sad, withdrawn, forgotten figure who had so captivated him: "Mephisto was the greatest worker ever in professional wrestling."

III. The Kindest Angel

It was the strangest tea party this side of *Alice in Wonderland*. In February 1940, famed Harvard University anthropologist Earnest A. Hooton hosted a gathering at his Buckingham Street residence near the campus. Hallam Movius Jr., curator of Harvard's renowned Peabody Museum, was there, as were several anthropology specialists. Boston wrestling promoter Paul Bowser was on hand along with Karl Pojello, a seasoned wrestler and trainer of Lithuanian origin. Another guest, Maurice Tillet, a recent arrival from Europe, wanted a little lemon with his tea, and naturally he got it because he was five-foot-eight and weighed 276 pounds with bones as dense as lead rods and a misshapen appearance that suggested an evolutionary false start.

Polite as could be, Tillet let the researchers probe him, prod him, X-ray him, and measure his 181-millimeter-wide head (twenty percent larger than normal), even though his gargoyle-like visage had caused spectators to faint during his Boston debut as wrestling's "French Angel" a couple of weeks prior. "He is a very friendly man who we found genuinely attractive. There is something unusually gentle and kindly about him, and he is furthermore a man of fine intelligence," Hooton decided. Of course, Hooton's afternoon tea had the whiff of a publicity event, and he warned Tillet's future rivals about what they were getting into. "Nobody is going to hurt M. Tillet in the ring," he said. "If an opponent succeeded in putting a full nelson on M. Tillet he might hurt his own hands but he would not hurt M. Tillet."

Such was the strange marriage of science, sports, and spectacle behind pro wrestling's first great curiosity. Wrestling had drawn performers from carnivals and circuses since its inception, but the Angel was the most remarkable of them. Billed as the world's ugliest man, he was the first sideshow-style attraction to claim a version of the world heavyweight championship. He was one of wrestling's top draws in the 1940s and begat the era of the freak show headliner, spawning a generation of pretenders and successors that would run in an unbroken line to Andre the Giant and maybe even Shrek.

"He had long arms hanging down to his knees and had long hair on his body, looked like a gorilla. At one time, they had him on the cover of *Life* magazine that he was the closest thing to prehistoric man," recalled long-time heel Rip Hawk. "But he was really a nice, nice man. I was just a kid barely making any money and my grandfather passed away. He called me over with his French accent, told me that if I didn't have the money to go home for the funeral, he would help me. So I was able to take a train from Chicago home."

The details of Tillet's life became as exaggerated as his looks once zealous promoters started twisting them into hyperbole. But most agree that Tillet grew up in Russia, where he was born on October 23, 1903, near St. Petersburg. His father, a miner and farmer, died when he was a child, and he fled to France with his mother, a French teacher, during the 1917 Russian Revolution. About three years later, his hands, neck, head, feet, and bones started to swell in unusual proportions. Acromegaly, a disorder of the pituitary gland, was transforming him from a blond youngster nicknamed "Angel" by his family. He continued to play rugby at a high level, worked in a circus, and served in the French Navy for almost six years as a petty officer. In 1937, Pojello encountered Tillet, then thirty-three, in a bar in Singapore, where he learned the big man had done some Greco-Roman wrestling. Pojello sat bolt upright. From then on, he would be Tillet's protector and handler; he also took a good chunk of his protégé's money — fifty cents of every dollar, the Angel once told "Tough" Tony Borne. But it never seemed to bother the generous Tillet. "He wasn't bitter about it at all," said Borne, who worked with the duo in Chicago. "In fact, Karl's wife told me, 'Karl doesn't love me, he loves the French Angel.' Dollar signs."

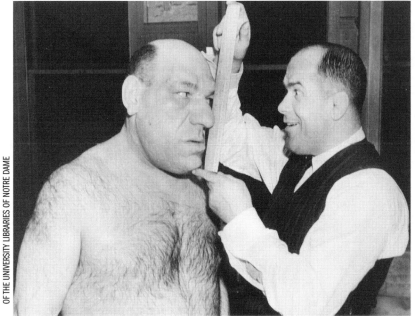

Karl Pojello puts a ruler to the skull of his wrestler Maurice Tillet, whom he managed around the world as the French Angel.

Pojello worked on the mat with Tillet and took him through England and France, where he became an immediate sensation. By one count, he had about 140 matches in five countries, with two draws the only black marks on his ledger. It was time for the main event, and Tillet arrived by ship in New York on January 14, 1940, on the *Rex*; his listed occupation was "artist." His North American debut on January 24, 1940, against Luigi Bacigalupi at Boston Garden nearly tripled promoter Bowser's normal house to 7,000 fans. "With his gargoyle head, bandy legs, suitcase feet and ham hands, he was more a nightmare than a human being," sportswriter Walter Gilhooly said. Tillet finished off Bacigalupi in seven minutes with his signature bearhug.

A star was born. Word spread like wildfire as newsreel clips of the match were shown in North American movie theaters. Pictures of the Bacigalupi beatdown appeared in sports sections across the country. In rapid succession, Bowser and Pojello ran the Angel five and six nights a week through cities such as Cleveland, New York, Montreal, Philadelphia, Buffalo, and Chicago. During his early travels, he appeared at a meeting of the Canadian Medical Association in Toronto as the most extreme example of acromegaly on medical record. In Hollywood, he escorted starlet Suzanne Ridgway at the Brown Derby restaurant. "Maurice Tillet (The Angel) is getting more publicity than any wrestler in years," said nationally syndicated columnist Eddie Brietz.

Not all of it was pleasant. Tillet wasn't a traditional good guy or bad guy wrestler; he was an oddity, a novelty, a mutant, and sportswriters had a field day breaking out every crude description in the book:

> ". . . the missing link between the Java man and whoever succeeded the Java man" (Victor O. Jones)

> ". . . the strangest two-legged human ever seen, including the Hunchback of Notre Dame" (columnist Walt Hickey)

". . . his big hideous head scared the women around the ringside, and probably would alarm even Boris Karloff" (sportswriter W.J. McGoogan)

To others, Tillet represented the tipping point at which a once-proud sport sank beneath vaudeville in believability. "Tillet is neither a superhuman in strength nor even an ordinary wrestler in real ability. He is 100 percent publicity of the kind built up with a tire pump," St. Louis sportswriter Ed Wray groused in June 1940. "And he isn't helping what remains of the wresting game."

The cruel words did nothing to rattle a cultured man, a devout Catholic, and a neatly groomed bookworm who became a U.S. citizen in 1947. "Since I was a little boy old enough to know what it was about, I have been an object of curiosity. Long ago I accepted my appearance for what it was," he said in 1943 as Oakland *Tribune* columnist Alan Ward molded his broken English into orderly sentences. "No, I have no inferiority complex. I have not let my looks get me — how do you say it? — down."

On May 13, 1940, Tillet won the Boston-based American Heavyweight Association world title when champion Steve "Crusher" Casey was disqualified for punching the referee in the third fall. "There was a burst of cheers from many of the close to 9,000 spectators who had sat out the long carnival," wrote Doc Almy in the Boston *Post*. The first freak titleholder remained unbeaten for nineteen months, felling some of the greatest champions of all time: Ed "Strangler" Lewis, Yvon Robert, Lou Thesz, Joe Savoldi, Ed Don George, Dean Detton, and "Wild" Bill Longson (five times). He didn't lose until January 19, 1942, when he was unable to continue after Casey booted him in the head in a bout in Portland, Maine. In May, Casey reclaimed the AWA title and beat the Angel in a pair of rematches.

Tillet continued to tour North America and Europe throughout the 1940s. His best city was Buffalo, where he drew ten crowds of more than 10,000 fans in a ten-year period. He provided the template

Was Maurice Tillet the inspiration for Shrek?

for nearly a dozen wrestling "angels," including at least one woman, most of whom were concoctions of promoter Jack Pfefer, who never met a gimmick he was afraid to usurp. A "Battle of the Angels" with the "Swedish Angel" (Olaf Swenson, neé Filip Olafsson), brought 10,000 fans to Toronto on December 17, 1942. Olafsson was taller and a better wrestler than Tillet. He also was less imposing and less interesting, and lost when he was counted out of the ring by the referee. "The French angel won a moral victory," wrote journalist Charles Lynch. "He was by far the uglier. He looked like nothing on earth — whereas the Swedish angel was seen to bear a considerable resemblance to Mussolini."

As most special attractions do, Tillet wound down, exposed by his age, his condition, and his lack of mobility, which was especially visible when televised wrestling gained a national toehold in the late 1940s. In January 1952, he plodded to a three-fall loss to ex–boxing champion Primo Carnera, another lumbering giant, in Hartford, Connecticut. "Speed is a word The Angel never learned," sportswriter Max Liberman wrote in the Hartford *Courant*. "His mobility was like a frozen bull-dozer. Even when covering The Angel back in 1942, when he was rated tops, he could never get around to satisfy himself." Later that year, Tillet was down to working middle school gyms in places like Carroll, Iowa, and Wausau, Wisconsin, in front of 400 fans. "His head was so big, you couldn't get your arm around his head. He was so weak at that time, he coached me on what to do," said Ed Francis, who was just breaking in under Pojello's tutelage. "If he went down to his knees, you had to pick him up, help him back up." His final match was a loss to Bert Assirati on February 14, 1953, in the same place Pojello had discovered him — Singapore.

Tillet and Pojello remained inseparable to the end. They lived in adjoining rooms in Chicago, where Pojello died of lung cancer on September 4, 1954. Sixteen hours later, Tillet was dead, just short of his fifty-first birthday. He is buried in the Lithuanian National Cemetery in Chicago. For many years, stories circulated that he died of a broken heart, a poignant if misleading diagnosis. Tillet had been bedridden for several months with a kidney disorder and spent three weeks in a Chicago hospital that summer with a respiratory ailment.

Tillet made a comeback of sorts in the 2000s when wrestling fans suggested he might have been the inspiration for Shrek, the animated movie ogre with a heart of gold. The online news site *Huffington Post* tried to pin down the uncanny resemblance in 2014 but got no confirmation from DreamWorks Animation, the film company. If true, it would have brought Tillet's career full circle; he had bit parts in three French films in the 1930s. And he probably would have gotten a kick out of it. As the Oakland *Tribune*'s Ward concluded, "No pity need be wasted on Maurice Tillet because he wastes none on himself."

Learning the Ropes

Introduction

How sweet it must be to have a full-scale training center in Orlando, Florida, with seven rings, the latest in video production facilities, modern conditioning equipment, and, say, air conditioning. Unlike current WWE hopefuls, Len Rossi didn't enjoy any of those things when he learned to wrestle as a teenager at a YMCA in Utica, New York. He did have cigarette smoke, though. When he was sixteen or seventeen, Rossi wrestled on unsanctioned smokers, so named because the all-male crowd around the mat at a Moose Lodge or Elks Club was smoking and drinking. "The spectators, the men, they'd throw fifty cents or a quarter, half a dollar, into the ring, and we'd all split that. It was chicken feed, but it was a lot of fun," Rossi said. "If an outsider jumped into the ring, you never knew what he would do, so you learned how to fight. Boxing, keep your hands up at all times, takedowns, go-behinds, things of that nature. It was more like a street fight at that time, and you just learned how to take care of yourself."

Rossi's story was not uncommon among wrestlers well into the 1980s. Well-stocked training facilities like the WWE Performance Center or the independent Monster Factory in New Jersey are a relatively recent development. There's no doubt that veterans like Rossi, who forged a long career as a top star in Tennessee, would have appreciated the modern conveniences when they were learning the ropes. Still, there was something to be said for learning the old-fashioned

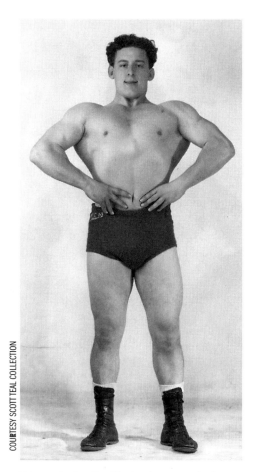

Veteran star Len Rossi had a glamorous physique, but there was nothing glamorous about the way he learned the business.

way. "Now that I look back, it was fun," he said, "but it wasn't fun at the time. You got beat up!"

I. Carnival Rides

Reggie Parks grew up on a farm in western Canada. He entered the carnival life at eighteen, tussling several times a day with burly lumberjacks who figured they could teach the kid a thing or two. "My mother, I'd come home and she'd always say, 'When are you going to quit the gypsy life?'" Parks recalled. "Yeah, you're living out of your suitcase. But it was a good education."

Long before he became Sputnik Monroe, Roscoe Brumbaugh was a fixture on athletic training (AT) shows that promoter Jack Nazworthy hauled in a thirty-six-foot-long trailer as part of carnivals, rodeos, and fairs. "He had a shower in the trailer and you washed your tights every Monday," Monroe said. "Nazworthy would come out and tell you you'd better wash them tights 'cause if you'd been doing a lot of wrestling and sweating, you smelled like a goat."

Eddie Sharkey started out on Chief Little Wolf's carnival in the Midwest in the late 1950s. His first opponent: Congo the

Wrestling Ape. "He'd come off the ground and scratch your face. But then you learned to cover your eyes and get down on the ground and let him play with your hair," Sharkey said. "We all had humble beginnings."

The number of wrestlers who cut their teeth on the carnival circuit at some point is staggering. Buddy Rogers. Harley Race. Clara Mortensen. Red Bastien. Joe "The Assassin" Hamilton. "Speedy" LaRance. Karl von Hess. Billy Edwards. Mildred Burke. Jim Londos. "Wild" Red Berry. Bearcat Wright. "Gentleman" Ed Francis. "A lot of wrestling internet talks about where did wrestling come from. 'It came from the snake pit,'" said carnival alum Billy Wicks, referring to the legendary English home of catch-as-catch-can wrestling. "That's bullshit. It came from the carnies."

Carnival and circus wrestling predates the Civil War; with much excitement, the Bowery Circus in New York announced in 1845 that the wrestler Mons. Leon would appear on its shows. By the early 1900s, AT shows were getting equal billing with merry-go-rounds, high divers, and two-headed cows. Captain Latlip's Exposition Shows United featured an athletic and wrestling show in 1913. American Exposition Shows and Sibley's Superb Shows advertised their "wrestling arenas." And how could a customer pass up the wrestling challenge issued by strongmen alongside trained bears at Elks Indoor Circus in 1910 in Canton, Ohio?

The symbiotic relationship got tighter when wrestlers started operating AT shows on their own, using them as a proving ground for young talent. James Strates, an immigrant from Greece, started wrestling in 1918 in carnivals and small venues along New York state's southern tier as "Young Strangler Lewis." In 1923, Strates used his wrestling savings and borrowed money to purchase a carnival with an AT show; in the winter, he used some of the same wrestlers while working as matchmaker in Elmira, New York. "The thing about Jimmy Strates is he knew his boxing and he knew his wrestling. So he had some quality on his show," said Frankie Cain, who worked with him for years. Gust Karras, another

Fans flock to an old-time carnival athletic show operated by veteran Jimmy Demetral.

Greek immigrant, was twenty-one when he started wrestling on AT shows; his performance on the World Bros. carnival was as well received as the showcase attraction of lions and pumas, the Macon, Missouri, newspaper reported in 1923. Karras moved into promoting and established Gust Karras' Greater Shows carnival in Kansas and Missouri.

The biggest name on AT shows was Nazworthy, a collegiate wrestler at Oklahoma A&M (now Oklahoma State) in 1935–36. He wrestled as a pro in Oklahoma and Texas but spent most of his time latching his AT shows on to the carnivals. Monroe bounced around a couple of AT shows as a boxer and wrestler — a combination man, in carny lingo — before settling in with Nazworthy in the 1940s. "Nobody had the kind of action, the banners, and stuff that Nazworthy had. It was all top-notch, first class," Monroe told historian Scott Teal in *Whatever Happened To . . . ?* "He'd just play the big spots; the state fairs and rodeos . . . We went to New

Mexico, Colorado, Wyoming, Montana, North Dakota, South Dakota, Nebraska, Oklahoma."

In some carnivals, two wrestlers squared off, usually for an audience that placed bets on who would win or lose. A born hellraiser like Monroe might stir the pot by cruising the carnival midway for game. "We'd stand at the gate and find a big sucker who looked like he might be able to fight. You'd whack him in the nose and then outrun him to the end where the AT show was," he said. More common was the bally and stick routine. The bally, short for ballyhoo, referred to the platform from which a barker would taunt the crowd and offer cash to anyone who dared to stay with a grappler for a given amount of time. The price of admission: usually twenty-five to fifty cents. "We stood up there on the bally and you had a guy hollering, 'Who wants to wrestle these fellows? Come up here and take your choice,'" remembered Rip Hawk, who started carnival wrestling in 1949 when he was nineteen. "I think they offered them twenty-five dollars or something to come up and wrestle one of the wrestlers. They had to stay with you five or ten minutes to get their twenty-five dollars, or it could have been fifty dollars. It was kind of shaky. You never knew what you were going to get up there."

That's where the stick came in. The stick was an ostensible audience member, secretly aligned with the AT show troupe. While the permutations were endless, often the stick would accept the challenge, get the crowd behind him, and darned near beat the wrestler. Case in point: Wicks traveled with carnivals in Minnesota with his good buddy Greg Peterson, an excellent wrestler who was a mite of a man at 160 pounds. "He would be the outside man. He was the stick," Wicks recalled years later. "If nobody came up to challenge me, Greg would. And we'd have a pretty competitive match. That got the big guys to thinking, 'Well, if this little squirt can do it, so can I.' You do it enough times, you make a little bit of money."

It was hard work, but you could do well for yourself. Gayland Shows, which ran circuses and carnivals in western Canada, recruited wrestler Tiger Tomasso to head its AT show. Tomasso reached out to

Parks, who'd been doing wrestling on local spot shows for a pittance — gas money here, beer money there. The big bucks, Parks found, rested with repeat carnival business — let his opponents think they had a legitimate shot at collecting the purse. "You'd beat him late or let him last and he'd say, 'Ah, I wanna make some more money.' 'No, you're too good. Get out of here.' The people say, 'Give him a chance.' 'Okay,' I say, 'double or nothing.' You'd fill up the tent again. I remember coming back with about three hundred, four hundred dollars in my pocket. That was really amazing."

From a storytelling perspective, there might not have been a better classroom than the carnival circuit, where young wrestlers learned how to work a crowd, think on their feet, make weaker opponents look like a million bucks, and defend themselves in tricky situations. There was always a blowhard or two, of course. Those were the easy ones to handle because tough as they might look, they seldom had the endurance to go the distance. "Most of the guys who wanted to challenge you were just drunk. In sixty seconds, they'd be tired and throwing up," said Sharkey, who operated carnival games as a kid before moving to the wrestling side of things. "That was a great experience. Young guys don't have that anymore. We'd get our ring time in and get paid a couple dollars for it, get used to the crowd."

Sometimes you had to take matters into your own hands. Monroe recalled a wild-eyed bull rider storming back and forth in front of the bally all night during a show in Cheyenne, Wyoming, declaring that he could lick anybody or anything. "Finally, about ten or eleven o'clock, it was getting cold and the people started to leave. I said, 'Normally, I don't box or wrestle derelicts or drunks, but since you think you're so tough, get up here,'" Monroe told historian Teal. "I whacked the guy and his leg went out. He went down and, as soon as he stood up, I hit him in the belly. From where I'm sitting, it's about twelve feet to my front door. That's how far that beer come out of him. It was like I tapped a wild keg. He went down and I told the referee to turn him over so he didn't drown in the beer."

Still, the tough guy braggart was the exception to the rule. Wicks estimated that he met sincere wrestlers, usually with an amateur background, in about eighty percent of the matches he fought during a five-year carnival run. He got to work with catch-as-catch-can legends like Henry Kolln and Doug Henderson, and the holds they passed on to him were instrumental in matches against wrestlers who knew what they were doing. "Say this local guy had some amateur background. You make a move. Then he makes a counter. Now you've got to make your counter. So I credit Henry Kolln and Henderson and these guys with teaching me top wrist-locks and side headlocks. I just can't imagine where I would have picked that up anywhere else," Wicks said. Nazworthy conducted wrestling classes every day, drawing on his college wrestling experience, then asked his men, such as Monroe, to practice the lessons. One week, a submission wristlock. One week, an escape known as a sit out. Wrestling on Strates' shows, the only railroad carnival left today in the United States, Cain picked up tips that he used for years to get himself out of tight spots. "On the AT show, I had a liver shot [boxer] Lou Bloom showed me. He showed me how to crossblock and parry a punch, and dip in, bend your knees and get the weight behind the punch and go to the liver," Cain said. "It would stop anybody in [their] tracks. So later on when somebody got fresh with me in the ring, I could use that."

Even as pros for Verne Gagne's American Wrestling Association, Sharkey and Harley Race occasionally sneaked into athletic shows. "I remember we had a match down there and the carnival manager gave us $175 a piece, which was an awful lot of money back in the early '60s," Sharkey said. "Verne never know about it, of course." In time, though, the bally and the stick became museum pieces. The purses for arena wrestling grew, and state athletic commissions cast a suspicious eye at an endeavor that operated without wrestler licensing, medical tests, and a ringside physician. Parks, who forged a long career as a pro and the industry's top maker of title belts, lamented the loss of the AT shows: "It was a great ride. I loved it.

I learned more than all the years I went to school. It was like being streetwise."

II. The Greatest Training Camp Ever

Jim Brunzell gave football everything he had, but football didn't return the favor. Brunzell played split end at the University of Minnesota from 1968 to 1970, spent a year with a semipro team, and then wrangled an invite to a Washington Redskins training camp in spring 1972. He spent $200 and traveled 2,000 miles, only to find himself in a muddy slog with eighty-one other prospective receivers. Three pass routes, a forty-yard dash, and the Redskins sent him home. But the competitive fires burned deeply. In addition to the gridiron, Brunzell had been a champion high jumper in high school at White Deer Lake, Minnesota, and continued his track and field career in college. Maybe there was something else he could do. Maybe wrestling.

So it was that Brunzell found himself in a frigid barn, floor coated with chicken waste, hay bales to the side, doing thousands of Hindu squats, jumping jacks, and push-ups until he thought lying down in the crap might not be such a bad option. Then Verne Gagne, the American Wrestling Association owner and icon, came in and rode the twenty-three-year-old trainee like a rented mule. "Basically, I had no idea what I was getting into, other than I thought, 'Well, I might as well continue something athletic; I can't make it in football,'" Brunzell said.

The days of learning to wrestle on the carnival circuit were over. Time to man up, and puke, while you were at it. The first wrestling training schools, the forerunners of today's advanced academies, had become the classroom for budding wrestlers, and nowhere was that more evident than in Gagne's dusty barn twenty miles west of Minneapolis. It was "a charm school with reverse English," quipped Minneapolis *Star-Tribune* sportswriter Larry Batson.

Gagne, who built the AWA and usually held its world championship, had been driving would-be grapplers into the ground for years at his property near Eden Prairie. Larry Heiniemi, later to earn fame as Lars Anderson, came to Gagne in June 1965 directly from St. Cloud State University. He'd placed third in the national AAU Greco-Roman championship and the national small college wrestling tournament that spring. Then he met his match. "I'd go out training at the farm in Gagne's barn and come home and sit down and I'd be crawling on my hands and knees trying to get to the bathtub to warm my body up," Heiniemi said.

In all, the paths of nearly 150 pro wrestlers passed through Gagne's barn. But nothing matched the productivity of the class of 1972. Ken Patera was the nation's premier Olympic weightlifter. Brunzell and Greg Gagne, son of Verne, were college football players while Bob Bruggers was an NFL linebacker. Khosrow Vaziri, the future Iron Sheik, was a skilled Greco-Roman wrestler. A tagalong named Richard Fliehr would become one of the sport's biggest celebrities. The roll call: five eventual world singles or tag team champions and two WWE Hall of Famers. "Verne had a good feel for talent," said Greg Gagne. "When people came into the camp, he made it hard on them at first. He'd have forty, fifty, maybe one hundred guys there for a tryout and when you'd get done, you'd have about two left."

Recruitment for the camp began in the fall of 1970. Patera was in Minneapolis visiting his brother Jack, an assistant coach with the Minnesota Vikings, after taking a bronze medal in the world weightlifting championships. When Patera expressed an interest in pro wrestling, Jack sent him downtown to AWA headquarters. Gagne looked him over and decided to invest in Team Patera, even at the risk of jeopardizing his amateur status. "Back then, American athletes were true amateurs to the core. So I got a deal with Verne where he'd help me out a hundred bucks a week. A hundred bucks a week back in 1971 was a lot of money," Patera said.

Along the way, Patera picked up a housemate — Fliehr, a prep school wrestling champion in Wisconsin, hardcore pro wrestling fan, and fellow bouncer at a Minneapolis nightclub. "Ric's problem was that he turned that place into an Animal House and I was training for the Pan-American Games and the Olympic Games. Well, every night after closing hour, 'We're having a big party at our house!' Next thing we know, there's twenty, thirty, sometimes forty people in that place . . . He was the 'Nature Boy' way before he started wrestling," Patera said. After the Olympics, but before the camp opened, Patera advocated for Fliehr as a potential pupil for Gagne. "Verne decided to let Ric come on board. At first, he wasn't going to. He felt he already had enough guys for training camp. But he let Ric in."

The six-week camp started in October and ran through December, mostly under the tutelage of Gagne and veteran Billy Robinson. From the outset, it was unlike anything the athletes had encountered. A typical five- or six-hour day might start at 10 a.m. with a half-mile jog along a makeshift trail and then proceed to nonstop calisthenics. Besides 200 push-ups, 200 sit-ups, and endless jumping jacks and neck bridges, the class worked up to an incredible ten sets of 100

PHOTO BY JOHN CROFT, COPYRIGHT 1973, *STAR TRIBUNE*

Under the eye of Verne Gagne (r) and Billy Robinson, Ken Patera picks up Bob Bruggers for a suplex during a 1972 pro wrestling training camp at Gagne's unheated barn.

freestanding Hindu squats. "That's 1,000 Hindu squats a day," Brunzell said. "My legs got bigger than they've ever been. You were sore the entire first week."

It was an awakening for Bruggers, twenty-eight, who played college football at Minnesota and was a veteran of five NFL training camps with the Miami Dolphins and San Diego Chargers. None of those compared with what Gagne cooked up. "He worked our butts off. I ended up in better shape than when I'd just gotten out of football," he said. Vaziri, the oldest of the group at thirty, was the lone exception. "In between whatever discipline we'd be performing, we'd all be laying in the ring. We didn't want to lay on the barn floor because it was all full of chicken shit and everything else," Patera added. "The Sheik didn't stop. He'd be doing jumping jacks, he'd be doing Hindu squats — for six straight hours, the man never stopped. He made us tired just watching him."

Ah, the chicken crap. Part of luxury, the Gagne way. "You'd look up and you'd see birds flying around, pooping all the over place," Brunzell said. Since the camp took place in an unheated barn, wrestlers sucked in cold air with each grunt and groan. Greg Gagne remembers wearing full sweats and a stocking cap in the ring. "It would be ten, fifteen degrees in that barn in the winter, you'd start shivering, and by the time you got back in the ring, you felt like one of those cartoon characters . . . like you were going to crack into pieces," he recalled. The wooden barn slats had loosened with age, so anytime a snowstorm passed through, it left drifts more appropriate for mukluks than wrestling boots. "You just had to keep moving, running in place, anything, or you'd freeze," Patera said.

It was almost too much for Fliehr, who was a no-show one day. "We were in about our third week in the camp when Ric decided he was going to quit," Greg Gagne said. "Verne left Billy [Robinson] with us and took off. Ric tells the story, he called him out of the house and when he came out, he knocked Ric on his ass. He said, 'You're not quitting wrestling. Get back in there. You have too much potential.'"

There was no character development, no dramatic interpretation in Gagne's camp. The majority of the ringwork consisted of running the ropes, getting a feel for the canvas, and learning how to spread the impact of falls across the entire body. "I very quickly found out the benefits of chiropractic," Brunzell said. "You'd take bumps and your back or your hip would get out of whack. If you went to a medical doctor, he'd just tell you to rest. That was not an option with us. I wound up really appreciating chiropractic." In one drill, the crew lined up to meet Robinson, who would turn each man on his back and challenge him to escape. In his autobiography *To Be the Man*, Fliehr said he kept shuffling around so Brunzell, who stood behind him, would have to meet Robinson first. "I'd spend the whole time thinking how can I get Brunzell in front of me? It was that bad," Flair wrote. By the end of the camp, though, it was clear that Flair was the star. "He was like a little minnow who jumped into the water and became a big whale. It gave him an opportunity to express himself," Brunzell said.

Except for Greg Gagne, who was recovering from an illness, everyone was a pro by December 1972. Seasoned vets like Tinker Todd, Johnny Heidemann, and Dennis Stamp came into the AWA to teach the newbies ring psychology in preliminary matches. In fact, no one sat down and actually explained the trade secrets behind the novices' new occupation. Flair kept wondering when Gagne would reveal how wrestlers simulated realism without injuring them-selves. "But everybody was so serious that I didn't dare ask one of the trainers; in fact, I didn't even discuss it with the other guys," he said. Added Brunzell, "They really didn't smarten me up until the day before my first match. It was like, 'Now you've done this; now here is what you need to do to be able to protect yourself and work with one another.'"

Gagne didn't run the camp for free; it was a long-term invest-ment. He paid Brunzell $300 a week during the camp and in return got ten percent of "Jumping" Jim's earnings for the next five years. "I repaid him and thousands beyond that," Brunzell said. By contrast,

Patera said he stopped paying Gagne's cut when he was wrestling in Shreveport, Louisiana, for $45 a match. "So Verne was supposedly going to get four and a half bucks. I showed the deal to a judge down at a gym there and he said there was no way it was enforceable, it was so one-sided."

Only Bruggers fell short of long-term main event status. In October 1975, he and Flair were in a plane crash en route to Wilmington, North Carolina. The accident ended Bruggers' career; Flair broke his back in three places but recovered to become a legend in the game. Meanwhile, Gagne continued to recruit prospective talent. Richard Blood, better known as Ricky Steamboat, showed up in 1974. "At the end of the first week, there were four of us; twelve had quit. Verne got his thousand dollars up front from each guy; of course, you had to pay a thousand bucks up front . . . and then at the end of the camp we had to pay him another thousand. There were four of us left at the end." Three years later, powerlifter Paul Ellering went through the torture, re-roofing Gagne's barn in his off hours to fulfill his debt. "It was just every day, we'd beat each other up, and then they'd beat you up, and we'd stand there and body slam each other for an hour straight," he said. "You've heard guys talk about paying their dues and that's what we did."

Under pressure from Vince McMahon's World Wrestling Federation, the AWA folded in 1991. By then it was clear that Gagne's training approach was a relic, as character-based wrestlers replaced talent-based wrestlers. A catchphrase, a superhuman physique, or an outlandish behavior became more important than the ability to execute a series of arm drags. Even with the chickens and the birds and the snow and the trips to the chiropractor, that represented a net loss for the profession, Brunzell thought. "It taught me respect for the business. They made it so darned hard, but they did it so that if you didn't want to be a pro wrestler, you'd quit."

III. Six Degrees of Keirn

When he started prepping for wrestling in the early 1970s, Steve Keirn hoped every playing card was a low number, like the two of clubs. Why? Because Hiro Matsuda, one of his trainers in Tampa, Florida, brought a deck of cards to practice, flipped them face up, and directed students to perform the specified number of squats. "My sister could have beaten me when I was done with just the squats," Keirn groaned years later. But that was not all. Push-ups, neck bridges, and running followed, then noted hardass Karl Gotch worked over trainees on the mat. When Keirn returned home after an arduous day of training, his mom saw the mat burns on his face. 'I thought wrestling was fake,' she said. I said, 'I did too. I don't know what I'm learning. But it's not what I'm seeing on TV.'"

Keirn never forgot that old-school attitude toward newbie wrestlers. When he started to share his knowledge, he knew that being stretched and beaten in a dark Florida gym, though it taught him respect for the business, was not the be all and end all. So when he started churning out future superstars from his Florida Championship Wrestling territory for Vince McMahon's WWE, he and his team of trainers knew a broader approach was in order. "Vince sat me down and said, 'Steve, you can't give me a good wrestler in one or two years. What I want you to give me is good people. I want good people in my business, I want good people representing the WWE.' So my job was not to go out and teach you movement because to me movement is not what made you. It's emotion," Keirn said.

Florida Championship Wrestling was the next step in the evolution of wrestling training from the carnival circuit and an unheated Minnesota barn. Like Ohio Valley Wrestling, Deep South Wrestling, Heartland Wrestling Association, and others in the 1990s and 2000s, FCW was more than a makeshift ring and some ropes. It was an actual promotion that offered regular local TV exposure, experience on small shows, and the shoptalk that comes with watching mile markers tick by. "They had to come to the building, FCW, for wrestling. Then they had to get in the car and drive forty-five minutes to an hour over to [the gym]," said Tom Prichard, head trainer at FCW for several years. "That means they had to get in their car, catch a ride with somebody, get a bite to eat, had to go train, had to come back, so in that car ride, what are you talking about? Wrestling. Then they would have to travel the towns, spot shows, get in the car, set up the ring, and take the ring down. That was great."

Keirn had the background to merge the old school with the new as wrestling's version of Six Degrees of Kevin Bacon, the name game connecting the actor to other Hollywood stars. "I'm kind of like the Kevin Bacon of wrestling. If you haven't worked with me, haven't been in a wrestling school with me, or if you haven't been on a card with me, you probably haven't been in wrestling," Keirn said in 2018 when the Cauliflower Alley Club honored him with its Trainer's Award. A wrestling fan growing up in Tampa, Keirn became friends with Florida promoter Eddie Graham's son Mike at Robinson High School. Others at the school included Dick Slater, Austin Idol, and Hulk Hogan. Eddie Graham took an interest in Keirn, giving him part-time jobs from working at a youth camp to picking up the likes of Harley Race and the Funk brothers at the airport. "Eddie didn't let you walk in front door until he felt confident you not only loved this industry but you'd fight for it," Keirn said.

The career-defining moment for Keirn as a wrestler came in 1982 when Tennessee promoter Jerry Jarrett married the new — rock videos, quick cuts, flashy outfits — with the old, bringing in the legendary Jackie Fargo to give his blessing to the Fabulous Ones tag team of Keirn and Stan Lane. Six years of magic followed until Keirn returned to Florida and Lane went to the Midnight Express with Bobby Eaton and manager Jim Cornette. Keirn's run as a Fab also was the beginning of his training career. With Jarrett's approval, Keirn placed a small ad in the Tennessee wrestling program soliciting clients, asking them to send in a picture along with their age, weight, and pertinent stats.

COURTESY PETE LEDERBERG COLLECTION

Mike Graham and Steve Keirn were high school friends.

"I got a post office box for the address and we'd go by there so excited on the way out of town for road trips, every day. Sometimes we'd have twenty, thirty letters in there," he said, remembering one prospect who was four-foot-eleven, weighed 110, and sent along a picture from his driver's license. "To me, it was funny at first and then I looked back and thought this guy must be really passionate about being in the wrestling business," he said.

Keirn's first school had twenty-four students; one of them was eventual pro Tracy Smothers. For all that he knew about pro wrestling, Keirn said he was still learning how to teach. He did understand he didn't want to inflict the punishment he received from Matsuda and company, dishing out beatings, and daring pupils to walk out the door and never return. Things were different in Tennessee; the angles were faster, looser, and often goofier. An anecdote sums up the mindset: walking down the hall, Jarrett put his arm around Keirn, sharing advice. Keirn took Jarrett's arm off and draped his own around his boss. Jarrett wondered why. "Eddie Graham taught me this," Keirn told him. "He said, 'If you're taking me to the cliff to push me off, I'm dragging your ass with me.'" Marrying the openness he picked up in Tennessee with the tradition and respect he learned in Florida and other promotions, like always wiping your feet on the apron before entering the ring, Keirn struck the right chord for the times. While his wrestling career continued post-Fabs, Keirn ran his School of Hard Knocks — "not an original name, but I thought it fit" — in Florida. Some young men came in as raw wannabes who needed to be taught and built up from scratch, such as Dennis Knight and future ECW world champ Mike Awesome. Others didn't seem suited for professional wrestling, like a young Dallas Page, who would later revisit his wrestling dream at World Championship Wrestling's Power Plant.

Keirn's relationship with McMahon and the WWE goes back to his early days when he competed for the WWE junior heavyweight and NWA international junior heavyweight championships. He took a break from teaching in 1991 to become the alligator-chasing Skinner in WWE (then WWF), which paved the way for some time on the road behind the scenes as an agent. FCW became the federation's official developmental territory in 2007, and McMahon set a goal. "Steve, if you can give me two new talent per year, I'll be happy," he said. More than a hundred came through and made the big-league roster. "Not everybody stayed, not everybody fit in," Keirn admitted. "The secret was that I knew what they needed. You need to be in front of a live audience. You've got to get a certain amount of experience in a gym, but the rest? You need to go out there and find out why you can't swim and why you can. And if you can keep the audience interested in your match and you're not going to freak out, then that's time to learn. Your real learning lesson is in the ring."

In the early days of Keirn's school, it was rudimentary, but by the end, it was not all that different from what would become the WWE's Performance Center in Orlando: modern rings, a video system to watch and critique matches, and a training staff that included Norman Smiley, Bill DeMott, Billy Kidman, Ricky Steamboat, Joey Mercury, and others at various times. Yes, there was conditioning and backdrops, but there also was psychology, character development, and microphone skills taught by the inimitable Dusty Rhodes. "We did make storytelling a priority. We explained that you had to have a beginning, a middle, and an end," Tom Prichard said. "We did that in practice and Dream was the best storytelling on promos and vignettes and things like that. In the matches, we stressed having a beginning, a middle, and lead up to the finish."

One product of that inclusive strategy? Thaddeus Bullard, who walked in Keirn's door in 2009 armed with a national college football championship at the University of Florida, time in the NFL and Arena League, and the encouragement of his neighbor Dave Bautista. Bullard simply asked Keirn, "Who do I need to see to get trained?" Following a fifteen-minute conversation, Keirn knew and told his boss John Laurinaitis, who headed the WWE talent relations

Steve Keirn is honored for his work as a trainer by the Cauliflower Alley Club.

department. "He had the athleticism, but there was no connection to wrestling. His body was the only tool he brought to the ring," Keirn told the *Tampa Bay Times* not long after Bullard started making big waves as Titus O'Neil in WWE.

In 2012, Triple H (Paul Levesque) informed Keirn that WWE was not going to renew the contract with FCW. Keirn hugged him. "I was so burned out," he said. With Triple H's dream of a centralized developmental complex and the accompanying NXT promotion in Orlando, Keirn opted out; he didn't want to move across the state. Keirn said he was happy to watch the wrestlers he helped along the way, whether it was polishing Natalya for the WWE or instructing Alberto Del Rio how to work from the left side of the body, not the right side as is done in his native Mexico. "I'd like to take credit for everybody that's said that I taught 'em, but I can't do that, because I know the truth. The truth is I gave them a basic knowledge and a concept, plus I gave them manners. I taught them manners and humility," he said. "This is the most humbling business you can be in, but if you're not humble, a lot of people aren't going to like you. If somebody you work against doesn't like you, they can ruin your career."

Voices of the Game

Introduction

Fans might have wondered what the truck and cables were doing outside of Brooklyn's Ridgewood Grove Athletic Club on November 16, 1939. New York's experimental NBC station W2XBS, which had been running boxing shows on Saturday night, was about to test a broadcast of something else — wrestling. Veteran boxing announcer Sam Taub was behind the microphone as Bobby Bruns went to a draw with Michele Leone in the main event. Though the details are lost to history, Taub apparently approached the telecast tongue in cheek. "Sam Taub deserves a plug for his amusing commentary on the wrestling matches delivered from the ringside," *Brooklyn Daily Eagle* media columnist Jo Ranson wrote. "Kidding wrestling is the only way to do it on television and that Taub did excellently." It was the first wrestling show broadcast over the airwaves and it changed the business forever. In February 1940, W2XBS patched together the inaugural out-of-town hookup, enabling viewers of WJZ in Schenectady, 130 miles to the north, to watch grappling on their TV sets. In Hollywood, W6XYZ showed a strip of news, interviews, comics, and wrestling in a one-hour block on Friday nights. Dick Lane typically handled serious interviews with wartime workers shifting to a peacetime footing and then called the action between Rube Wright and "Wee" Willie Davis. "Occasionally," *Billboard* noted, "Lane would integrate plugs with his regular patter, comparing a hold with the power of a Ford."

"TV found the perfect vehicle in this constant, flying-around action that was perfect for the small screen television and wrestling did change to accommodate it," said Ted Lewin, one-third of the famous Lewin brothers. "People no longer laid in holds for twenty minutes. There had to be a lot of moving around and a lot of flying and acrobatics to keep people's interests. I think they kind of grew up together."

Sam Taub was behind the mike when wrestling first appeared on TV.

I. The First Storyteller

When Dennis James walked into the Jamaica Arena in Queens, New York, on November 8, 1946, he had never seen a professional wrestling match. But at the ripe young age of twenty-nine, the New Jersey native had been in TV since 1938, so he knew he needed some familiarity with the event he was to call for WABD, a DuMont Network station. At a local bookstore, James picked up a volume authored by Frank Gotch, a champion of the early 1900s, which included twenty-nine instructional plates on wrestling holds. He went on the air with the book at his side, a CliffsNotes for calling the grunt-and-groan action. "I learned as I worked," James explained. "There I'd be at ringside, looking up at the wrestlers in action and then I'd glance down at the illustrations in Gotch's book. 'Why, sure enough,' I'd say to myself, 'there it is, just like in the book — a hammerlock.' And then, like a real authority, I'd announce to the TV audience, 'Folks, there you see a beautiful hammerlock.'"

If James was learning, so too was his audience, which grew from a few thousand at the outset to millions by the time he concluded his wrestling run in 1952. "James was just another struggling TV announcer who was told to go out and do the commentary on the telecasting of the wrestling matches from Jamaica Arena," wrote King Features columnist Mel Heimer. "He did as he was told — and did it so entertainingly that he fashioned an enormous personal reputation and he made wrestling so fashionable on TV that to this day it seems to be on the screen any time you look."

In fact, at one point, you couldn't turn on the TV without seeing a flying dropkick. At various points between October 1948 and March 1952, the DuMont Network ran wrestling on Monday, Thursday, Friday, and/or Saturday. ABC showed Wednesday night matches from the Rainbo Arena in Chicago for six years. NBC and CBS got in

COURTESY JAMES FAMILY

Broadcasting pioneer Dennis James was the voice of wrestling during the early days of television.

the game too. But James was wrestling's first national voice, an audience demographer, and a one-man special effects department. He was "the monster's high priest," as *Pageant* magazine dubbed him.

Born Demie James Sposa on August 24, 1917, James planned to go into medicine but switched his career path when he fell in love with theatrics and performance at St. Peter's College. He started out at a radio station in his home of Jersey City, New Jersey, before moving to a disc jockey slot at WNEW in New York. Given the embryonic state of the industry, he was taking a gamble when he hooked up in 1938 as on-air talent for Allen B. DuMont's experimental TV station. "There were only about 300 sets in New York at the time and 200 of them didn't work," he joked in 1951. James' first brush with wrestling cost him a chunk of change when he hosted a group of nine men led by 300-pound Man Mountain Dean on a TV show. The gig paid James twenty-five dollars a week. "It cost me $100 a week to feed the guests on the sports show," James said. "Six of those nine were wrestlers. How they could eat!" During World War II, James had a three-year absence from the airwaves; he produced, directed, and emceed shows for troops before returning to the expanding DuMont Network.

Initially, the audience for those first wrestling shows was tiny — only about 7,000 sets were in use in the entire country in 1946 when James called his first main event of Primo Carnera versus Milo Steinborn. But he had a major advantage that today's broadcasters would envy — no competition. "It was early in TV's career and no other station was on the air during wrestling time. I had 100 percent audience. What guy in show business could ask for more?" he said. Audience analytics were in their infancy, yet James had a keen sense of who was watching wrestling and how to increase the numbers. From the start, he targeted female viewers, a demographic that wrestling promoters would pursue with various ploys for the next half century. James understood that watching pro wrestling amounted to a guilty pleasure. Men could downplay their interest in it by simply explaining that they were watching what their spouses wanted to see. "When a member of the male sex talks to a wrestler or one of us connected with the sport, he never says, 'I love wrestling.' With his eyes sparkling and a big grin on his face, he says, 'Boy, oh boy, my wife goes crazy over wrestling,'" James wrote in *Billboard* in January 1949.

So James marketed his commentary to the mother of the family. "In those days, there was only one television in the house. By gearing his comments toward women, it made them feel included. And it made the husband look like the hero," his son Brad James said. "If my father said, 'Hey mother, that hold is called a hammerlock,' he knew the wife would turn to her husband and say, 'Is he right, dear; is that a hammerlock?' To which the husband could confidently say, 'Yes dear, it is.' It made everyone a winner." The strategy paid big dividends. Appreciative women brought him pies, darned socks for him, and brandished signs imploring "Save Dennis" at a TV match after wrestler George Lenihan hoisted James by his lapels and hurled him to the floor. In October 1950, *Business Week* magazine attributed a surge in wrestling viewership and arena attendance mainly to women. "If your grandmother can tell a right cross from a right hook, and our mother can distinguish between a half-nelson and a hammerlock, the chances are they have been pupils of Dennis James," concluded Jack Tell of the *New York Times*. The emphasis on the fairer sex paid off for James, as well. He spun off the concept into a hit daytime show aimed at women called *Okay, Mother* that featured games, stories, and prizes.

Gotch's book on holds wasn't the only aid at James' side. Early on, he realized he couldn't call wrestling matches with a straight face, though he was ultra-careful never to suggest that they were orchestrated. From Abercrombie & Fitch's pet department, he purchased a rubber dog bone with steel bands inside that crackled when twisted. A perfect audio accompaniment, he thought, when a wrestler wrenched an arm or a leg. He dug up a slide whistle for when wrestlers tossed one another out of the ring. If a grappler ripped at his opponent's trunks, James tore a window shade. And when his subject went flying high, James played a cadenza on a harmonica. "After a few bouts I knew wrestling wasn't meant to be taken seriously but I also knew I'd better not get too cute for two reasons — the fans get mighty zealous and the wrestlers themselves don't look kindly on us kidders," he said. In fact, Ted Tourtas and "Dangerous" Danny McShain conspired one night to silence James' party favors in New York's Columbia Park. "I told Danny, 'If you get a chance, throw me at the son of a bitch, or I'll throw you at the son of a bitch.' He won the tossup, so I had to throw Danny at Dennis," Tourtas said. "At the appropriate time, I took Danny up and threw him at him. His equipment was on the floor, transistors on top of him. The match was over and we went in the dressing room, here comes Dennis, limping in there. 'What are you guys trying to do, kill me?' I said, 'I didn't want to kill you, Dennis. I wanted to kill that nutcracker!'"

James' penchant for talking in rhyme got him in hot water with Frank "Tarzan" Hewitt. "Look at the suet on Hewitt," James told his audience, referring to the wrestler's ample midsection. Backstage, Hewitt took exception, grabbing James and ordering him to cease and desist from the obesity references. "Mr. Hewitt was kidding so much it still hurts my bones when I think about it," James recalled more than a decade later. "He got me in a hammerlock — right then, believe me, I really knew what a hammerlock was — and he said, 'Listen, you, say anything you want about me but never mind that Hewitt-suet business or else." Comical, yes, but there was a serious side to things. James asked the public one night to say a prayer for the son of wrestler Gino Garibaldi when the boy was hospitalized with suspected polio. "From that point on, he could do no wrong as far as Gino was concerned," James' assistant Sam Laine told TV historian Jeff Kisseloff. And though he favored tongue-in-cheek commentary, James never exposed the business. Fake, staged, worked, predetermined . . . he shrugged it all off. That was not the point. James always extended respect to his subjects, silly as they might be. "He never mocked wrestling or put it down.

He said he always referred to it as 'entertainment' and never would say it was fake or rigged," said his son Brad, a communications executive in Los Angeles. "The same was true of game shows. He never made a disparaging comment about them."

Network TV moved on from wrestling by 1954, and James moved on to game shows, TV shows, movies, variety specials, commercials, his own production company, and a spot on the Hollywood Walk of Fame before his death from lung cancer on June 3, 1997, in Palm Springs, California. Nothing matched his support for the United Cerebral Palsy Foundation. He hosted annual telethons for forty-seven years, helping to raise more than $700 million. The national organization honored him as Humanitarian of the Year in 1965. The Dennis James United Cerebral Palsy Center in Cathedral City, California, is named for wrestling's first TV storyteller. "Sometimes I think I was lucky to escape without bodily injury," he reflected in 1962. "Looking back, I can only say it was a ball."

II. The Professor

For more than forty years, Bill Mercer helped train broadcasters as a professor at the University of North Texas in Denton. But there was no one around to teach him when he was assigned to ringside to call wrestling matches from the City Auditorium in Muskogee, Oklahoma — on radio. Growing up there, he didn't remember attending matches and pro wrestling wasn't a part of his three years in the U.S. Navy in the South Pacific as World War II ended. He suspected he might have seen wrestling once on TV while going through Chicago. So what was a recent grad from the University of Denver, early in his career at KMUS, to do?

"I went down and the promoter was just great in Muskogee and he taught me. I met 'Wild' Red Berry, Danny McShain, and they showed me the holds," recalled Mercer, who jotted notes as his new instructors spoke. "I fumbled around with the legal pad at my side

"Wild" Bill Irwin takes Dallas announcer Bill Mercer for a ride.

for the first bouts. I would talk with wrestlers before we'd go on the air and get some other ideas. But nobody ever told me how to broadcast it or what to say or anything. I guess they just thought I'd do a simple job and that would be okay. But I got into it; I really liked it." But "Bill Mercer" did not call the action in Muskogee. Gardo Plutnik described the bouts. That was Mercer under a *nom de radio* created by the literary, artsy engineer at the station, who looked down on wrestling and considered Mercer's future. "'Why did you call me Gardo Plutnik?' He said, 'Oh, I don't think you want to be known for this.'"

Quite the contrary. As the voice of Dallas-based Big Time Wrestling and later World Class Championship Wrestling, Mercer brought impeccable credentials that would earn him recognition as far away as Israel. After wrestling left the national airwaves in the 1950s, regional TV picked up the slack with each territory having its own broadcaster, who became as closely identified with the promotion as a local football or baseball announcer. Mercer knew all about those roles too, as play-by-play man for the Dallas Cowboys, Texas Rangers, Chicago White Sox, and North Texas State. As a newsman, he covered the assassination of President Kennedy for KRLD, the Dallas CBS-TV affiliate. "Bill Mercer gave a lot of credibility to World Class Championship Wrestling, and he was an asset to the show," manager Gary Hart, his friend and on-air nemesis, wrote in his autobiography.

Mercer moved from Oklahoma to Dallas and KRLD in 1953 because of wrestling. "They wanted somebody to do wrestling live on Tuesday nights. All the stuff you try to prepare for, and you never know what's going to happen. I don't know if I'd ever gotten out of Muskogee if it hadn't been for wrestling." It wasn't long before he took his first big bump, courtesy of Bull Curry. Mercer was ringside, doing the radio side on a card for KRLD at the Sportatorium with another announcer handling TV. "Bull Curry was running around and had been disqualified, if I recall. He gets out on the apron. Well, I'm sitting right at the edge of the ring, right below the apron. He's running up and down, slamming against the ropes. He's running around and people are screaming. All of sudden, he looks down and I'm looking up, and he kicks me in the face. My first thought was 'Oh, I hope I didn't say some bad word.' But I was just stunned." Mercer later filed a complaint with KRLD to get compensation. "It was kind of just a joke. They said, 'Well, we can't give you any bonus money for being kicked in the face. It was part of your job.'"

Mercer wasn't in Dallas the entire time; he called White Sox games for six seasons before returning in 1976. But he was there for the groundbreaking run of the Von Erich boys in the early 1980s and the equally innovative work of the television production crew. With his day job offering an introduction to developing technology, Mercer was able to capitalize as broadcasting changed, especially in pro wrestling. Things that fans today take for granted, like a close-up shot, weren't always standard. The routine was to have a wide shot and a medium shot from cameras bolted in place for stability and maybe a third camera for interviews. Mercer saw his students tinkering with new, less cumbersome handheld cameras. When KXTX took over the weekly wrestling show and invested in even better equipment, professional wrestling broadcasting changed for the better. Two cameramen roamed ringside to the annoyance of the stars. "It bothered the wrestlers at first," Mercer said, adding that they discussed signals to indicate they were ready for their close-ups. "We ran a show and did it and they realized how great it was to show their muscles and good looks. They realized quickly, 'Oh man, this is going to make us look great.'"

The mobility helped with more than just the ringside action. World Class became known for its colorful segments that furthered storylines and bolstered already outsized personalities. "You get these sidebar things like we made and you really get to see them away from the ring and how they are somewhat the same, but not the same," Mercer said. "I thought that was one of the really selling features of World Class, plus the production." There were filmed lunches with Mercer and the Fabulous Freebirds, who always stuck him with the bill, and a trip to "Gorgeous" Jimmy Garvin's home, where valet/wife Precious answered the door in a black negligee. Mercer took another bump hunting for Kamala, the Ugandan Giant, in weeds along the Trinity River. "I'm out there giving this spiel about looking for Kamala and all of a sudden, he comes crashing through there. It wasn't intended, but he bumped into me, and I was off balance and fell over into this pile of weeds on my back. He was just mortified, afraid that he'd hurt me. We stopped the cameras and he came over. He was just so upset about it. I said, 'Hey, it was my fault. I was leaning or something.'" As "Freebird" Buddy Roberts concluded, "He was a good interviewer. He was with the program; he was very, very good. He did his job."

Mickey Grant from KXTX came up with much of the technical innovation, including adding microphones at ringside to hear more of the action and the roar of the crowd. Grant's Continental Productions syndicated World Class Championship Wrestling as well, meaning that the Von Erichs, Skandor Akbar, the Freebirds, and Mercer gained an international audience on Pat Robertson's Christian Broadcasting Network. "We were really big in Lebanon; the war would stop when we were on the air," Mercer said. "Businesses would shut down in Israel while World Class aired." Though WCCW promoter Fritz Von Erich wouldn't pay to take production to Israel, Mercer gained a measure of fame there anyway, as he learned years later at a wrestling convention in Charlotte, North Carolina. There, he was told that a woman from Israel had come from Chicago just to meet him. "I look up and here is obviously the woman, the Israeli, a very short, attractive lady, and she's just looking at me and smiling. I said, 'Are you . . . ?' and she said, 'Yeah,' and she came over and we hugged. We talked about how she watched it all the time and her mother thought she was going mad. It was so great to see her and touch somebody who had watched it over in Israel. It's like being there, and that was a great moment in my post-wrestling life."

Behind the scenes were the matchmakers and bookers like Red Bastien and Hart with their creative ideas and penchant for mischief. Hart called Mercer "The Professor" for obvious reasons, and Mercer dubbed him Simon Legree after the evil slave owner in Uncle Tom's Cabin. One of their most recounted bits was Mercer asking if the sneaky, streetwise manager from the streets of Chicago had ever matriculated. "Sure! Two or three times a week. In fact, I was just matriculating in the bathroom before I came out here for this interview," Hart shot back. "I tried not to laugh. I could hear in my ear, the guys were laughing in the truck," Mercer recalled. "So they broke us up."

Through it all, Mercer stayed out of production meetings and called wrestling without the preparation he'd devote to his baseball or football assignments. "I didn't know what was happening or what was going to happen. Maybe because I was a sports announcer, I could react quickly to that and understand it. That's what spontaneously came out," he said. His job as wrestling announcer for $100–$150 a shot wasn't to pass judgment. "I never put either side down. I just let it ride. I'm thinking, 'If they still believe all this is real, there's not a thing that I can do to change it and why should I want to?' Because we filled up the Sportatorium, everybody was having a great time, they liked it . . . they hated the right guys, they loved the good guys. It's not up to me, I'm just the announcer, I'm just the guy that's driving this, so let them make up their minds if they think it's real or not."

III. Return to the Front Lines

Like Captain America frozen in ice waking up decades later in a world he had trouble recognizing, Tony Schiavone walked to ringside to call the action for Major League Wrestling in April 2018, seventeen years after World Championship Wrestling shut down and put him out of a job. He'd gone cold turkey on pro wrestling. Like "Cap" Steve Rogers, he'd fought in the wrestling wars and was now faced with something completely different. "I think wrestling has changed a great deal since I did it last," Schiavone confessed, talking about violent hardcore action, nonstop high spots, and the fast pace. "I could see it was changing back when I was right at the end of WCW."

What he's referring to is how different professional wrestling is compared to his days as a fan in Virginia in the 1960s and 1970s, and as a young announcer for Jim Crockett Promotions, the Charlotte, North

Tony Schiavone.

Carolina–based promotion that had a national reach on superstation WTBS. Those were the days of regular enhancement talent matches, and it was equally important to talk about the fall guy, so the star could be seen as beating someone of consequence. There was a post-match interview to conduct or a taped segment of ranting and raving from the wrestlers promoting an upcoming match at the local arena.

That's all gone. With its collection of hungry grapplers on the way up the ladder to the big time, paired with a few names released from the onerous WWE schedule, MLW has been as good a place as any for Schiavone to play catch-up. Court Bauer ran MLW before joining WWE as a writer and, like Schiavone, found himself starting anew years later after he'd left the big company. Bauer convinced Schiavone to do a podcast, *What Happened When*, which debuted in January 2017, and then sold him on returning to TV for his monthly MLW TV taping for the beIN sports channel.

"I love his calls; it feels that he's calling a sport and that's part of the persona of this TV show we have, is Tony calling it like a sport," Bauer said. "He's not shilling; it's not so plastic. It feels warm and throwbacky." The action and move sets were a challenge at first. "We used to know what a suplex was and we used to know the brainbuster and Ric Flair's figure four, but now everybody's got a move; it's called something and you got to learn those," Schiavone said. Unlike the live *WCW Monday Nitro* broadcasts, though, there's an opportunity to fix things. Sitting at home in suburban Atlanta or in a hotel room while on the road with the Gwinnett Stripers of the Class AAA International League, Schiavone can rerecord any commentary and email it to be patched in. A trained ear, like his, can hear the difference, but fans would never know.

It's a long way from Radio 101 at James Madison University, where he spliced audiotape by hand. Schiavone's broadcasting career started in his college days, when he did play-by-play for high school football and basketball on WTON in Staunton, Virginia. After graduation, he became a minor league baseball announcer, handling the call for the Class A South Atlantic League Greensboro Hornets, followed by the Charlotte O's of the AA Southern League. That became his connection to wrestling. Jim Crockett Sr.'s daughter Frances Crockett was the team's general manager and hired Schiavone to do baseball before he drifted into the family's wrestling business.

Schiavone started with interviews and promo segments, and began sitting alongside David Crockett for NWA World Wide Wrestling in 1984. Ever interested in the backstage producing, Schiavone described the setup. "They had a truck; that's all they had when they videotaped their promos during the week," he said. "They didn't have a studio and everything was done live to tape. They didn't have an edit bay or they didn't have the edit suites."

Imagine the culture shock when he jumped to the WWF in April 1989, when he was thrown into the fray immediately, conducting interviews backstage with wrestlers at WrestleMania V. While many fans remember him from hosting duties on *WWF Wrestling Challenge* and *WWF Prime Time Wrestling*, he also was the play-by-play announcer for SummerSlam and the 1990 Royal Rumble. What most fans don't know was his role with Coliseum Video, where he was the producer shepherding concepts for tapes from start to finish, his team outfitted with better equipment than he'd ever seen. "I had an editor and basically any type of idea I had for a videocassette, budget-wise, they approved it," he said. "I was really letting my creative juices flow as the cliché goes and really, really enjoyed that work."

After his one-year contract was up, Schiavone jumped to WCW, which Turner Broadcasting had purchased when Crockett went belly-up. He immediately regretted the decision, but WWE owner Vince McMahon told him to make it work, that it wasn't fair to his wife Lois and their five young children to move yet again. "I was really distraught when I came back," Schiavone said. "I came to Turner and it was kind of just a step above the old Jim Crockett mom and pop organization that we had," he said. "It was not a good time for me that year."

There were plenty of highs and lows in WCW. For a time, Schiavone was the lead play-by-play announcer on the number one show on cable television, *WCW Monday Nitro*, which bested WWE's *Monday Night Raw* in the ratings for eighty-three consecutive weeks. The competition raised both companies, Schiavone said. "There's no way to recapture what we had back in the '90s because it was real live competition and we both benefited from it. And that's gone," he said. The lows were obvious to fans when the wheels came off and WCW began spiraling down, leading to its 2001 acquisition by WWE. "It got more and more exhausting for me and thus the fun element was out of it," he said.

As WCW became more corporate, it represented a far cry from the wrestling that had corralled a young Schiavone. "I grew up with [announcer] Bob Caudle from Mid-Atlantic Championship Wrestling, where they just put over the stars and told stories. They didn't have to promote about 'By the way, the pay-per-view is coming up this Saturday or make sure you watch *Monday Nitro* coming up this week.' They talked about the match and that was it. It made those guys seem bigger than life. So that's what I grew up on and that's the stuff that's magic in the business." Instead, in the late 1990s, there were always producers in his ear while he was live, telling him what to talk about, what to promote, and to show some emotion. "I never minded that. I still don't. I would rather them tell me what to say than to let me try to say it on my own and then afterwards say, 'Tony, we didn't want you to say it that way,'" he said. But the pressure grew as WCW fell behind WWE in the ratings and turned to hoopla and hype to make up the difference. Schiavone remembers producers and bookers exhorting him to show more enthusiasm. "I would have Ed Ferrara in my ear or Kevin Sullivan or I would have Terry Taylor in my ear, and I remember them saying 'You need to get more excited, you need to be more excited.' And I got to thinking to myself, 'I can't get more excited. I can't push it any more than I'm pushing it now.'"

To Schiavone, there was no better example of the shift from broadcaster to carnival barker than WCW's million-dollar giveaway in September 1999. He was in the announcer's dressing room in Miami with color man Bobby Heenan when WCW head Eric Bischoff revealed the big plan. "He says, 'I want you to promote during the course of the event tonight that one fan is going to be able to win a million dollars just by watching *Nitro*.' Then he paused for dramatic effect and I said, 'Oh, great.' And a rage flew out of him. He said, 'See that reaction right there? That's the kind of reaction I expect from you and you probably won't sell it the way I want to sell it,' and he stormed out of the room. So I looked at Heenan and I said, 'Okay, watch this.'" For most of the three-hour show, Schiavone hawked the million-dollar contest like a local radio DJ giving away tickets to a boat show. "A hip toss, yeah, but somebody is going to win a million dollars!" he joked. "Near the end of the show, I'm thinking, 'Boy, that sucked' . . . Then after the event Eric came up to me and said, 'I apologize; you did a hell of a job.' I'm thinking, 'But that was a shitty broadcast.' But that's what he wanted and again that's how wrestling announcing has evolved or changed through the years."

Schiavone was a producer on the afterthought program *WCW Saturday Night*, which filled the hallowed time slot of 6:05 p.m. on Saturday nights. It was a retro program in many ways, with superstars appearing only sporadically and mid-level talent being given a chance to shine as highlights from *Nitro* and *Thunder* filled up airtime. Schiavone worked on taking the product and storylines and making the show mean something in connection with the angles on WCW's other TV programs. "No one gave a damn about it except me, Arn Anderson, and Jimmy Hart," he lamented.

The "real" sports connection never left Schiavone, though, and he's done a myriad of different jobs, including hosting pre- and post-game Atlanta Braves radio broadcasts, working as a producer on the Georgia Bulldogs Radio Network for football games, and anchoring sports each morning on Atlanta's 92.9 The Game. "I love sports," he said, calling baseball games relaxing, especially compared with wrestling. Concerned with the demands placed on his vocal cords, Schiavone visited the Emory Voice Clinic in Atlanta to see a voice therapist. Upon hearing some *Nitro* clips, the doctor quipped, "You used to scream for a living!" As a result, it's a different Tony Schiavone than in the past. "I work on my voice all the time now so it's probably helped me out," he said. There's a warm-up session, and he has learned to pace himself. By his own admission, he is his own worst critic. Watching a MLW YouTube clip, he'll think, "Boy, that old man's voice is cracking."

Conrad Thompson, Schiavone's co-host on the *What Happened When* podcast, has had to deal with that insecurity. "He thinks I'm good every week, and he's bad every week," said Thompson, who met Schiavone through Flair, with whom Thompson once hosted a podcast. "He definitely lacks the confidence that we all would imagine that he has. I think, if I'm honest with you, that's what makes him so good."

After seventeen years in the wilderness — at least from the perspective of rasslin' fans — Tony Schiavone is back and happy. "His story's great," Bauer said. "How the modern era of wrestling revitalized him in many ways — the podcast and now back on weekly national TV. If you had asked him two years ago if this would happen, he'd be like, 'There's no way you could have gotten it into my head I would even do it, let alone be enjoying it.'"

Sideshows

Introduction

Since pro wrestling originated in the carnivals, it only made sense to bring the carnivals to pro wrestling. Terrifying creatures of the wild and little people all made the transition from the midway to the ring as promoters turned to special attractions to beef up lagging attendance, cultural sensitivity be damned. Take Ginger, a black bear that Reuben Ray trained to perform stunts at the World's Fair in Chicago in 1934. Ginger passed from Ray to a Tennessean service station owner named James Downing to wrestler/promoter Roy Welch, who paraded the bear around the South with a muzzle and a pair of specially made mittens. For a night's labor, Ginger got hard corn, a hamburger with onions, and a beer. That payoff wasn't much considering Ginger's ample skill level, which Associated Press sportswriter Will Grimsley compared favorably with a more established wrestler known for bursting into tears after a defeat. "The manner in which she groans and grimaces during a performance would make George Zaharias proud," he wrote.

When midget wrestling hit the U.S. airwaves in 1950, promoters and fans couldn't get enough of it, though in a less sensitive era, some of the writing about people of small stature might make today's readers cringe. "The bantam battlers have been gaining in popularity," syndicated columnist Omar Garrison wrote in admiration. "Several have achieved national prominence and have built

Ginger, one of the original wrestling bears, toys with a masked man under the direction of Pat Malone.

personal bankrolls that are in inverse ratio to their physical size." Whether the small wrestlers actually made more than a few bucks plying their trade from town to town every night is debatable. But the sideshows set a wrestling pattern that would hold for years, from the WWE push for Hornswoggle to a generation with a bent toward critters, such as Jake "The Snake" Roberts and his slithery pal Damien, or Koko B. Ware and his macaw Frankie.

I. The Monkey in the Ring

When it came to the wrestling game, Sambo gave new meaning to the term "monkey business." That's because Sambo was a thirty-pound chimpanzee who screeched at opponents, nipped at referees, entertained ringside fans, and coached his human, Trader O'Neill, in matches throughout the Southwest and Midwest. Referring to O'Neill, promoter Mike London once quipped, "I don't know how good he is. But the monkey is sensational. Laff a minute."

O'Neill and Sambo set foot — er, paw — in a wrestling ring for the first time in 1953. They mostly stayed on the undercard as a special attraction, and their run was relatively brief, only about six months long. But even diehard fans would be pressed to name a more entertaining sideshow than the only wrestling second who walked on all fours. "Now that Trader O'Neill is in the United States, he has, as we said, given new medicine to the box office," Dick Axman wrote in *Wrestling As You Like It* magazine.

It's unclear whether O'Neill was any kind of wrestler, or simply a sportsman looking to make a few bucks off a particularly clever chimp. Chicago promoter Fred Kohler might have been the brains behind the simian silliness. London, who ran shows from his Albuquerque, New Mexico, headquarters, worked closely with Kohler and at one point noted Sambo and O'Neill were biding their time in warm weather before heading to Chicago to fulfill a wrestling TV contract.

Sambo first appeared with O'Neill in March 1953 in Tucson, Arizona, drawing more than a few curious glances when the two paraded around a post office and a Sears store. Their in-ring debut came on March 25 in Tucson, but not before one of the most clever publicity builds of all time. Transcribing notes the chimp had supposedly scribbled, the *Daily Citizen*'s Dave Feldman authored an account under Sambo's byline that traced his origins, his opinion of tight blue jeans, and his expectations for a new career.

"I guess you know the boss thinks this is going to be a big thing," Sambo said. "Wrestlers have used pigs and snakes and raccoons and alligators with them, but I'm the first chimpanzee in the racket. I'm a little worried about Trader, though. He's had an arm and a shoulder and a nose broken, and his knee is banged up."

The alleged word on Sambo was that he was one of about twenty chimps picked up by O'Neill, an exotic animal merchant, during a 1952 swing through Sierra Leone. O'Neill sold all of them

Trader O'Neill briefly created a stir with Sambo, his trained chimpanzee and valued ringside assistant.

except the two-and-half-year-old Sambo, who cost him $2,000, and another chimp. The housebroken monkeys lived in a thirty-five-foot trailer with his O'Neill's wife Kiko, a daughter, a dog, and Benjy the parakeet. "Most conceited bird I ever saw," Sambo scoffed to Feldman. "Has two mirrors in his cage and won't come out till dinner time."

Unsurprisingly, Sambo stole the show during his first match before a crowd of 2,500 at the Tucson Sports Center, even though Rocky Hessel and Chris Tolos donned padded gloves in a special boxing grudge match as the main event. Wearing bright red trunks and a striped T-shirt, Sambo antagonized O'Neill's foe Tony Falletti throughout the contest and was treated as a wrestler by referee Monte LaDue, who "unthinkingly waved him back to his corner, like half of a tag team combo," Feldman wrote under his real name. O'Neill pinned tough guy Falletti for the victory.

O'Neill was more than willing to play second banana to Sambo, though he was probably even more shocking in appearance. The shallow-chested O'Neill had a long tangle of dark, mangy hair — he looked like Russell Brand on a bad day — and wore a leopard-spotted, one-strap leotard and sandals. According to Axman, one of the sport's legendary concocters, a grappler in Africa taught O'Neill the rudiments of wrestling. From there, O'Neill went with Sambo to Hong Kong and China; in the United States, he was alternately billed as from Wang Poo, China, and Singapore. "I kept Sambo because he's exceptionally good-natured," O'Neill said.

Promoter London discovered most of his wrestlers were lukewarm about squaring up with a lesser species, even though Sambo was chained to a ring post for the duration of the bout. In fact, Falletti and Ben Sherman were O'Neill's standard opponents during his three months in the Southwest. Part of the stock routine was for O'Neill to guide his opponent into Sambo's reach, "depending on the chimp's inhuman or subhuman tactics to take it from there," according to Arch Napier of the *Albuquerque Journal*. In one match in Santa Fe, New Mexico, Sambo got the crowd howling when he tickled Sherman in the ribs. London was delighted with the monkey business uptick. "I'd like to hire him just to have him around," he said.

In late June 1953, O'Neill and Sambo headed to Kohler's territory, appearing several times on Chicago TV shows, once with singer/actor Jimmy Durante, and working cards in Illinois, Indiana, and Wisconsin. A wrestler and his monkey manager was a tailor-made feature for small-town sportswriters. In Janesville, Wisconsin, O'Neill went to a draw with Carl Engstrom while Police Chief Jasper Webb served as the monkey's ringside custodian. "The chimp performed all kinds of stunts, from applauding to trying to assist O'Neill when the latter seemed to be getting the worst of it," the *Daily Gazette* said.

As in the Southwest, O'Neill worked with a small set of opponents in Kohler's promotion — Milt Olsen and Treach Phillips accounted for at least half his matches. O'Neill's finishing hold was, appropriately, the African monkey flip. Still, the outcomes were unimportant — O'Neill lost as many as he won — since Sambo was the star of the show, as the *Belvidere (IL) Daily Republican* reported after one match: "The chimp, entering the ring on O'Neill's shoulder and attached to a leash in the Singapore slugger's corner, tugged and nipped at the wrestlers and the referee, whenever the opportunity presented itself, and generally entertained the younger fry in the audience throughout the thirty-minute match."

By the fall of 1953, the act had apparently run its course. There are no recorded matches for O'Neill, at least under that name, after early September. He disappeared as quickly as he arrived, and researchers are still trying to find out what happened to him. The same cannot be said of Sambo. We know exactly what happened to him.

In late 1953, O'Neill sold the chimp to the St. Louis Zoo. Sambo took over as the lead in the zoo's chimpanzee production. Dressed as Davy Crockett, he skated, rode ponies, clowned around, and petted little kids on the head. Zoo director George Vierheller called Sambo the most photographed animal he had in his collection. "Sambo seems to like children almost as much as he dotes on attention," wrote John Stipe of the St. Louis Post-Dispatch.

It sure beat sharing a house trailer with a stuck-up parakeet.

II. Bearly Getting By

Would Victor the Bear go to jail? Would he be sentenced to do hard time, whatever hard time might entail for a bear? It seemed like a concern in June 1965 when police in Pasadena, California, found Victor breaking the law by wrestling Tuffy Truesdell, his owner and trainer, in front of a crowd in a used car lot.

Truesdell pulled out all the stops to get Victor — and himself — off the hook for violating a ninety-two-year-old ban against teaching animals to fight for fun and profit. "Victor looks to me as a mother and father, and I never show him anything but parental devotion," Truesdell told jurors, who watched as the bear ate marshmallows from his handler and flushed them down with two bottles of a strawberry-flavored concoction. "He can't drink soda pop. It makes him burp," Truesdell explained. A municipal court jury took fifteen minutes to deliberate. Truesdell and Victor were free man and bear. Truesdell wept. "I've got to go home and tell Victor the good news," he said.

A love story? In a way. Victor loved to eat and to wrestle. Truesdell loved publicity as North America's foremost proprietor of wrestling bears and alligators. And maybe there was more to it than that. "Somewhere I came to believe in reincarnation and the Navajo belief that the bear is a sacred animal that carries the spirit of your grandfather," Truesdell told the *Philadelphia Inquirer* in 1975. "I lost my grandfather a few months before I got Victor, and I believe that bear did carry the spirit of my grandfather."

More than anyone, Truesdell was responsible for popularizing animal acts as a pro wrestling sideshow and sometimes as the main event in the post–World War II era. Part P.T. Barnum and part Jack Hanna, Truesdell's animal kingdom consisted at times of dozens of alligators, all named Rodney, and multiple bears — at one point, three Victors were competing simultaneously in rings across the continent. "It is a high level of civilization that Tuffy presides over," wrote Frank Deford, who traveled with him for a 1970 *Sports Illustrated* profile. "The man who has his wife, a redhead, mixing martinis in the middle seat of his limousine and a contented bear who responds quickly to his orders domiciled behind her may be said to have found law and order."

At first, Truesdell was interested mostly in wrestling humans. Born September 8, 1916, in Nokomis, Illinois, to a painter and his wife, Truesdell claimed to have thrashed a school bully when he was six years old, earning the nickname of "Tuffy," which he much preferred to his given name of Adolphus. He quit school in eleventh grade, started wrestling for cash in Missouri around 1936, and worked at a St. Louis bakery to make ends meet. Compact and stocky at five-foot-five and 165 pounds — he'd hit 195 in time — Truesdell worked lower-card matches until he headed to Louisiana's Fort Polk during World War II as a U.S. Army recreational director. After that stint, Truesdell took his skills to Mexico City, where he beat Carlos "Tarzan" Lopez for the country's middleweight title. Truesdell defended the championship through early 1947 and showed off the belt to visitors for years, but never broke into the top rank of wrestlers. Jimmy Houghton, a friend and promoter in Wilmington, Delaware, put it simply: "He didn't have the weight for the pros."

In October 1946, Gil Woodworth started a rage in pro wrestling by battling ten-foot-long alligators in cages enclosed by chicken wire. The slender Woodworth was not a wrestler by trade, but was affiliated with a Florida reptile center and doubled for actor Johnny Weissmuller in underwater gator scenes. Fans held their breath as Woodworth routinely placed his head between reptile jaws. Some 7,300 showed up on January 21, 1947, in Louisville, Kentucky, when "The Alligator Man" followed up his wrestling act by marrying Perma Crook in the ring. "The doubleheader novelty outdrew even the largest basketball crowds of the winter season," the Courier-Journal reported.

Truesdell couldn't help but notice Woodworth's success. "One night I was sitting in a promoter's office and looking at my take," he said to the Chicago Tribune in 1969. "I told him, 'The hell with wrestling for the championship for purses like this. I'm going to wrestle

COURTESY CHRIS SWISHER COLLECTION

Before he wrestled bears, Tuffy Truesdell cut his teeth grappling with alligators.

SIDESHOWS **105**

an alligator.'" How exactly he got into the gator biz is murky; Truesdell's tales often got bigger than an alligator's tail with each retelling. At one point, he said he inherited Woodworth's gig when the incumbent lost several fingers to an unplanned chomp in Texas. Another time, Truesdell said he prowled for gators in the Louisiana bayous during his service years; he also claimed to have learned the ancient art of gator wrestling from the Seminole tribe in Florida. In any event, he stocked up on alligators and was off and running. In 1947 alone, he wrestled Rodney(s) in Ohio, Mississippi, Kentucky, Connecticut, Massachusetts, Maryland, and Michigan. He swapped out gators often because they didn't take travel well. Veteran wrestler Phil Melby remembered the time Truesdell and one of his props came to town. "He had it under the seat of his car, it was cold, he was froze stiff like a Popsicle. Then he'd bring him in the room where it was warm and he'd be okay. I'd never seen that before." Truesdell made no bones about the danger involved in his new line of work. "Alligators may be dumb and they usually end up as handbags, but they're better than some of the guys I've met in the ring," he told a Connecticut newspaper in 1950.

Love pulled Truesdell from his itinerant life. After about five years of gator wrestling, he fell for Mona McEwan, the bookkeeper for promoter Frank Tunney at Maple Leaf Gardens in Toronto. The marriage produced two children but didn't last. Meanwhile, he built a roadside refuge east of Sarnia, Ontario, near the Michigan border, with gators, monkeys, a zebra, a lion, and a brahma bull alongside a go-kart track. On the lookout for a cub to add to his menagerie, Truesdell was in northern Ontario in 1958 when he heard about a bear that had ripped up a logging camp. Loggers shot the offender, who was said to have left two six-week-old cubs behind. Truesdell hightailed it to the site, tracking for nearly five hours until he found the den. "There was a little female cub out front, frozen to death," he recalled a decade later. "We were gonna leave, but I remembered the people saying they had seen two cubs, so we crawled inside. Way in the back, I found Victor, unconscious. I thought he was dead too, but I put my tongue in his mouth and felt him quiver so I tucked him inside my jacket and let him warm up."

The bear was not the only thing Truesdell took under his wing. Larry Serratore was among several local youngsters who hung around the Truesdell spread, doing odd jobs, feeding gators kept in the house basement, and sparring with the desexed, defanged, declawed Victor. "Tuffy was almost like a father figure," Serratore said. "He'd keep you out of trouble, make sure you didn't get in any trouble, and he'd give you lots of good advice." Serratore regularly visited Victor's barn to roughhouse outdoors on the grass, though Victor hightailed it back indoors if he caught a glimpse of the brahma bull. "Victor was like a pet, like a pet dog. He was calm, cool, and collected, and anything we were afraid of, he was afraid of," Serratore said. He and his pals rewarded Victor with bagfuls of day-old donuts and an adult beverage. "We always brought a bottle of beer with us. He'd down that beer like you wouldn't believe. He'd put it up and he'd just roll back with the bottle."

In 1962, Truesdell and a professional square dancer named Lee Ann who, as a side job, dodged knives hurled by a blindfolded thrower, took three gators and Victor on the road. Wrestling had its newest superstar, a Canadian black bear that would grow to be six-foot-five and 450 pounds, thanks to a daily intake of lettuce, apples, dog food, and bread. In Austin, Texas, a boastful Tony Borne signed an open contract to meet all comers. Enter Victor. After an eight-minute struggle, Borne reached for Victor's muzzle and pulled it off. Exit Borne, whose boots barely touched cement as he skedaddled to the dressing room. Truesdell was confident enough to put Victor in a battle royal in Hawaii in 1965, just before the California court fracas. Intimidated by seeing ten wrestlers at once, Victor rolled on his back and was counted out. "Victor, you're a lazy bum," yelled King Curtis Iaukea. Shrugged Truesdell, "Victor is used to wrestling one man at a time, or at the most, two."

In addition to wrestling shows, Truesdell brought Victor to county fairs, children's hospitals, car dealerships, and outdoor shows, and let anyone spar with him as long as they signed a liability waiver. Before he became a top wrestling historian, Steve Yohe was a high schooler in Montebello, California, mustering up the nerve to challenge the bear. Yohe scouted Victor in a car lot and watched his moves, but balked at paying the entry fee of $15 or so. Three weeks later, he learned Victor was overnighting in a garage stall where his brother worked. As a trade, Yohe got to wrestle Victor for free and test out his carefully designed strategy. "My plan going in was to be nice to Vic and not piss him off. So I reach out to pat him on the head, he knocked my arm away. It was on and that's all he cared about," Yohe said. At one point, Yohe went for a double-leg takedown, thinking he could knock Victor off balance. "He didn't move and I don't think Andre the Giant could have taken him down. Animals are so much stronger than humans," he said. "After what seemed like twenty minutes, Tuffy came over and said, 'Okay, that's it.' Maybe I was boring Vic . . . I don't know; he never said anything." What Yohe recalled most nearly forty-five years later was the stink — "the smell was terrible." Pat Williams, the colorful basketball front office executive, had a similar experience. He booked Victor at halftime of a Philadelphia 76ers doubleheader and introduced him as the "bear of a forward" that the 76ers craved. Williams then wrestled Victor, who whacked him three times inside a minute, and had the same stinky recollection. "He wasn't using Scope, either," he said. "The big thing I'll never forget was his breath. It was really brutal."

Victor's fame spread far and wide. He had a role in the Lee Marvin movie *Paint Your Wagon*, did guest spots with Mike Douglas and Ed Sullivan, and appeared on TV's *Let's Make a Deal, Truth or Consequences, Lassie,* and *To Tell the Truth*. Truesdell, never particular about the count, put Victor's undefeated streak at 3,000 to 50,000 contests, including a victory against The Destroyer (Dick Beyer), who was disqualified for slugging the bear. "I won't say he's never lost, but he's never been beaten," said Truesdell, who cited powerful Don Leo Jonathan as Victor's toughest adversary. According to Jonathan's wife, Rose, that might have had more to do with the time of year. In 2014, she recalled a match between Victor and her husband during one winter in California. Jonathan tried to rouse Victor, who was more interested in hibernating than in playing, when his daughter stood up on her ringside seat and yelled, "Don't hurt the bear, Daddy, don't hurt the bear!"

Victor died in March 1975; he was in the back of a converted Cadillac hearse going from Mobile, Alabama, to Portland, Maine, when he suffered a heart attack. Truesdell tried to revive him, but the animal was gone by the time he could get to a vet. "You know, it wasn't until two years after Victor's death that I could talk about him at all," he later said. "He was a part of the family. Hell, I loved that bear. He was almost human." Even before Victor's demise, Truesdell had expanded his furry empire in 1970 by adding Sonny, a 585-pound Alaskan brown bear, and bringing on former wrestler George Allen as a trainer and supervisor. In 1978, Truesdell and Lee Ann settled in Cherokee, North Carolina, where he was bearmaster emeritus for a traveling troupe of about ten bruins. Truesdell also housed some thirty others at his Bear Land, which operated under federal permits amid regular protests from animal rights activists. "I'm not ashamed of my outfit," Truesdell sniffed. "They can go up there and see for themselves — if they pay the admission." The bear business slowly dried up, though. In 1983, Maine barred Victor from performing, and in 2012, the U.S. Department of Agriculture suspended the zoo's license and hit it with a $20,000 fine. By then, Truesdell had been dead for eleven years. While a man-versus-bear match pops up now and then, no promoter in his right mind would regularly sanction the kind of entertainment that sustained Truesdell and fans for many years. It's probably just as well he wasn't around to experience the cultural shift. "I'm happy. I feel lucky," Truesdell once said. "When I was growing up in St. Louis I had to work because my family was poor. I never had time to play."

III. Size Doesn't Matter

The hay bale never knew what hit it. Time and again, sixteen-year-old Roland Barriault tried to impress his straw man trainer in a dirty, musty barn, mustering up all of his four-foot-seven body to throw dropkick after dropkick at a tin can he strategically placed on top of the hay as a target. It took time, figuring out this pro wrestling thing, no matter one's size.

What didn't take any time at all was Barriault's decision to pursue the nomadic life of a pro wrestler. He was eight years old in 1954, attending the wrestling matches in Sudbury, Ontario, for the first time. It was eye-opening. There were other little people like him, and they were stars, larger than life. He turned to his mother and told her that he was going to be a midget wrestler too, and an evil one.

It's hard to dispute the success of Barriault, who used myriad names throughout his forty-eight-year wrestling career; his best-known moniker was Frenchy Lamont, the alias he wrestled under when he was world midget champion in the 1970s. A championship is one thing, but the proof of his commitment, of his youthful folly, is in his broken-down body. His legs struggle to support his weight, let alone lift two full-sized men on his shoulders, as he did on many occasions to drum up publicity for an appearance.

Yet, like so many colleagues, big or small, Barriault swears he'd still be performing, riling up the crowd if he physically could. He called it quits at age sixty-six. "If it hadn't have been for my legs messing up on me, I'd still be doing it," Barriault said.

That he got to do it at all is one of those twists of fate that make life interesting. Born July 22, 1946, in the mining city of Sudbury, about four hours north of Toronto, he was three years old when learned that he wasn't going to grow big and tall like his five brothers or his sister. His mother, Corrine, broke the news to him; his father, Wilfred, found humor in it. "I'd make my dad laugh, because I'd tell him he didn't finish his job. He should have given it an extra stroke," Barriault laughed. His family members looked out for him and after the fifteen-year-old "Rollie" worked up the nerve to approach wrestling star Lord Littlebrook (Eric Tovey), who working the matches in town, they gave him their blessing to leave town for 'Brook's farm in Havelock, Ontario. Littlebrook picked him up in a car jury-rigged with longer pedals so he could drive.

Littlebrook, who hailed from England and had been in the circus before heading to North America, wasn't in the first batch of little people who started appearing as special attractions after World War II, but he was pretty close. The promotional genius behind midget wrestling was Gabriel Acocella, who followed his older brother, Luigi, known as Lou Kelly, into the sport in the early 1930s. As a wrestler, Gabriel was known as Jack Britton, and the name stuck. His son and grandson later wrestled and promoted as Gino Brito Sr. and Jr. Based out of Montreal, most of Britton's early little wrestlers were Quebecois; if they weren't from *la belle province*, they certainly got to see it. Sky Low Low (Maurice Gauthier), Little Beaver (Lionel Giroux), Pee Wee James (Raymond Sabourin), and Pancho the Bull (Ferdinand Tucci) captivated an eight-year-old Gino Brito Sr.

"My dad tried them out in little towns like Sorel and Drummondville, a couple of matches, not even in the big arenas, to see how it would work out," Brito Sr. explained. "Then he would

London, Ontario's finest pose with Brown Panther and Little Beaver.

bring them to the Stade Exchange; that's where they had a ring and they would all work out; that's where everyone started." Before he was the famed "Mad Dog," Maurice Vachon saw it for himself. He was there when Sky Low Low wrestled Little Beaver in Montreal, the first time they had ever come into a ring. "After two, three minutes, Little Beaver was huffing. After that, he could wrestle well and he never got tired. But that was his first time ever, and he became one of the biggest attractions in the world."

Based in the Montreal Park Avenue Hotel, Britton booked his contingent of little people everywhere. Writers had a field day. "Tito Infanti, who from a distance looks no larger than a fifth of Scotch, is one of the nation's fastest, smartest, and richest midget wrestlers," wrote Gay Talese in the *New York Times*. Upon seeing the midgets Pierre Raymond and Billy Bowman (later Major Tom Thumb) debut in 1949 at Toronto's East York Collegiate Memorial Stadium, wrestler Joe Perlove quipped, "It's like wrestling seen through the wrong end of a telescope."

As with Barriault years later, getting the diminutive grapplers in front of an audience attracted other small people. "Then they started coming, Mighty Schultz, Mighty Fritz, Little Brutus, which was Tiny Tim in those days," Brito Sr. said. Sky Low Low was the de facto leader. "If Sky Low Low said, 'Yeah, this guy's going to make it,' my dad used to keep an eye on him, and say, 'Okay, we'll train him more,' and get him going and put him in the show. A lot of midgets went through."

They also put a lot of miles on their cars, their bodies, and their livers. Once asked about Sky Low Low, Littlebrook said he had his issues. "Until he had a few drinks, he was all right. But once he had a few drinks, he was pretty obnoxious. He became Mr. Tough Guy." Asked to name where in the world he had wrestled, Littlebrook, born in the heart of London, countered with where he had never worked: China and the Soviet Union.

Midget wrestlers were best used sporadically, said late promoter Bob Geigel, who controlled the Kansas City, Missouri, territory. "If you had midgets on the card every night in every town, they wouldn't draw because they'd be old hat. But if you just bring the midgets in two, three times a year, and worked them around your territory, then they'd draw like hell," Geigel said.

Brito Sr. said there was more to it than that. The idea was to think ahead, whether booking the midgets out of Montreal or later

Frenchy Lamont drops a knee during a tag team match.

Detroit, where his father partnered with promoters Burt Rubi and Harry Light from the end of 1960 to 1967. "Everybody wanted Beaver all the time," Brito Sr. said of the fan-thrilling babyface with his trademark Mohawk haircut. Britton would say no, sending in other wrestlers instead, building those months out of the territory for the payoff bout of Sky versus Beaver.

The midgets were their own self-contained show, said Barriault. "We could get away with murder," he said. "It wasn't up to the promoter to arrange the matches, we'd arrange it ourselves, what we're going to do, the routines." The formula was familiar to fans: the referee, a key part of the shtick, got down to make the count, and the pinned wrestler pressed up, launching his foe into the arms of the surprised ref, who dropped him back down to start counting again; rinse and repeat.

At various points, Britton would have four or five groups of midgets working for him, often under the care of his son. "When I first started, just before I got married, I was on the road with them continually," said Brito Sr. "The proof is that I bought a car and seventeen months later, a new car had 144,000 miles on it — that's how much we traveled." However, he did not book the handful of women midget wrestlers like Diamond Lil, Baby Cheryl, Dolly Darcel, Darling Dagmar, or Cuddles Anderson, who was married to Barriault for nine years. The Fabulous Moolah (Lillian Ellison) handled their business.

Barriault and others Littlebrook trained, like Beau Brummel, made up the second generation of midget wrestlers and carried on the legacy established by their older peers. Littlebrook went on to train many wrestlers, big and small, male and female, out of his home in St. Joseph, Missouri, and then take over the booking of midgets worldwide when Britton called it quits. Little Tokyo, also a former world champ, served as a second trainer in St. Joe.

Acting as talent agents, Britton and Littlebrook took a share of the paychecks of their charges; therein was the friction. Eventually, Barriault had enough of the shorted paydays and struck out on his own. He would call around to promoters and book himself and a partner into town. Like the small-sized grapplers who inspired him, a young four-foot-two Paul Richard in Hamilton, Ontario, saw Frenchy Lamont in the ring and decided he wanted to get into it. "I would talk to Frenchy," said Richard. "He would take me in free." Throughout the 1980s, across much of Canada, the pairing was Richard as Farmer Pete against Frenchy Lamont.

While midget wrestling never again hit the heights it had in the 1950s, it also never left the wrestling world. For every high-profile little person moment, like Hornswoggle and El Torito tearing it up on WWE Television, or King Kong Bundy squashing Little Beaver during a WrestleMania III match, there were bouts in gymnasiums, arenas, and bars. Phil Watson, son of former National Wrestling Alliance world champion "Whipper" Billy Watson, hired little people for his Canadian Half Pints Mini Hoops Basketball team in the 1980s and 1990s. TV shows in the 2010s, like The Half Pint Brawlers and Hulk Hogan's Micro Championship Wrestling, boosted profiles.

Short Sleeve Sampson (Dan DiLucchio) was one of those who benefited from the new exposure, but he lamented how publicity opened the floodgates. "Let's put it this way, there are a lot of midgets out there. I don't know if I'd say that there's a lot of midget wrestlers out there," he said. "The reason I categorize it like that is because unfortunately there are a lot of guys out there that figure because of the fact that they meet the height requirement that that automatically puts them in the category of being a midget wrestler. But they've never taken the time to be trained, to learn the sport the right way, even to have proper ring attire."

Looking back, Barriault has tinges of wonder and regret in his voice when reminiscing about his various characters. He debuted as Rolly the Rocket; was Golden Boy Lamont when he had blond hair; worked as Little Hawk with a Mohawk haircut; seemingly joined a motorcycle gang to be Frenchy Rider; tried to work under a mask as Dirty Morgan; and has a wolf tattoo on his left arm to prove he was Lone Wolf. And, during a swing through Florida and Alabama in 1967, he donned a mask and kept his decades-long bad guy vow to his mother. He was Little Evil.

Adventures in Storytelling

Introduction

In the old days, you might mosey on down to the fair to drum up a little attention for your storyline. At least that's what Sputnik Monroe was thinking when he paraded around the Mid-South Fair in Memphis in a black suit, derby, and championship belt on September 27, 1959. Gene Barry, TV's Bat Masterson, was a featured fair guest and Monroe told friend and wrestling foe Billy Wicks that he intended to raise a little hell. "Sputnik called me up and said, 'Hey, Wicks. I'm gonna get us some national publicity. I'm going out there and I'm taking Gene Barry's cane away from him and I'm going to break it over my knee and hand it to him.' I said, 'Well, go ahead, baby, whatever you want to do.'" Things didn't go as planned. An ill-advised wisecrack got Monroe in a scuffle with a cowboy named Ray Marley. The tough guy wrestler ended up on his back with a cut under his eye, and egg on his face thanks to a front-page newspaper story. Monroe later downplayed the incident but admitted to Wicks that he'd had second thoughts about grabbing Barry's cane. "He said, 'I couldn't get enough nerve to do it, Wicks.'"

An arena marquee and a newspaper advertisement are seldom enough. Wrestlers have long pushed the envelope on out-of-the-ring publicity adventures from real news, in Monroe's case, to reality TV, as

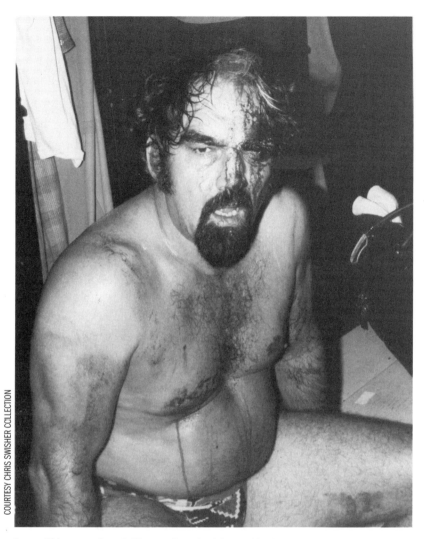

Born rabble-rouser Sputnik Monroe always had time to bleed.

in the 2016 "Broken" Matt Hardy angle. Sometimes they've attracted law enforcement, sometimes they've skirted it, but they've all been designed to get fans in the seats or, in the twenty-first century, clicks on a video. Very often, the stories behind the publicity ploys are more interesting than the plays themselves.

I. The Great Detroit Barroom Brawl

If Dick the Bruiser had decided to stop in and simply whet his whistle at one of Detroit's most prominent watering holes, then he wouldn't have been Dick the Bruiser. Instead, during one night in April 1963, the buzzcut madman of the ring busted up the Lindell Athletic Club bar, smashed a TV set and a vending machine, sent two policemen to the hospital, took five stitches under the left eye, and landed a night in the hoosegow. Oh, and he reaped coast-to-coast headlines for his upcoming main event with suspended football star Alex Karras of the hometown Lions. No wonder Lyall Smith of the Detroit *Free Press* exclaimed, "If this was a publicity stunt, it definitely deserves a Gold Cluster for action above and beyond the call of duty."

It was a publicity stunt, of course. Mel Butsicaris, son of John Butsicaris, who owned the bar with his brother Jimmy, recalled that sportswriters and TV reporters were seated well before Bruiser's entrance, poised to report on the ploy. "In fact, there was a news-paper article that talked about this fight in the bar before it even happened," Mel said. "It was 100 percent staged ahead of time." Yet even though it had all the salacious elements of a box office gold-mine — a hard-hitting football hero and a villain who ripped up kids' autograph books — the Bruiser-Karras affair became a classic example of how not to build a wrestling storyline.

When Bruiser confronted Karras in the early morning hours of April 23, 1963, the two were already larger-than-life figures in the Motor City, with contrarian streaks as thick as their chests. In 1959, William F. (Dick) Afflis began a five-year run as the snarling face of wrestling in Detroit, drawing crowds of more than 16,000 to the Olympia Stadium for promoters Johnny Doyle and Jim Barnett. Karras also did some pro wrestling — at the behest of promoter Pinkie George,he quit the University of Iowa after his senior football season for the grappling game. Undefeated in about thirty matches in 1958, Karras wrestled in the off-season through 1960 as he developed into

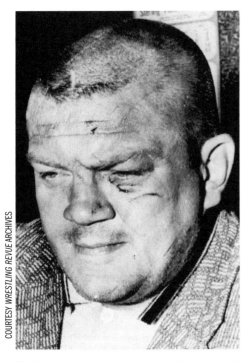

COURTESY WRESTLING REVUE ARCHIVES

Dick the Bruiser took a beating before his match with Alex Karras thanks to a publicity stunt gone awry.

an All-Pro defensive tackle for the Lions. But Karras was his own worst enemy. In 1962, he agreed to buy one-third interest in the Lindell bar for $40,000 from the mother of the Butsicaris brothers. When the Lions' front office took a dim view of his involvement with a saloon, Karras dug in with Bruiser-style obstinacy. "If the Lions are going to stop me, I'll fight them. I'll sue them," he roared. Then, during an NFL gambling investigation, Karras, twenty-seven, committed career suicide.

In a clip that appeared on NBC News' *Huntley-Brinkley Report*, he admitted to placing bets on pro games. Karras howled that the clip had been truncated to omit the trivial stakes — a cigar here, a few bucks there — and he said he never gave less than 100 percent on the field. No matter. NFL Commissioner Pete Rozelle put Karras on a lie detector at league headquarters in New York, and then suspended him indefinitely on April 17, 1963.

The big guy needed money, and he needed it fast. Karras started negotiating for a match with Bruiser even before Rozelle's verdict and weighed a $40,000 full-time wrestling contract from Doyle. He later called it "a reflex action on my part; a gut feeling to grab some outside income while my name still meant something in the sporting world." Doyle and Barnett set the Bruiser-Karras bout for April 27. In the meantime, he was a humble barkeep at 1519 Cass

Avenue. In a candid moment, he told a reporter he thought he could pocket $5,000 from the match with Bruiser "and maybe another five from a rematch." Milking the moment for all it was worth, he named a second — a forty-three-inch-tall bar regular named Major Little. "You and me, together, all the way to the top. I'm going to be undefeated heavyweight champion of the world," Karras told his buddy.

On a national level, the match got more attention from mainstream sports editors than just about any wrestling event of its day. Yet the buildup in Detroit was strangely quiet. Rob Bauer, an authority on Michigan wrestling, said the booking puzzled fans because Karras and Bruiser had no history between them. Nor was there any attempt to create one. Two weekly TV wrestling shows passed without Karras or Bruiser in warm-up matches against prelim wrestlers or on-camera interviews. "Nobody saw Karras wrestle," Bauer said. "Bruiser did some taping, but it was not part of the wrestling program. They put it on the news a few times."

Perhaps that's why Bruiser decided to take matters into his own hands. Accounts of what happened at the bar that night differ; even Karras gave conflicting versions in subsequent interviews. But it's certain that things did not turn out as intended. "They came with this idea about having Dick the Bruiser come into the bar and pick a fight with my uncle Jimmy, and then Alex was going to step in to defend my uncle's honor and embarrass the Bruiser in front of people," Mel Butsicaris said. "Everybody knew this was a setup." Sure enough, Bruiser, thirty-three, entered the bar just before 1:30 a.m. on April 23. Jimmy Butsicaris was tending bar and wearing an old shirt, knowing what was to come. Bruiser started mouthing off, propping himself on the bar for emphasis. Some reports say Bruiser was swearing at Karras, seated in a corner of the bar, but Mel Butsicaris said the invective was aimed at his uncle, who was refusing to serve a rowdy patron. "He was yelling, 'You fat grease-ball' and stuff like that," Mel said of Bruiser. Instead of horror, customers laughed and egged on Bruiser, who took a couple of swings at Jimmy, pinned him against the wall, and ripped his shirt off, as scripted.

But Uncle Charley had not read the script. Charles Kelly was an uncle of Jimmy Butsicaris' wife. A quiet Texan, he walked into the bar to see Jimmy locked in the grip of an apparent psychopath with no one pitching in to help. Kelly grabbed a pool cue and shoved it at Bruiser, gashing him under the left eye and knocking him off a stool. In a flash, the drinking haunt turned into the Royal Rumble. Bleeding profusely, Bruiser tore the establishment apart, busting chairs and tables. On one wall, a peanut vending machine was bolted into the counter with a piece of plywood. He ripped out the device and threw it against the wall. Some patrons jumped on Bruiser, trying to subdue him, though Karras was not among them. "Alex sees all the blood and sees this fight is for real. Alex doesn't want any part of Bruiser when he's really mad. Alex leaves the bar, gets in his car, and goes home," Mel Butsicaris said.

Andrew Meholic and James Carolan, a pair of policemen walking their beat, arrived to exercise authority. At that point, Bruiser had a choice, he later told wrestler Jim Lancaster — he could back down in front of a bunch of reporters and fans, or he could stay in character. One does not become a legend by backing down. Bruiser flung the policemen against a wall like a pair of movie extras, breaking Mcholic's wrist and tearing a ligament in Carolan's elbow. Jimmy Butsicaris chimed in, encouraging Bruiser to wreck a black-and-white TV above the bar since it was insured for more than it was worth. Done and done. Six more policemen arrived, locking Bruiser in handcuffs and ankle manacles, charging him with criminal assault, and hauling him away. At Detroit Receiving Hospital, Bruiser told a scribe that he intended to confront Karras for allegedly calling him a third-rate football player. "Let anyone who says this is a publicity stunt get all beat up like this and be taken by the police to the hospital," he yelled. The next day, Bruiser called Karras. "Oh man, they killed me. Killed me . . . but we're sold out tomorrow night." Dollar signs flashed in the eyes of promoter Doyle. "This looms as the match of the century," he said gleefully. "It's obvious that my boys are really up for this one. I can hardly wait for the rematch."

There would be no rematch, though. The brawl at the Lindell was as entertaining as it got. Bruiser pummeled Karras on April 27, 1963, before about 10,000 fans at the Olympia Stadium — some estimates put the crowd as small

COURTESY WRESTLING REVUE ARCHIVES

Dick the Bruiser drops a knee on football star Alex Karras in a match that didn't live up to its hype.

as 6,500. The contrast between the two was startling. "Karras was puffing away. Dick the Bruiser was all suntanned, looked good. Karras looked like a football player in the off-season," said Bauer, who watched from the second row. Major Little accompanied Karras to ringside, as did Jimmy Butsicaris; after all, they had a pub to promote. Early on, Bruiser started bleeding profusely from above his right eye, perhaps the residue of a match the previous night in St. Louis, when a referee ruled he was bleeding too badly to continue against Lou Thesz. Karras tossed Bruiser through the ropes three times, while Bruiser responded by kneeling in a three-point stance in a football-style challenge. The end came when Bruiser choked Karras and climbed to the top rope. Butsicaris jumped on the side of the ring and tried to swipe at Bruiser's leg, but missed. Bruiser dropped a knee across Karras' throat and pinned him easily. "It was a horrible match," Bauer said. "The match was about eleven minutes. Karras didn't look like he was going to make it for five, and he was blowing wind after three."

Karras hung up his boots a few days later. In 1984, he boasted that he made $17,000 for his showing, but that seems unlikely given the size of the gate — Detroit sportswriter Jerry Green reported the payday at $4,500. Bruiser, who got five stitches above the right eye to match the five from the bar brawl, suggested why the match was so short. "He can do all right if he would get in shape. He's strong and he knows all the moves," he told Green. Looking back a year later, Doyle admitted the match didn't pass the smell test. "The fans knew that Karras was no match for Bruiser," he said. "They knew that Karras was a fine football player, a great one. But they didn't feel he had a chance in the ring. So they stayed home and waited until we put on a bout they liked." In the judicial aftermath, a judge dismissed the assault charge as long as Bruiser paid $400 to a police fund, though police refused to accept it, labeling it "blood money." Officers Carolan and Meholic sued him in federal court; in separate rulings, judges awarded $10,378 to Carolan and $15,000 to Meholic for the damage Bruiser inflicted. Bruiser's lawyer later offered to settle with Meholic for $7,500, but there is no public record of the disposition.

After a year in the penalty box, Karras returned to the Lions in 1964. He retired after the 1970 season to launch a long and successful career in TV and movies, including a scene-stealing role as the illiterate brute Mongo, who knocked out a horse in the movie Blazing Saddles. The accumulated football and wrestling thumps took their toll; he battled dementia for a dozen years and died in 2012 at seventy-seven. Bruiser never stopped being Bruiser, even when he recast himself as a fan favorite in the mid-1960s. Almost until his death in 1992, he never tired of talking about the time he was tough enough to go hand-to-fist with an entire police force. "It was my fault. I was looking for trouble," he conceded. Bruiser left a little souvenir behind. Later in 1963, the Lindell bar moved to a larger location down the street. For several years, it maintained an exhibit on a wall — a TV with a gaping hole in the middle of the screen. A sign perched above the busted set read, "Dick the Bruiser was here."

II. Bridge over Troubled Waters

The closer Paul Jones got to the bridge over Tampa Bay, the bigger the crowds got. People lined his route along Gandy Boulevard by the dozens, then by the hundreds. Boaters circled in the bay. When he slowed his car, more people ran to catch up with him. TV news trucks were on hand as witnesses. It was, Jones thought, like he was the Pied Piper except his magical instrument was the Florida heavyweight championship belt, which he planned to chuck into the water. "I get up all the way to the top of the bridge and I look out. I've got the belt. I'd already took out the phony diamonds. There were, it seemed, like thousands of boats down there and they wanted to catch it. So cocky me, I take about three practice swings and boom! I just let it go. It hit the water. Nobody caught it."

Jones should have trademarked the move. Growing up in Tampa, David Sierra watched the heave-ho unfold and called on it nearly a decade later during a turnstile-busting program in Portland, Oregon. Ronnie Garvin tossed the Southeastern title off an aging bridge in Knoxville, Tennessee, as authorities hustled people away, fearing the structure would collapse. In 1997, WWE resurrected the angle when Steve Austin threw The Rock's intercontinental title — actually an old tag team belt — off a New Hampshire bridge. Countless belts pollute North American waterways, with the Arkansas River, Pensacola Bay, and Long Island Sound among the final resting places for titles discarded in copycat skits. But only a select few carried the elements of legitimacy and believability that Jones brought to his belt toss. "Even though it has been recreated, it was the first and there was a seriousness to it," said Florida wrestling authority Barry Rose, who watched it go down as a young fan. "There was no comedy involved. Paul Jones was mad, he said so, and he went to the top of the bridge and he threw the belt off."

A native of Port Arthur, Texas, Jones (real name Al Fredericks) had just finished a four-year run in the Carolinas as a good guy

In this 1898 poster, Ernest Roeber publicizes his athletic training shows that were a staple of the carnival circuit.

Prince Bhu Pinder (l) shakes hands with Sandor Szabo after they battled in ankle-deep mud in Los Angeles in 1937.

Count Pietro Rossi (r) did a bang-up job managing the Great Elmer (l) in the ring, but appears to have lost control of him at the diner.

COURTESY FAMILY OF COUNT ROSSI

They lost more than they won, but no one doubts Kenny Jay (l) and Jake Milliman were among the most important building blocks of the American Wrestling Association.

PHOTO BY JOYCE PAUSTIAN

It's not enough to attend a live WWE show anymore; you can watch it in the stands on your phone.

PHOTO BY JOE HRYCYCH

Irate fans tell the villainous Spoiler (Don Jardine) just how little they think of him at the Will Rogers Coliseum in Fort Worth, Texas.

Traditionalists were miffed when World Championship Wrestling put its title on actor David Arquette. They probably weren't any happier when Arquette lovingly put the strap on a doll of his grandfather Cliff, known to generations as Charley Weaver.

Though he didn't win the match, Mark Henry's dual ladder shakedown was a highlight of the 2010 WWE Money in the Bank card.

PHOTO BY MIKE MASTRANDREA

Frenchy Lamont readies Smokey for travel to a match as one of wrestling's most prominent sideshows.

COURTESY FRENCHY LAMONT

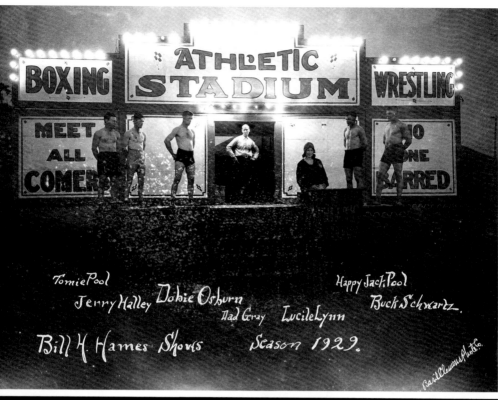

TomiePool
Jerry Halley   Dobie Osburn
Dad Gray   LucileLynn

Happy Jack Pool
Buck Schwartz.

Bill H. Hames Shows   Season 1929.

Basil Clemons Photo Co.

A stable of wrestlers stands ready to take on anyone with the gumption to test their skills as part of the Bill H. Hames Show in 1929 in Breckinridge, Texas.

Two hardcore artists, Necro Butcher (l) and Mad Man Pondo, celebrate a victory in Detroit as World Juggalo tag team champions.

PHOTO BY BRAD MCFARLIN

Though he was an arch heel in Florida and the Carolinas, "No. 1" Paul Jones had a sweet side too.

PHOTO BY PETE LEDERBERG

A TV camera brings it home to viewers as Jimmy Garvin staggers with his wife/valet Precious after a match in Fort Worth, Texas.

COURTESY CIRRUS BONNEAU AND ANA BEAULAC PHOTOGRAPH COLLECTION, SPECIAL COLLECTIONS, THE UNIVERSITY OF TEXAS AT ARLINGTON LIBRARY, ARLINGTON, TEXAS

Jeff (l) and Matt Hardy return to WWE after their Ultimate Deletion storyline in Impact Wrestling created a buzz among viewers and on social media.

PHOTO BY RICKY HAVLIK

In the world of WWE, fans have their own place in the production.

PHOTO BY JOE HRYCYCH

The controversial Paul Jones with the controversial Florida heavyweight belt.

when he went to Florida in March 1972. He quickly became one of the hottest heels in the business, beating Jack Brisco, a close friend in real life, with a banned karate chop for the Florida title in May. "I don't think I ever saw anyone draw so much heat so quickly," Brisco wrote in his autobiography. "Jones was a great heel, arrogant and unbeatable." That set up Jones' excursion to the three-mile-long Gandy Bridge, which connects Tampa Bay and St. Petersburg.

Some accounts say Jones junked the belt to prevent it from falling into Brisco's clutches, but the real impetus came from Buddy Fuller, an old-time promoter working in the Florida office. Jones said he clashed on and off camera with Fuller over rules and policies. "Mainly, they brought him in to control me," Jones said. During a TV interview, Fuller threatened to yank the Florida title from Jones if he persisted in his rule-breaking. Jones did what any good heel would do. He got in Fuller's face. "I told him, 'I'll just take this belt and go back home to Texas and that'll be the last you ever see of it.'" When Fuller continued to push, Jones upped the ante by announcing he planned to feed the belt to the fishes. The taping was done on Wednesday but aired on Saturday, meaning Jones scheduled his action for Sunday, July 16, 1972. "Paul told me when he said it, he didn't even know what he was saying. He said, 'I just said it to show my cockiness,'" said veteran wrestler George South, his top fan and a long-time friend. "He had no intentions in the beginning to go to that bridge, but as the day went by, the TV stations and the police and the news started getting phone calls like 'Is Paul Jones really going to throw this belt off this bridge today?'"

Around 4:30 p.m., Jones headed to the bay with a friend who could drive away the car if police detained the miscreant. "I was looking to go to jail. Fuller wanted me to go to jail, which would have made it even a bigger deal," Jones said. He figured WTOG-TV in Tampa would be on hand since the station televised the Florida promotion's matches. But the size of the crowd caught him by surprise. "The TV was just the previous day and I couldn't believe all these people were coming out almost overnight." Where others saw waves of people, Jones saw opportunity. By slowing down, he encouraged onlookers to block the road behind him — the bridge did not have emergency shoulders at the time — to prevent a police pursuit. "People were screaming at me, 'Brisco's gonna kill your ass!'" After he sent the belt to its watery grave, Jones jumped in the car, nudged aside his friend, grabbed the wheel, and hightailed it toward the St. Petersburg side of the bridge. "The cops are at the bottom of the bridge on the Tampa side," he said. "They can't get up, so St. Pete cop cars are hauling ass up the bridge toward Tampa. I got down into St. Pete, made a U-turn, come back to my apartment, get home, and watch it on the 11 o'clock news." The Florida wrestling office played it to the hilt. The next week's match programs featured a column by John King, a manager known as "The Old Gray Fox," commenting that Jones had "testicular fortitude" to pull off such a feat. "If I'd have done something like that, I'd have wound up sweeping out Sam Muchnick's office to work off my fine!" he said, referring to the National Wrestling Alliance president. Barry Rose, who worked with Jones collecting his wrestling memories, said the belt fling boosted the already thriving business in the Sunshine State. "It's immeasurable the amount of tickets that were sold off of that angle because everybody wanted a piece of Paul Jones then."

Some of those tickets were snapped up by David Sierra, a teenager so obsessed with wrestling that he and referee-to-be Bill Alfonso often skipped school to slip into the Wednesday TV tapings in Tampa. Sierra remembered saying, "Wow!" when he saw Jones cast off the belt.

By 1981, he had launched his own career and was wrestling in Portland as the masked Destroyer, part of Buddy Rose's Army. On the road one day, Rose mused that he'd like to find a way to ratchet up his rivalry with fan pinup Jay Youngblood. Sierra had a flashback. "I'm telling you something. I've seen Paul Jones take the belt and throw it off Gandy Bridge, which is just a low bridge. The heat that he got! If you did this the right way, we could get a bunch of sellouts out of this," he told Rose. Rip Oliver, another member of the army, was from Florida and recalled the gambit, and he seconded Sierra's notion. Rose won approval from promoter Don Owen, fending off veteran star Dutch Savage, who wanted to put the retired belt in his trophy case.

On January 10, 1981, Rose stole the Northwest belt from Youngblood, raced to the TV interview platform, and announced his intention to throw it from the Fremont Bridge into the frigid waters of the Willamette River. Five days later, Sierra, TV announcer Frank Bonnema, and other members of the Legion of Buddy got in a limousine to execute the plan. They had to pass by the bridge in order to pick up Rose, and Sierra couldn't believe his eyes. An hour ahead of schedule, hundreds of people were walking up to the structure. As the heels doubled back to the bridge, the crowd continued to grow. "There was all kinds of boats down there waiting for him to throw the belt. I mean, there had to be twenty, thirty, forty boats down there. There was kids up there crying, saying, 'Don't throw the belt.' I was saying, 'Wow, this is huge. This is definitely going to draw some money,'" Sierra said. It also was a dangerous proposition. The bridge was not designed for pedestrian traffic, and the crowd started to close in on Rose's Army. A false step, an inadvertent move, and it was 175 feet down to the water. "Buddy kept hesitating and talking and I said, 'Buddy, throw the belt.' Finally, Buddy threw the belt and I'm getting in the limo because the next thing that was going to happen was we were going to get pushed off the bridge by accident or get arrested," Sierra said.

Arrested they were. As fans spat on the limo, a police corporal told the wrestlers to drive off the bridge and report to the local precinct. Sierra figured they were going to jail. "He was so mad, oh my God," he said of the corporal. "Some people had dogs with them and he said, 'You know even if one of those dogs got killed by accident on that bridge, you all would be liable.'" By a stroke of fortune, the officer's supervisor was a wrestling fan. Rose invited him and his family to the matches after a stern admonition against a repeat of the antics. In the wrestling storyline, Rose had to pay $2,500 to forge a new belt and present it on TV to Youngblood. Naturally, a fracas ensued, and Youngblood had to go through Mike Miller, Oliver, and Destroyer/Sierra for weeks before he got a solid crack at Rose. "It was unreal," Sierra said. "People believed too. When you've got little kids crying and adults up there begging you not to throw the belt off the bridge, they believed it 100 percent."

Sierra and company got off easy compared with Garvin's 1978

chuck from the Gay Street Bridge in front of a TV camera in Knoxville. He'd gotten the Southeastern title belt from The Mongolian Stomper and announced the time and place of its demise. "When I threw the belt, they had already removed people. They were afraid the bridge would collapse because density is heavier than cars," he said. "I'm glad, I was right in the middle of it. I would have been the first one to go." As soon as the belt hit the current, Garvin felt a tap on his shoulder. It was the same officer who worked the matches in Knoxville. "He said, 'Hey, Ronnie, I'm sorry but you broke the law. Here's your ticket.'" Garvin paid a $15 fine for littering.

That was the key to the belt throws — they were genuine reality TV. "People really believed. Five TV stations believed," said Jones, who died in 2018. "Nowadays it would be an organized publicity stunt and it wouldn't work." In fact, the Gandy Bridge in Tampa has become a sort of unofficial wrestling landmark, though there's no historical marker to commemorate the drowning of the Florida heavyweight belt. After Jones retired to Florida, George South visited him and egged him to return to the scene of the crime. "He thought I was nuts. There was traffic everywhere. I said, 'Paul, I've got to get out. You've gotta take a picture of me at this bridge,'" South said. "So here it is. I'm with No. 1 Paul Jones on that bridge. I'm standing out with rush hour traffic and he's taking a picture out of the window. I wish I'd had a picture of him taking a picture of me, standing there on that bridge."

III. Delete! Delete!

Say what you will about the Final Deletion storyline with a "Broken" Matt Hardy striving valiantly to rid the world of his real-life brother Jeff, aka "Brother Nero." It was inspired. It was visionary. It was insipid. It was vapid. It changed storytelling forever. It was a nonsensical blip on the radar, part Blair Witch Project and part backyard wrestling. But what can't be denied is that it breathed life into the Total Nonstop Action promotion, which was in its final tailspin under the ownership of Dixie Carter and Panda Energy. All of a sudden, people were talking about TNA, which hadn't happened since it brought in Hulk Hogan and ceded creative control over its product to him in 2003–04. ShowbuzzDaily.com reported that TNA Impact hit its highest-ever rating on Pop TV for the Final Deletion show on July 5, 2016, with 410,000 viewers, 90,000 more than the previous week. All the buzz and social media hype helped the company and demonstrated how short-form wrestling storytelling could go viral among users of shareable media.

"The ratings of the following week usually reflect what you did the week before, and if you watch a lot of the Hardy stuff, you saw the rising trends for the Impact numbers during that run," said Mike Johnson of PWInsider.com. "They tried to do all kinds of off-the-wall things. Over the top, ridiculously silly stuff, but if you're going to present pro wrestling as this sort of quirky action-adventure, you've got to go all the way with it. I think that's what they did."

For those who never saw The Final Deletion or The Ultimate Deletion, its successor mini-movie in WWE, a little background is necessary. Matt and Jeff Hardy had both finished up with WWE and were on the sidelines battling addiction issues, with time in rehab for both, and briefly prison for Jeff. Come July 2014, Matt was back in TNA (he was there for a few months in 2011) and had kept himself in the wrestling stratosphere with a series of bizarre, buzz-worthy videos that veered from fascinating and weird to something that appeared to be a cry for help. The duo won the tag championship and each had a turn with the TNA World title. A feud between brothers in spring 2016 ended with a no-contest finish in an "I Quit" match with Matt wheeled away on a stretcher.

The TNA creative team considered its options. With Billy Corgan and Jeremy Borash, David Lagana was one of the writers involved in the storyline. The pitch to the returning Matt was simple: What if you come back broken? What if you come back in a dark manner? Matt agreed, though he nixed the idea of bleaching his hair blond in favor of a single Sweeney Todd–like white strip, as though he'd been struck by lightning. "Matt came to TV and did the first version and it was quite god-awful," Lagana said. But it grew on everyone. "Then Matt had made it so campy that we all started contribute to it. So for example, the characteristics of that character were honed by Matt Hardy. The story was done by all of us together because there was always conflict to it."

In a 2018 WWE documentary, Matt said he appreciated the space he was given to develop the "broken" character. "I had so much wiggle room just to play with, be creative, do different things. 'Okay, cool, here's a blank slate, what do you want to do?'" he said. "When I had that downward spiral, I almost rendered myself obsolete and deleted myself out of the game. Having that burnout, physically, mentally, and emotionally, that's where the whole 'Broken' Matt Hardy character started."

Dressed in more regal attire, with the streak in his hair complimenting his graying beard, Broken Matt spoke oddly, emphasizing irregular syllables in words, with a grandeur and conviction that helped it shine. He acted with a spiritual side, as he felt that he had escaped death during his darkest days, but included elements of the supernatural and mystical, not unlike TV shows such as True Blood, True Detective, and Game of Thrones.

The entire gimmick of Broken Matt built to a bout at the Hardy family's compound in North Carolina. The presentation was pure genius or extreme silliness, depending on your point of view, and maybe both at the same time. The Final Deletion opened with a birthday party for Matt's one-year-old son, Maxel, who received a lovely toy xylophone from Señor Benjamin, Matt's handyman and real-life father-in-law. Matt promised an even better present for his son — to rid the Hardy family tree of Jeff/Brother Nero. Through holographic drones, he challenged Jeff to a final confrontation, though not before running a riding lawnmower over his brother's carefully manicured lawn. The two wrestled a hardcore match in a ring in the woods; highlights included Matt jumping twenty feet from a tree onto a ladder, but missing his prone brother, and the two shooting fireworks at each other. Matt apparently drowned Jeff in a pond, but the victim turned out to be Jeff's alter ego, Willow. In the end, Matt's wife, former wrestler Reby Sky, arrived to hand him the baby's birthday candle; Matt proceeded to light a gasoline pit, down his brother, and get a three count from a well-placed referee.

On Chris Jericho's podcast in June 2017, Jeff said that he and his brother financed much of the shoot, which lasted about fifteen hours with two cameramen and an audio technician. "I spent $3,000 building a clay volcano just to dig a hole on top of it. They brought some power and shot nice stuff on it and made a big ole flame out of it. They put a lot of money on it, but other than that, it was all on us. That's what makes Final Deletion so cool because there is no budget," Jeff said. Matt tried to explain The Final Deletion in the WWE documentary: "It didn't have any traditional wrestling format to it. It had a tree set up that my brother could jump out of. I had to run and block fireworks from a dilapidated boat. My wife was involved in it, my father-in-law."

Jeff Hardy talks with Reby Sky as Matt Hardy lurks in the background during the Final Deletion storyline.

Reaction to the display was immediate and mixed. "People thought it was amazing or they thought it was the worst thing that ever happened to wrestling. We evoked so much emotion," Matt said. "I just remember that night my Twitter feed was insane. It was on video-sharing platforms that had millions of views. It became like a viral deal. People would come up to me and go, 'Oh, man, when you doing another one of those Final Deletion matches?' And that was insane." Wade Keller of the Pro Wrestling Torch said the viral buzz worked for the YouTube generation but left traditional fans shrugging their shoulders. "I don't think it had any lasting effect," he said. "It was inspiring to others to think that they go viral with something, but I'm not quite sure that it had any kind of high impact or lasting effect beyond what we already knew, which is that something kind of different . . . can catch fire briefly and put your name on the map and maybe give you a little boost going forward."

It did boost the career of the Hardys, who were far removed from the high-flying, daredevil ways of their youth. After other "broken" storylines, including a feud with the team of Decay (Abyss, Crazzy Steve, and Rosemary), who tried to kidnap the baby, and an entire episode filmed at the Hardy compound, the brothers left TNA in March 2017. They hit the independent circuit, moved plenty of merchandise, and eventually landed a deal with Ring of Honor. They were decidedly back on the wrestling map. But initially, they lacked permission to continue the "broken" angle. After the Hardys left TNA, now renamed Impact Wrestling and owned by Toronto-based Anthem Sports & Entertainment, Matt's wife, Reby Sky, posted news of friction between the brothers and new management on social media. She complained about poor contract negotiations and the way the company treated the Hardys. Anthem responded by issuing a cease-and-desist letter preventing the Hardys or ROH from referencing Broken Matt or Brother Nero at all. In a sign of the times, Matt continued to be "broken" on his own social media accounts, though not on wrestling shows. In November 2017, Anthem changed its tune and allowed all talent, not just the Hardys, to retain their names and gimmicks in and out of Impact Wrestling. Scott D'Amore, a vice president at Impact, said the decision would ensure wrestlers could invest fully in their characters. Plus, it added value to Anthem's Global Wrestling Network video archive, which licensed the "broken" footage to its competitor, WWE, for the 2018 documentary.

With the Hardys hot and the lawsuit settled, WWE signed the brothers again. The duo worked a ROH show against the Young Bucks on April 1, 2017, in Lakeland, Florida, and then were surprise entrants in a tag team title ladder match at WrestleMania 33 the next day in nearby Orlando, where they won the titles. The fans chanted "Delete! Delete!" at the returnees, but WWE took its time acknowledging it. Shoulder surgery sidelined Jeff in December 2017, which allowed the creative team to revive Matt, now "Woken" and not Broken. In a subsequent storyline with Bray Wyatt, including a far more slickly produced movie-like match at the Hardy residence, Matt found renewed life and even won WrestleMania 34's Andre the Giant Memorial Battle Royal.

But WWE version of Deletion wasn't the same, said PWInsider's Johnson, and it showed the limits of exotic storytelling. "When they tried to play off a lot of the same elements, and even did their own version of Ultimate Deletion, it didn't work as well because it was something that was perfect for the time and place," he said. From the start, Matt was totally committed to his "broken" persona, much the way wrestlers of the 1960s and 1970s never let their guard down in public. That dedication to character didn't work the same way in WWE, in part because he wasn't allowed to use it at first. According to Lagana, Hardy didn't connect with fans because there was "no story to his character . . . and honestly it's not new anymore. They did the style once and they gave up on it."

Not everyone could have pulled off the Deletion storyline, said Sonjay Dutt, then an Impact Wrestling producer, but other wrestlers might be able to draw on the innovation for their own purposes. "I don't think anybody went down that route to try to tell a story or to present professional wrestling in that type of a medium and an environment," said Dutt, who has since moved to WWE. "In that respect, yeah, I think it was revolutionary and it's opened the doors to tell people, 'Hey, you can think outside the box. It's okay.' There's always thinking outside the box, and there's thinking way outside the box. I think it told everybody that's okay, and people enjoy it."

Celebrity Jeopardy

Introduction

Jerry Lawler was borderline frantic. On the mat beneath him, Andy Kaufman, star of TV's *Taxi*, lay nearly motionless, the victim of Lawler's deadly piledriver. Lawler didn't give a hoot about Kaufman's condition, though. It was getting close to the bewitching hour of 11 p.m. at the Mid-South Coliseum in Memphis, Tennessee, at which point the arena would charge the wrestling office an additional $750 for overtime. Lawler strutted around the ring, soaking up the applause for whipping the ultra-cocky Kaufman even as he whispered to referee Jerry Calhoun, "Go ahead and get his ass up and get him back to the dressing room." Calhoun did as ordered and reported back to Lawler. "He says he wants an ambulance." No go, Lawler said. From experience, he knew an ambulance would cost another $250. "So Calhoun goes back over and talks to him, comes back, and he says, 'Andy says he'll pay for it,'" Lawler said in 2016. "So I said at that point, 'Okay, call an ambulance.' This is how far Andy would go to make the thing believable."

Promoters always have wanted an extra dash of celebrity, the lure of a big name to attract casual fans to their shows. Babe Ruth as a referee in Maine and Massachusetts. Pete Rose taking Kane's tombstone piledrivers at WrestleManias XIV and XV. Jay Leno (Jay Leno?) in the ring at WCW Road Wild in 1998. Kevin Federline, Britney Spears' ex-hubby, beating WWE star John Cena

Andy Kaufman has Jerry Lawler at a distinct disadvantage during their well-publicized celebrity wrestling feud.

in 2007. Having a star like Jon Stewart, former host of *The Daily Show*, on *Raw* means he talks about it to his own audiences pre- and post-appearance, reaching new eyeballs, his obvious love of pro wrestling shining through. Relying on celebrities can draw short-term attention to a promotion and maybe provide a brief ratings bump. But unless the celebrities have a thought-out purpose, like Kaufman's memorable heel run in 1982 and 1983, experience shows their contribution to storytelling is decidedly hit and miss.

I. Put Up Your Dukes

Of all the boxers who left the sweet science for the squared circle, no one was more equipped to be a star personality than Tony Galento. He had the pedigree, challenging for the world title and knocking down the legendary Joe Louis, and sported a larger-than-life nickname: "Two-Ton." It wasn't due to his considerable girth, either. Late for a bout early in his career, he was questioned about his tardiness. "I had two tons of ice to deliver on my way here," he said.

The man was made for publicity stunts. On a bet, he ate fifty-two hot dogs the day before a fight. "On some, I didn't eat the rolls," he rationalized. He raced famed swimmer Buster Crabbe despite resembling a bloated whale more than a sleek salmon. He boxed a kangaroo on the Atlantic City boardwalk. He tried to stay atop a bucking bronco in Albany, New York. He fought Teddy, a 550-pound Russian bear, in a cage in Newark, New Jersey, and grappled an octopus in Seattle. "Tony was told he was fighting an octopus and he thought it was the name of a local wrestler," said Carmine Bilotti, his PR guy. Galento gloated when his vanquished eight-tentacled foe died days afterward. His single line from the classic film On the Waterfront was memorable too. Cast as a thug, he watched as a snitch got tossed off a roof and quipped, "The canary could sing but couldn't fly." As Galento's boxing career wound down, how could wrestling not take notice of him, given its reliance on non-wrestlers as gate attractions? "Tony'll be the next wrestling champion. There just ain't anybody around to throw him. He's 275 pounds of solid man — like a rock," crowed his manager and promoter Willie Gilzenberg as he waved a list of eighteen holds Galento had mastered in a mere four months of training. "Tony knows 'em all perfectly . . . We made up the list during training. It helps to have 'em written down, just in case Tony forgets."

Boxing came first, though. Domenico Antonio Galento came into the world on March 12, 1910, in Orange, New Jersey, to parents originally from El Barona, Italy. Growing up, professional boxers were mythic figures and fans crowded around the radio to hear the fights. Jack Dempsey's clash with Georges Carpentier got Galento interested in the sport, and at age ten, he built a makeshift gymnasium in the backyard of his home. In reality, the gym and Galento didn't mesh. He was five-foot-eight and started boxing at around 200 pounds — then 220, then 240, and by the time he was done in 1947, he tipped the scales at 275.

According to BoxRec.com, Galento fought 112 times from 1928 to 1944, winning eighty with fifty-seven knockouts, and gaining a reputation for fighting dirty, especially with a dangerous thumb to the eye. The ring record leaves out many unsanctioned brouhahas, including fisticuffs in a bar he owned with his brother, who once hit Tony with a broken glass the night before a fight. The ultimate smackdown was when his hero, Dempsey, retired from the ring

Tony Galento goes airborne, at least briefly, as he transitions from boxer to wrestler.

and, dressed to the nines, came by Stillman's Gym on 8th Avenue in New York City in 1932 to consider taking on Galento as a protégé. Disgusted by the overweight, lazy Galento, Dempsey slipped on a pair of boxing gloves and entered the ring to teach Two-Ton a lesson, splitting his lip and then breaking his nose. To many, Galento's crowning glory came not during the June 28, 1939, world title fight against champion Joe Louis at Yankee Stadium, where he managed to knock down "The Brown Bomber" in the third round before a TKO loss, but prior to it. That's when he entered the popular lexicon of the time with a crude, bold prediction that he would "moider da bum."

Galento didn't start the boxer-to-wrestler career switch, nor was he its most prominent specimen — former heavyweight champion Primo Carnera beat him to the punch in the 1940s. Instead, he started on the mat circuit as a special referee brought in to maintain order when a conventional ref wasn't up to the task. In January 1942, he was the arbiter for the tag team tussle pitting Bad Boy Brown and Eddie Davis against Finis Hall and Carlos "Babe" Rodriquez in Alton, Illinois. Brown took a swing, so Two-Ton swung back. "Galento, having waxed exceeding wroth at Brown's rassling, biffed Brown in the kisser, knocking out two teeth and also Brown," as the Evening Telegraph eloquently described the action. Back in the dressing room, Brown vowed revenge as soon as he could track down Galento. "They next met at the Columbus hotel and Brown forthwith walked up to Galento and let fly a wide haymaker," the paper said. "Bystanders halted things at this stage. Later, Galento blustered that: 'I'll moider dat bum! He hit me with me overcoat on when I wasn't lookin'!'"

Dollar signs were on Galento's mind when he started wrestling full-time in April 1947. He said he refereed a match in which Carnera wrestled, walked with him to the box office, and found the "Ambling Alp" collected $3,606 for a night's work. "When old Tony sees money being waved under his nose, he ain't going to run away," he told reporters. Wrestling promoters also saw a way to replicate Carnera's moneymaking prowess. "Every time it appears that wrestling fans are getting tired of grapplers in the pro game, mat promoters come up with a new attraction to give the sport a lift," quipped New Jersey sportswriter Sam Siciliano, who correctly foresaw a Carnera-Galento match on the horizon.

Galento's first two opponents were "Dutch" Rohde, the future heavyweight champion as Buddy Rogers, and former world champion Dave Levin. Those two could make anybody look good, even an obese ex-boxer who had trouble keeping his wrestling trunks above his beer belly. Galento took down Rogers on April 29 in Baltimore in a surprisingly clean contest where he used flying mares, armlocks, and headlocks to win in ten minutes. The next night, Levin did the honors for Galento with 2,800 crammed into Washington, D.C.'s Turner's Arena and an estimated 2,000 turned away. "Levin was patient. When Tony couldn't get a half-nelson and couldn't think of another hold, Dave moved conveniently into place and winced appropriately," the *Washington Post* dryly noted. Decades later, Levin shared a memory about Galento that tells you everything you need to know: "We were in the locker room and this very muscular fellow came in and Tony Galento said to him, 'You a weightlifter or you a wrestler?' And the kid says, 'Oh, I'm a weightlifter.' 'Oh, so am I,' Galento said. 'How much can you lift?' Well, the kid said, 'I can clean and jerk 320.' Clean and jerk in weightlifting is to pick it up from the floor, get it to your chest, and throw it over your head. Galento didn't know that at all. So Galento says to him, 'Yeah, that's about what I can lift. How much can you put over your head?'"

Once Galento got away from the skilled likes of Rogers and Levin, he was considerably less impressive. On June 4, Galento and Bull Curry sold out the auditorium in Hartford, Connecticut, going to a no-contest, three-fall brawl with Jack Sharkey, another former heavyweight boxing champion, as referee. Bill Lee of the *Hartford Courant* called the fight a joke, saying he could have absorbed the lefts and rights that Galento threw at Curry without flinching. "Curry, Galento and Sharkey appeared as advertised, but their performance was so awful, so odoriferous, so utterly lacking in amusement, entertainment or excitement, that all three should have been arrested for obtaining money under false pretenses," Lee concluded. That November, Galento and Carnera fought their inevitable boxer-meets-boxer match at Laurel Garden in Newark and it went about as expected — a thirty-minute draw with more slugging than wrestling. "This epic struggle was conducted along lines that would have nauseated Bothner, Hackenschmidt and Gotch," the United Press reported, referring to three early twentieth-century wrestling greats.

"But the capacity crowd of 2,500 apparently got a kick out of it, despite the fans' bewilderment."

Bob Geigel was just breaking into the business in 1950 when he worked with Galento in a mud match in Lake Worth, Florida. It was not exactly the professionalism Geigel envisioned for his wrestling career. "'Two-Ton' Tony Galento . . . was about half smashed. He was a lousy performer anyway, but exciting because he fought Joe Louis. He got down in the mud and couldn't get up. So I figured, what the hell — the match is going about four or five minutes, or six. So I covered him." For a decade, Galento wrestled, armed with fame, his dangerous left hook, and even a polka composed by a fan to get to the ring:

> Heigh-Ho, Tony, he's champion wrestler, number
> one!
> Heigh-Ho, Tony, see how he's got them on the run.
> Heigh-Ho, Tony, he will give the crowd a thrill!
> First a left, and a right, then a tackle and a bite, until
> his foe is lying still!

In a first-person magazine piece written early in his wrestling days, Galento said that he'd rather wrestle than be a boxing champ, that he enjoyed the travel if not the work itself: "There's a funny thing about sportswriters and a lot of other bums that are all the time saying wrestling is a phoney. I wish every one of them could feel the bumps, sprains, black-and-blue spots and other misery I've felt so they'd know that wrestling is much tougher than boxing." Neither boxing nor wrestling was as tough on Galento as he was, though. He had a hair-trigger temper and ran up countless infractions outside the ring. In December 1951, Galento knocked out four of promoter Bill Johnston's teeth at a gas station for allegedly shortchanging him on a payoff from a show in McKeesport, Pennsylvania. Johnston dropped the assault charge after Galento agreed to pay $250 for his hospital stay and false teeth.

Galento tended to his various bars and even starred in *Guys and Dolls* in summer tent theater in Valley Forge, Pennsylvania. His prodigious appetite for a good time was a constant throughout his life, but booze and diabetes were not a good mix. Galento lost one leg to circulatory problems in 1967 and the other just before his death on July 22, 1979. Two-Ton lived on for wrestling fans, though, in an advertisement for a "Sport" hairpiece that ran in *Wrestling Revue* for months after his death. In the first image, dressed in prison stripes and cap, he said, "I tried wearing a hat . . ." With an eye patch and sword, he admitted that "Bald . . . I looked like a killer." In the final image, wearing the hairpiece and chomping on a cigar, he referenced Cassius Clay, the birthname of Muhammad Ali. "Now . . . I'm more beautiful than Clay!"

II. The Fugitive

At the age of twenty, Roger Vest found himself lying prone on the floor of an Ohio high school gymnasium, being kicked by one of the most celebrated convicted murderers in the country. The ambush surprised Vest because Dr. Sam Sheppard, the inspiration for *The Fugitive* on film and TV, wasn't even part of his match. But, as Vest recalled, Sheppard was equally surprised by what happened next.

"I got tossed out of the ring and when I went out, I was laying on the gym floor and Sam comes up and kicks me hard as he could in the middle of the back," said Vest, who was in a tag team match with partner J.D. "Killer" Kent. "J.D. didn't take to that very well. In the scuffle, he took out a TV camera. He either tackled Sam or threw him into the camera, and the camera went down."

Such was the scene when national reporters and TV crews descended on Waverly, Ohio, on August 9, 1969, to witness the wrestling debut of Sheppard, a Cleveland osteopath who spent ten years in prison for the brutal murder of his wife, Marilyn, a crime he said he didn't commit. During the next eight months, Sheppard would travel the country, elope with his manager's twenty-year-old daughter, drink heavily, get flattened by wrestlers who resisted his fingers-in-the-mouth nerve gimmick, and die. It was a bizarre case study of wrestling's infatuation with notoriety that left everyone scratching their heads, wondering what that had all been about.

"I've done some crazy stuff," said Jeff Walton, veteran publicist for the Los Angeles wrestling office, who was on Sheppard detail during an October 1969 tour. "This was the craziest, in terms of trying to rein him in, and you couldn't rein him in because he had been in jail for I don't know how many years. He was a free man now, and he was going to do whatever he wanted to do and with whom he wanted to do it with."

Sheppard was O.J. Simpson before the advent of cable news. In December 1954, a jury sentenced the physician to life in prison for bludgeoning his pregnant wife just before dawn on the Fourth of July that year. Sheppard claimed he was innocent, insisting that the real culprit was a mysterious bushy-haired man who knocked him unconscious during a skirmish at the family's suburban Cleveland home.

He spent a decade behind bars while his lawyers, notably F. Lee Bailey, later part of O.J.'s defense "dream team," argued that Sheppard was the victim of a hit job by the Cleveland media. His story was considered the basis for The Fugitive, the Emmy Award–winning show about a doctor falsely accused of murdering his wife. In 1966, the U.S. Supreme Court overturned Sheppard's conviction, saying a "carnival atmosphere" had prevented him from getting a fair trial. In a retrial, a second jury found him not guilty.

Sheppard thus bounced from one carnival atmosphere to another. He returned to practicing medicine, but was named in two wrongful death suits for accidentally cutting arteries of patients, who bled to death. A German woman he married in prison divorced him, saying he threatened to beat her up. The Internal Revenue Service was after him for $11,000 in back taxes. As for wrestling, choose your story: Colleen Strickland, the daughter of wrestler George Strickland, said she brought Sheppard to her dad's attention when the doctor visited her Columbus hair salon. In another account, Sheppard said he was grappling on the side with Strickland when Big Bill Miller saw him and suggested he turn pro. Dr. William W. Wiltberger, who wrestled professionally from time to time, wins "most likely" honors for recruiting Sheppard into the business. Wiltberger was a surgeon in the Ohio penitentiary system when he met the inmate and he arranged Sheppard's debut performance. In any event, Strickland became Sheppard's manager and announced that his charge had been a fiend on the mat as a prep student and collegian. "The truth is, Dr. Sam had to make a hard decision in college between entering medicine or become a professional wrestler," Strickland declared without documentation.

That set the stage for Sheppard's first match, which attracted two national networks, both major wire services, and a host of reporters to Waverly, population 4,800. "I'd never been around anything where all your big network TV stations were there and I mean they were all there," Vest said. "It was pretty chaotic. Before the matches started, in the dressing room, you couldn't get near Sam. It was packed in there." To a skeptical reporter, Sheppard demonstrated his new finisher — a mandibular nerve hold in which he pressed two fingers under an opponent's tongue and his thumb against the bottom of the chin, a maneuver later employed by Mick Foley. Silly? Yes. But it made a believer out of the reporter. "Sam stuck his fingers in this guy's mouth and he went down to his knees," Vest said

In addition to kicking Vest, Sheppard scored a singles victory that night against "Wild Bill" Scholl. He followed that up with wins around southern Ohio, Cleveland, and Buffalo, all in tag team matches. Strickland would soften up the foe and Sheppard, slim at 195 pounds, would clinch the contest with his nerve hold. All the while, Sheppard maintained he was simply getting some exercise and raising money for cancer research, telling the Cincinnati Enquirer in September that his purse, less expenses, went to the Sloan-Kettering Cancer Research Foundation. "Of course my expenses come pretty high," he added.

Dollar signs flashed in the eyes of The Sheik (Ed Farhat), who owned the Detroit territory and handled Sheppard's bookings. It was time to go national. In Los Angeles, promoter Mike LeBell was running a show on October 24 to benefit the City of Hope Cancer Research Fund. Sheppard headed west with Strickland, his wife Betty, and daughter Colleen for a tag team match against Magnificent Maurice and Don Carson. "The Sheik wanted to make Sheppard like Andre the Giant and have him go all over and he would be an attraction," Walton said. "Mike did a favor for The Sheik, saying 'Okay, I'll bring him in and get a lot of publicity out here about it.' And we did. We got a ton of publicity because here was the guy, this was the original Fugitive, the guy saying he didn't kill his wife. Did he or didn't he?"

After four tumultuous days, Walton and LeBell concluded Sheppard was anything but innocent. First up was a huge mainstream news conference in which Sheppard professed his devotion to cancer fundraising. "That was bullshit. Typical wrestling thing in those days. They wanted to make the money and that's why Strickland was with him," Walton said. Unstated was his devotion to alcohol. Sheppard was drinking vodka and orange juice like, well, a condemned man. Walton estimated he brought him a fresh bottle of each every ninety minutes to two hours. "I was not only trying to babysit him, but bringing him booze constantly," Walton said. As it turned out, Sheppard, forty-five, also had a devotion to Colleen, who was twenty, making goo-goo eyes at her and suggesting to a writer that she might make a fine Mrs. Sheppard No. 3.

Which she became, under unusual circumstances. Sheppard snuck Colleen out of her hotel in the middle of the night and across the border into Mexico. He claimed later that the secret nuptials were on October 21, but the date doesn't quite line up since they spent that afternoon with a *Los Angeles Times* columnist — the marriage might have been a day or two later. Colleen later explained her impetuousness by saying she felt sorry for Dr. Sam. "The ceremony was real quick too — and in Spanish," she said in 1974. "For all I know we

Sam Sheppard applies his in-the-mouth nerve hold to Magnificent Maurice during an October 1969 tag match in Los Angeles.

might have got divorced that day." Regardless, when Sheppard showed up at the Olympic Auditorium for the match with his new bride on his hip, it equaled any battle royal LeBell had promoted. Strickland was apoplectic; he wanted to cancel the match, leave Los Angeles, and kill Sheppard, not necessarily in that order. Several wrestlers restrained him from tearing into his son-in-law. Strickland's wife was crying hysterically. Somehow, the show went on, and Strickland and Sheppard emerged victorious, managing to score a win against Carson and Maurice. "It was terrible," Walton said. "It was the first time I had encountered something like that. I was just learning the wrestling business as it was and to have to do this was just like, 'Oh, my God!'"

The bloom was off The Sheik's ambitious plans, but Strickland and Sheppard still had obligations to fulfill. They headed to Tennessee as part of a deal with The Sheik and promoter Nick Gulas, one of his closest allies. On November 5, the partners lost in the ring for the first time, falling in Nashville to The Black Menace and Saul Weingeroff, a fifty-three-year-old manager. Atlanta was next on the dance card, with a November 28 semi–main event in the City Auditorium. This time, Strickland and Sheppard were lined up against the Assassins (Joe Hamilton and Tom Renesto), one of the greatest tag teams in history and a duo unamused by a jailbird turned nerve grip specialist. "They told me who I was with and everything, and I said, 'I hope he's in the mood for an ass whipping,'" Hamilton remembered nearly fifty years later. "I went out there to whip his ass and that's basically what I did. Tom said neither of those guys could throw a fit if a mad dog bit them." At one point, Sheppard entered the ring to administer his famed tongue press to Hamilton. The Assassin responded by coldcocking his opponent, knocking him out, and winning the easy pinfall. "I didn't know where his fingers had been. So I knocked the shit out of him," Hamilton said. Asked why he didn't just bite down on Sheppard's fingers, Hamilton laughed. "Hitting him was much, much more satisfying."

That was it for the tag team of George Strickland and Sam Sheppard. Sheppard and his wife returned to Ohio and, transgressions forgiven, moved in with her parents. He operated a small general practice near Columbus and donned the trunks occasionally to diminishing fanfare. Vest's dad, Hank, who promoted in southern Ohio, tagged with Sheppard a few times, and Roger was on several cards with him. He said he was never certain whether Sheppard was supposed to be a hero or a villain in the ring, especially after he ran out and kicked young Vest in the side that first night. "There's a good guy and a bad guy in wrestling. I'm not sure and I don't know what he was supposed to be. He'd be a heel today."

On April 6, 1970, Sheppard died at his in-laws' home in Columbus. Betty Strickland said he had been battling the flu for three days but refused to be treated by a doctor. "He had been drinking some lately but he wasn't on any drugs as far as we knew," she said. Sheppard frequently told friends that he had developed cancer from volunteering to be a cancer cell guinea pig in prison, but coroner Robert Evans rebutted that notion. Instead, Evans said April 15 that Sheppard died of liver failure brought on by drinking or a bad diet. His death led to the reshuffling of an April 18 card in Chillicothe, where Sheppard was scheduled to wrestle. In the days leading up to the show, a stand-in was named for the deceased grappler. The story came full circle. The replacement was Roger Vest. "I never did see the guy smile," Vest said. "To me, he was hardened in prison."

III. Ready to Rumble

For the record, David Arquette doesn't think he should have been World Championship Wrestling world heavyweight champion either, and agrees that it was ludicrous for an actor to follow in the footsteps of Lou Thesz and Harley Race. But that doesn't mean he fails to relish the memories. Jovial and never defensive about his two-week title reign in 2000, he launched into a tale: "There was one time, we were all at the bar, and everyone was pretty fed up that I was the champ, they all hated it, you know what I mean?" Arquette and Ric Flair began talking, and "The Nature Boy" came away with an appreciation for the Hollywood star, who bought a round for the bar. Shouting over the din, Flair addressed his colleagues, "Hey guys, he's one of us!"

Given that his family history in entertainment goes back to the days of vaudeville, it's unsurprising that Arquette referenced a bizarre 1932 movie with circus oddities welcoming an outsider with a creepy, pulsating chant around the dinner table. "Literally, at that moment, I was so happy. It was like my Freaks moment, 'One of us, one of us.'"

Arquette formed friendships that continue to this day with the likes of Diamond Dallas Page and Jeff Jarrett and is still in awe of the skill set required to succeed in professional wrestling. He's relished the few opportunities to appear on WWE TV in recent years — once with a "Former WCW World Champ" sign while in the SmackDown crowd.

"I cannot say enough good things about the human being that David Arquette is," said Jarrett. "He's just like me in one aspect . . . we're both big, big wrestling fans. So that's something that we definitely have in common. His family business is Hollywood, my family business is professional wrestling, and we've had conversations, multiple conversations about that."

The Arquette acting legacy runs deep. Charles Arquette performed in vaudeville. His son Cliff was a regular radio voice actor until TV came along and he created the character Charley Weaver — chances are you saw him on *Hollywood Squares*. Cliff's son Lewis was an actor and he married an actress/poet, Mardi Nowak. They had five children, all of whom acted: David, Rosanna, Alexis, Richmond, and Patricia.

Born in 1971, David was a wrestling fan and attended WWE shows featuring Hulk Hogan and Andre the Giant at the Los Angeles Sports Arena. In the 1990s, he was a full-time actor, making guest appearances on TV and in many films such as *Buffy the Vampire Slayer*, *Airheads*, and *Never Been Kissed*. On the set of the first *Scream* horror movie, he met his first wife, Courteney Cox, who propelled him into a different kind of stardom as she was part of the TV mega-hit *Friends*.

Then along came a new project, a pro wrestling movie written by Steven Brill and directed by Brian Robbins. The Warner Bros.– produced *Ready to Rumble* tag teamed with WCW for access to some of the sport's hottest stars like Bill Goldberg and Page. "It was just another film. The director, I'd known forever," said Arquette, not really recalling how it all came about. "I also knew [co-star] Scott Caan forever, so it was just like it made sense and it was fun."

In his posthumously published autobiography, Chris Kanyon recalled meeting Arquette, who wanted to play around in the on-set ring. Kanyon taught him the basics and was floored to be invited to the home that Arquette shared with Cox. "On my way over to the Arquettes' house, I thought about David. He was funny, but also nutty at the same time," Kanyon wrote. With so many WCW wrestlers appearing in *Ready to Rumble*, Arquette was in nirvana and asked a lot of questions. He credited Kanyon, Page, and Gregory Helms as being especially patient as he learned about the in-ring and the behind-the-scenes details.

No one thought that the goofy film would spill over the way it did into WCW storylines, he said. Synergy made sense: promote the movie on TV, just as the movie put over the WCW wrestlers as personalities deserving of the big screen. "The Turner organization put millions upon millions of dollars in the movie *Ready to Rumble*," Jarrett said. "It's a business, no different than any other business that you want to broaden your platforms and so there was an opportunity there." WWF tried something similar in 1989 with *No Holds Barred*, a Hulk Hogan vehicle, but unlike WCW, the federation never put its world championship around the waist of Zeus (Tiny Lister), Hogan's antagonist in the flick.

Arquette debuted on *Thunder* on April 19, 2000. "The first time I went, I just went in, I jumped in the ring, I was supposed to bust something up, and then it got such a big pop, or whatever, that they're like, 'Why don't you stay and do the pay-per-view?' And that's kind of how it all started."

With a brown belt in karate, Arquette was young and fit, though at five-foot-ten, he was dwarfed by all but the cruiserweights in WCW. A convoluted storyline — chief writer Vince Russo had a hand in it — had Jarrett blaming Arquette for costing him the WCW world title that Page held, even though Arquette hadn't been involved in the match. A tag team bout was set for *Thunder* on April 25 with Jarrett and Eric Bischoff, a power broker on- and off-screen, against Page and Arquette. The winner of the pinfall would be declared the new champion. Page hit the Diamond Cutter on Bischoff, Arquette scored the pin, and referee Mickey Jay (who came in after original ref Kimberly Page took a bump) raised his arm, handing him the title belt. "He was just living in a wonderland," Jay said. "He was, 'Hey, okay, whatever.' To me, in WCW, there were a lot of things that really didn't make a lot of sense."

The two-week reign went by quickly — who really remembers Arquette defending the title against Tank Abbott and winning in a couple of minutes? The ratings were terrible. At the Slamboree pay-per-view on May 7, a triple-decker cage was erected to mirror the one in *Ready to Rumble*. Jarrett emerged as the champion after Arquette clocked Page with a guitar, turning heel and then disappearing from storylines. "At best, it was a very difficult situation," Jarrett recalled. "Dallas injured his back the day of, so there was a lot that went into that." As well, only a year before in the same venue, Kansas City's Kemper Arena, Owen Hart had fallen to his death. Jarrett, who had been pals with Hart, was being interviewed on screen when Hart died.

WCW wrestler Maestro (Rob Kellum) spoke for most "perplexed" wrestlers. "It really was nothing against David Arquette because he was a great guy and he donated his salary to charity," 'Stro said. "It was the whole principle of it, honestly. For a lot of us, the heavyweight championship is sacred ground. You disrespect the heritage and the prestige and the history of that championship, then what is there to go for? From their point of view at the time, it would give the belt publicity and all that stuff, and they're playing off the film, *Ready to Rumble*. But a lot of us from the old school, it didn't sit too well with us, just the fact as a belt, it was something we all should go for."

There was no plan, Arquette noted. "It seemed so cavalier and I treated it kind of cavalier. I was just going along. They didn't want me to do any wrestling because I could get hurt," he said. "They wouldn't let me do any stuff. I had to beg 'em into the final cage match to let me jump off the top rope." It's an understatement to say that it was more random than what Arquette was used to in Hollywood. "It was really super difficult. I could have used more direction. I didn't know what I was doing. No one was really guiding me on that part. So I kind of went with it, but I'm dyslexic, I've been dropped on my head too many times."

Dyslexia, injuries, age, a heart attack; none of it was a deterrent for Arquette to get back into the ring in 2018; if anything, it was justification for a renewed health regimen. It started with an angle on *Championship Wrestling from Hollywood* with RJ Skinner that culminated in a bout in July. Following that, Arquette and Skinner (who often wrestles as RJ City) took their act on the road to select promotions. As in his first run, Arquette got a lot of grief, but had his defenders. Promoter David Marquez hosted the first Arquette-Skinner bout, and quashed any debate about the Hollywood star's qualifications. "The bottom line is Arquette is a pro and has great respect for what we do. Also, in my opinion he's more qualified than the majority of the shit I see by the minute in Independent Wrestling," wrote Marquez in a Facebook post.

David Arquette grabs a kendo stick to go after Bubba Ray during a House of Hardcore bout in December 2018.

Like a great heel, Arquette relished the negativity, and took to Twitter to address the trolls:

> I love all the hate I'm getting here. It baffles me that these people can love wrestling just like I do but I'm a joke in their eyes. That's why I'm doing what I'm doing. 8 months of training. Two surgeries, 3 broken ribs, traveling across the US, getting . . .
>
> Stiffed by promoters, helping shine a light on talent I believe in that aren't getting recognized, doing little things I won't mention to give back to both wrestling and individual wrestlers and I'm the asshole? Wrestling is for the people and by the people . . .
>
> I may have grown up in Hollywood but I'm not some stuck up punk. I had an opportunity to be a part of WCW when I was in my 20's to travel with some of my heroes in the ring and I took it. I'm done apologizing. Now I just want to kick some ass . . .

It nearly ended tragically for Arquette, during a Death Match against Nick Gage at Joey Janela's LA Confidential in November 2018. During the bloodbath, a piece of broken glass lodged in his neck. "I'm thinking, 'I just got cut in my neck, and if that's my jugular, I'm going to die,'" Arquette told SI.com. "Pretty quickly after that I exited the ring and had someone look at it." He was back in the ring three weeks later.

What was the legacy of Arquette's WCW title reign? The stunt got some mainstream publicity and Arquette worked the title belt into the 3,000 *Miles to Graceland* movie he was filming at the time of his wrestling dalliance, clocking star Kurt Russell with a chair. In short, though, the brush with celebrity didn't advance the fortunes of WCW, which closed shop in 2001. "When David Arquette won the belt, all the times I had won the WCW belt just went out the window. That belt absolutely meant nothing," Kevin Nash told wrestling journalist Wade Keller.

"*Ready to Rumble* didn't work right either when it first came out, but people have come to like the movie, or love the movie. But yeah, sometimes things just don't work," said Arquette. "I don't care, though, I'm in the record books! . . . I might have been the WCW killer, but I'm still in the record books. I don't know why WWE doesn't relaunch that brand; they have it in their back pocket."

Jarrett won't let Arquette take the fall for WCW. "You're still talking about it to this day, so it was a lightning rod of emotion, good and bad, and obviously a lot of the fans took that on it. The environment, and I've said this on multiple, multiple, multiple interviews, it's impossible and it's not fair to point the finger at one act or any one person. It was truly the culture that was created in a corporate environment that it was destined to fail . . . When a wrestling organization is run by non-wrestling people, it's just a matter of time before failure."

Helping Hands

Introduction

Frankie Williams. Tom Reesman. Randy Barber. Randy Hogan. Randy Mulkey. Bill Mulkey. Mike Fever. Al Johnson. Al Schiller.

Rich Landrum was usually an announcer, but this time he was a listener. Outside an arena in Richmond, Virginia, he came across police officers and security guards placing playful penny ante bets on who would win the matches that night. They noticed Landrum and figured he had the inside scoop. Everyone loves an underdog, but to pick veteran Charlie Fulton would be throwing money away, one man argued. Landrum didn't say anything. He just looked like he knew something, and the bet was changed: Fulton to win. "Charlie Fulton won that night. He had never won in Richmond. He won, and he just went berserk," Landrum said. Fulton jumped around the ring yelling, "I won! I won!" The fans too were going nuts, a feel-good story, since there is more Charlie Fulton than Hulk Hogan in most of us.

"Iron" Mike Sharpe. Tom "Rocky" Stone. "Golden Boy" Apollo. Vincente "Bull" Pometti. Ron "Bull" Johnson. Jeff "The Gambler" Vann. David "Cowboy Hondo" Novak. George "Scrap Iron" Gadaski. "Silent" Brian Mackney.

The roll call of wrestlers who spent their careers on the short end of things is much longer than the list of champions. Some were consigned to opening match status because they were too small, too bland, or held better-paying day jobs. Others never got a promotional push that often seemed like the luck of the draw. The life of

Charlie Fulton gains a rare upper hand.

undercard guys could be funny, artistic, dangerous, and irresistible, all at the same time. But there's no question they were essential building blocks of wrestling storytelling.

Rusty Brooks. Keith Eric. Joey Maggs. Lee Wong. Rocky King. Rujet Woods. Barry Hardy. Mario Mancini. Chuck Cell. Steve Lombardi. Barry O. Curt Hawkins.

I. Unsung Heroes

Reno Riggins was in a bad way, his body limp in Lex Luger's agonizing "human torture rack." Luger draped Riggins across his mighty traps like a sack of flour, flexed his muscles, and bounced up and down. The pain! The agony! As he contemplated his woebegone fate at the upside-down arena around him, Riggins noticed something out of place. He whispered to his conqueror.

"Hey, superstar. Why don't you turn around and face the camera?"

So Luger turned, step by step, still holding Riggins, still flexing, still displaying his physique, until the main World Wrestling Federation TV camera could show him in all his musclebound glory. A small moment, but one that speaks volumes about the little guys, the whipping boys, the down-on-their-luck losers who sometimes looked like they ran past GNC straight to the food court — they were the unsung heroes of wrestling storytelling.

"I knew with every spot I called, the end result was me getting my butt kicked," said undercard veteran George South. "But I always told people if you have an opportunity to make those top guys look good, then we are all going to look good because people are going to come and see the matches."

That's what the starmakers reliably did during the second half of the twentieth century. Take a dive. Offer a helpful hint during a match. Provide feedback to the office on newcomers. Make your opponent look invincible. Do whatever was necessary to advance a storyline, even when that work involved loss of blood.

Journeyman Peppi Dipasquale of Canada agreed to go head-to-head with The Sheik (Ed Farhat) on October 27, 1973, on Pittsburgh TV when his colleagues demurred, sensing a likely bloodletting. Wrestling as Dino Nero — a quicker signature with which to dispatch autograph hounds — Dipasquale was willing to endure a blade job since The Sheik had helped him get a green card to wrestle in the United States. Next thing he knew, Eddie Creatchman, The Sheik's manager, flicked ashes from his cigar on Dipasquale's chest. "That was bad, then The Sheik started cutting me," Dipasquale recalled. "I said, 'Ed, you cut me four times; that's enough.' I grabbed his arm and finally he let me go. A couple guys came in and pulled me out. That ring was soaked almost total red."

Outrageous, especially by today's hygiene standards? Sure. But incidents like that built Dipasquale's reputation as a dependable hand to the point that other wrestlers showed their appreciation by handing him a win in a January 1974 battle royal in Akron, Ohio.

Early in the contest, Dipasquale slid under the bottom rope and hid by a corner of the ring. When six-foot-nine Ernie Ladd was about to claim victory, Dipasquale crawled up the steps and threw a dropkick that barely grazed the big guy. "Somebody threw a cup, okay? So you could hardly tell what hit him first, but I knew I didn't touch him. That goddamned rolled-up cup hit Ernie — good timing — and he took the bump over the top rope. They did that for me, those guys. It was planned."

Boxing has always had its tomato cans and Joe Palookas, but in wrestling, the idea of the perpetual fall guy really took root in the 1950s with the growth of television. Promoters saved name-brand matches for paying crowds and developed an entire class of stepping stones, or, in industry lingo, "carpenters," since they couldn't draw a house on their own but could help you build one. The late Frank Thompson, who broke into wrestling in Brantford, Ontario, in the late 1940s, realized that at 225 pounds, he was too small for any

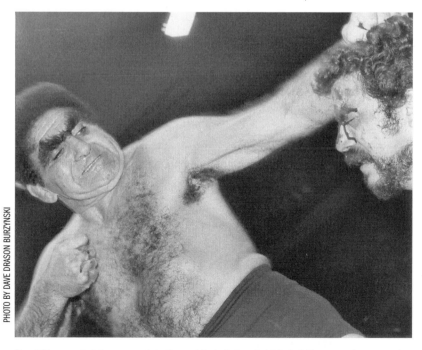

PHOTO BY DAVE DRASON BURZYNSKI

Peppi Dipasquale takes a punch to the noggin to help establish Bull Curry as a fearsome star.

heavyweight-dominated territory. So for fifteen years, "Scotty" did his job as cannon fodder to the stars.

"From Sky Hi Lee to Hans Schmidt, Fred Atkins, Don Leo Jonathan, and down the line, those were just a few of the boys that I had the opportunity to put over," he said. "I distinctly remember working with Hans in Buffalo. I put him over in about two minutes. I must have done a good job because my wife got called at one in the morning to see if I was all right." In 1954, Schmidt returned the favor when he worked with Thompson at the famed Marigold Arena in Chicago. "This was the big time and he made me look good for about twenty minutes before he dumped me."

For Kenny Jay (Kenneth Benkowski), no experience was needed, but that kept him largely relegated to carpenter status for nearly three decades in the American Wrestling Association. He wrestled steers on the family farm in Holdingford, Minnesota, but never knew about the pro game until he was about twenty and saw it on TV at his sister's place in Milwaukee. "It wasn't that I put them over, it's just that the guys I had were a lot better. Most of the guys were amateurs before they become professionals," he said. "I didn't have the experience for professional wrestling. What I got is what I just picked up on the way." Known as "Sodbuster" for his Minnesota landscaping business, Jay wrestled mostly as a good guy, figuring no one would want to employ a heel landscaper. "I'd go on TV and I'd hear Mad Dog [Vachon] say, 'Gimme Kenny Jay!' And I thought, 'Uh, oh,'" Jay laughed. "I struggled. I took the beating and kept on ticking."

Gene Ligon showed up at a 1983 tryout in Charlotte, North Carolina, hoping to do better than his substitute teacher's salary of twenty-five dollars a day. Ligon had wrestled with the small International Wrestling Association in 1977, but it had been the better part of six years since he stepped in a ring. Sparring partner Mike Rotunda was being a little uppity, so when he charged, Ligon dropped to the canvas, grabbed Rotunda's crotch, gave a little squeeze, and rolled him up. "I slapped the mat fast as I could, one, two, three times. Got up, crawled out of the ring. He said, 'Get back up here.' 'Nooo. I gotcha!'" As Ligon told Sandy Scott, who hired him following the wily crotch maneuver, "I just want a job. I'll do whatever I can. I'm a company man. If you want me to fall down five times, I'll fall down five times . . . If you want a guy that'll do everything he can to make the star look good, I'm your man."

Sometimes you were allowed to put up a fight, sometimes you were not, and sometimes you were unsure which way to go. Jim Lancaster learned the fine art of lying down on command at Lou Klein's low-rent training center in Allen Park, Michigan. "I would go to Detroit and they'd say, 'You're working with Fred Curry and you're going to go four minutes. Just hit him a couple times and he'll do his flying thing and you'll die and he'll be the greatest thing walking on water,'" Lancaster said. So it was a shock when former NWA heavyweight champion Gene Kiniski approached him before their May 1973 match on St. Louis TV, and asked what he wanted to do in their ten-minute timeframe. "I had no clue what the guy was talking about," said Lancaster, noting St. Louis promoters liked competitive preliminary matches. "I didn't know what to say to him. I didn't have any moves. I get in and I die. Hollywood stuntman." But Lancaster said the incident was the first time he learned the importance of telling a story in the ring, which served him well during a twenty-year career.

Storytellers they were, even if fans didn't appreciate the skills of the down-and-outers. "I had to learn the psychology more so than a lot of the guys that were getting the push to begin with," said Dusty Wolfe, a lower-card fixture in the WWF and WCW in the 1980s and 1990s. "Not only did I have to know what the office wanted out of them, but I had to know what my role was going to be, whether it was to go one minute and I never raised my fist, or to go five, eight minutes and compete with them. You had to understand the big picture; it wasn't just in the moment."

That's what Ligon was thinking when he wrestled Owen Hart, working as the Blue Blazer, on WWF TV in October 1988. "Nobody could do anything with him because he had so many stunts he could do. It was hard to enhance him." An ex–college gymnast, Ligon knew he was just what the Blazer needed. "If you want me to help you walk those ropes, I know what to do. When do you a flip, I'll flip you high and I'll do it just right because we used to do this in gymnastics," Ligon told him. Sure enough, the Blazer walked across the top rope, jumped in the air, and landed a flip. Another flip and a dropkick. Perfect. "He goes, 'Thank you. That was great. That was fun.' That's how I got over," Ligon said. "If a guy who was a star recognized me and said you made me look better, I said, 'Thank you.' That's all I was trying to do."

Above all, the utility men of wrestling had to be nimble because they might work with a smooth operator like Curt Hennig and then someone less mobile, say, The Warlord (Terry Szopinski), the muscular colossus who debuted for Jim Crockett Promotions in 1987. Warlord never had a match until he entered the ring with South. "I'd come up with something where I'd try to run from him, not because I was afraid of him as a shoot, but I had to make the ten or fifteen minutes last," South said. The first time they wrestled, South bounced off the ropes to take a shoulder tackle. Warlord went down. "I said, 'No, Warlord, I don't think you're the one that's supposed to be going down. We won't tell nobody. I'm the one who's supposed to be going down.'" To add insult to indignity, South swung by a drive-thru restaurant after a show in Macon, Georgia, to hasten the five-hour return trip to Charlotte. Warlord announced he couldn't eat in the car, got out, and went to a restaurant next door. "Here I am putting my order in and I'm looking at Warlord sitting," South said. "He ate, took his time, put a napkin on his shirt. I didn't get home till like eight in the morning."

Few undercard wrestlers exuded more personality than scruffy-bearded Jake "The Milkman" Milliman, so called because he downed a gallon of milk every day for a year to gain the 100 pounds that AWA owner Verne Gagne demanded before he'd consider him for a tryout. Milliman had never wrestled the legendary "Crusher" Lisowski until they met on TV. During the match, Crusher told

Milliman to watch out for the double barrel. "I'm thinking to myself as I come off the ropes, 'What in the hell is the double barrel?'" Milliman said. Turns out it was Crusher's rubric for a double thumb poke to the eyes. "He'd hold his thumbs up and you had to run into them. People don't realize that you'd go way out of your way to get the guy over." The payoff? Milliman said Crusher congratulated him on one of his best TV matches ever, and when he attended Lisowski's funeral in 2005, he was surprised to see a video loop of the match. "Why in the world of all the main events he was in would they be playing that over and over? Then I found out from his son that was the last match he had on TV."

Then there was John "Earthquake" Tenta. Riggins wrestled with the 468-pounder — at least that was his billed weight — in arenas and on TV as the office built him for a program with Hulk Hogan. Earthquake had to be a force of nature — he couldn't go down, even on one knee, for anyone but Hogan. "So I had to be on the creative babyface side of things. I did a lot of chasing, a lot of Jack and the Beanstalk. I'd go through his legs, dropkick him in the back, and he'd almost lose balance. It was David and Goliath, except Goliath was going to sit on David in the end," Riggins said. "There is a form of artistry and creativity in laying all that out, whether it's a three-minute match or a one-hour time limit match. And that's what wrestling is. It's a ballet. It's a song. It's storytelling."

By no means were the little guys always losers. Many of them had successes in territories in North America. It's just that the money wasn't as good. "I knew what my role was," Riggins said. "I could go wrestle in Memphis and make fifty bucks a night or I could come here [the WWF] and make 300 bucks a night. What do I want to do? When you go to the bank, they don't ask you, 'Sir, did you win or lose?' They ask you, 'Sir, how may I help you?'"

By the time of the Monday Night Wars in the 1990s, the enhancement guys of old gave to more competitive matches designed to boost TV ratings. Some hung up their boots to pursue other ventures while several found a niche as wrestling trainers. There remains a fondness for the lost days of the starmakers. Milliman, living near Milwaukee, remembered a conversation with Jerry Blackwell about life as a lesser light. "Blackwell came up to me one day and said 'Jake, if I was to propose to you that there's $200 sitting down in Kansas City, would you drive down and get it and drive back?' Well, hell, no, I wouldn't. But you're not only driving down there, you're getting beat up! That'll kind of put it in perspective how much fun we had, like in any sport, the locker room, everybody's ribbing everybody. It's just laughs, camaraderie in the locker room."

II. The Perennial Candidate

Long before WWE Hall of Famer Donald Trump won the presidency, long before Jesse Ventura became governor of Minnesota, long before Jerry Lawler ran for mayor of Memphis, Dominic Doganiero was on the ballot, election after election.

While managing a pharmacy. While saving a drowning child. And while wrestling as a doctor, an Indigenous person, and a Hindu star. In the post–World War II era, Doganiero was representative of a group of undercard wrestlers whose duty was to build up the main eventers, occasionally venturing from their home territories to other regions, but always keeping a traditional job in their back pocket. Except nothing about Doganiero was traditional, unless you can name another wrestler who ran for office more than a dozen times under the Socialist Labor Party banner. Win or lose, the stocky native of Camden, New Jersey, was delivering a message whether it was in the ring or in the political arena. "He was very personable, yet very private, very simple, yet he was a very complicated guy," said his youngest brother Enrico. "My brother 'Doc' is the kind of guy I wish I could write a book about."

Born December 11, 1921, to Italian immigrants, Doganiero was raised in an ethnic section of Camden and started wrestling at the local YMCA at ten. He had good company, growing up with Dutch

Rohde, the future Buddy Rogers, who was a blocking lineman when Doganiero played halfback at Camden High School in the 1930s. But their careers took different paths when Doganiero's father died of a heart attack. With two brothers in college and two younger brothers at home, Doganiero quit school at sixteen to take over the family barber shop and assume the role of man of the household. At the end of World War II, when his brother Bernardo opened a pharmacy, Doganiero managed the front end of the business, which still operates today.

So he was relatively old when he first got into the wrestling game at twenty-eight, lured by "the call of the wild," as his brother Enrico laughingly referred to it. "Wrestling is something he always wanted to do and unfortunately, he was never able to give it his full attention because of the family situation at the time. So every once in a while, Doc got that urge to go off and to wrestle for a while."

His earliest recorded mat appearance was in December 1950 in New Jersey, and he stuck close to home for the first few years of his career, wrestling regularly on the undercard at the Camden Convention Center as "Doc" Doganiero, a play on the pharmacy connection, with Billy Darnell and Rogers usually as headliners. He wasn't long into his career when he was in the headlines for another reason. On August 6, 1951, the twelve-year-old son of Mr. and Mrs. Arthur Miller of Camden was waiting for a swimming class at the YMCA. Through a misunderstanding, the boy entered the water during a break between classes, tried to get out, slipped, and fell. Doganiero was there and applied artificial respiration. The mom and dad thanked Doc and others in a letter to the editor of the local paper for preventing a drowning.

Despite his good deed, Doganiero was the heavy in the ring, with a roughhouse style that suited his appearance. "He could never wrestle as anything but the bad guy," Enrico said, noting his brother had a scar over his eye from an auto accident. "He had the look of a villain and even when they tried to make him the good guy, he was always the villain. He had a dark complexion, maybe five-six or five-eight, and he had that gangster look about him, gentle as he was."

Doganiero stepped out into Ohio and Indiana for promoter Al Haft in 1953, billed as a South American and appearing regularly on Haft's TV shows. The 220-pounder feuded with Jackie Nichols and got disqualified in Marion, Ohio, for roughing up a young Ray Stevens. He also did a stint as Chief Thundercloud in 1954. Upon his return east, he

Wrestling journeyman Dominic "Doc" Doganiero takes a swing at a baseball, like he took a swing at politics and the mat.

announced that he was claiming the Italian junior heavyweight championship of North America and wrote *Ring* magazine to let the editors know. Dan Parker, the New York newspaper columnist hypercritical of wrestling, was surprised New York promoter Toots Mondt didn't think of Doganiero's title angle first: "This will make Toots Mondt seethe . . . How did Mondt ever overlook that title?"

Through the mid to late 1950s, Doganiero was a fixture on from cards from Massachusetts to Florida with bouts against stars like Argentina Rocca, Pat O'Connor, and Ricki Starr. He carried on a bit of a feud with Stevens and his wrestling brother Don (Don Kalt) with their February 1956 tag match, described by the *Baltimore Sun* as "one of the wildest tag team matches ever to take place at the Coliseum." Mostly, he was the perfect foil for a babyface just entering the territory — Doganiero was the first opponent for wrestlers like Chief Big Heart, Adrian Baillargeon, and Jim Bernard in Baltimore. "Rocca and those guys got the big gates, but the wrestlers like Doc got very little at the time. Doc never made much money wrestling, but he just loved to wrestle. That was his job — to build them up a little bit," Enrico said. In 1959 and 1960, Doganiero worked in Ohio as Indian Bamba Tabu, not to be confused with the Bamba Tabu who wrestled in the 1930s and 1940s. He worked a little bit of his real life into the Tabu character, telling Ohio sportswriter Steve Bulkley that he was an ex-football player based in New Jersey where his brothers were doctors, lawyers, and pharmacists. On the other hand, he proclaimed himself to be a master of the sleeper hold, which he learned as a tot growing up in Calcutta: "Why every boy that is over ten-year-old in India knows how to put this hold on someone. We used to do it just for fun." Ethnic subtleties aside, Tabu/Doganiero earned a main event match against former world champion Lou Thesz in Cincinnati that drew a packed house of 3,300. He returned home for good later in 1960 but continued to wrestle part-time from Connecticut to Maryland through 1963.

At the same time Doganiero was trying to rouse fans through his actions on the canvas, he was trying to rouse voters in support of his political goals — replacing capitalism with a system oriented toward the working class. Doganiero considered the two major political parties to be exploitative peas in the same pod and favored a system of industrial congresses made up of working men and union delegates. With his brother Bernardo, he became active in the Socialist Labor Party in the 1950s. Doganiero was on the ballot for the Camden County Board of Freeholders — county commissioners — in 1954 and the New Jersey state legislature in 1955. He ran for freeholder unsuccessfully again in 1958, and to make matters worse, he was squashed by 600-pound Haystacks Calhoun in a handicap match a few days later.

Among other attempts, he ran for the state legislature in 1959, 1961, and 1963; freeholder again in 1962 and 1964; and for the U.S. House of Representatives in 1966 and 1972. His last race was for the state senate in 1973. He never came close to winning; as a minor party candidate, he did well to win several hundred votes in most cases. But losing did not dampen his enthusiasm or his view of the inequalities in capitalist society. "Either we have spread the message enough to enable the workers to make the right choice or we are doomed," Doganiero said after one election. As his brother Enrico put it, "He was very devoted in what he believed and he would welcome a good debate with anyone who was willing to listen."

Because they saw him on TV or at the arena, teens flocked to Doganiero like a magnet, and he spent years giving wrestling lessons to Camden youths, training future pro Les Morgan. He also owned one-quarter of the family pharmacy when three of his brothers merged two stores into one, and was active in the business until he died on February 27, 1994, at seventy-two. He's remembered by praise that his friend Vince Salerno heaped on him at the height of his wrestling career. Doganiero was "a villain in the ring but a polished gentleman and a wonderful guy with a heart as big as the Rock of Gibraltar out of the ring."

III. The Cutting of Dr. Beach

To this day, the thought of it makes Dave Drason Burzynski sick to his stomach. Burzynski was a lanky teenager photographing a meaningless match between Dr. Jerry Graham and Dr. Beach in Detroit's Cobo Hall for The Sheik's promotion. A couple of ring-side snapshots for the record and he retreated to a hallway perch to talk to friends. Beach was going to lose — he always did — and Graham was so obese and past his prime that the match was a certain stinkeroo.

Then came the scream. Then came Dr. Beach. Then came the blood. "The match wasn't over," Burzynski said. "You just hear him screaming and running through the hallway. And as he comes running, it's like, 'Wow, that's a weird finish.' And the next thing you know, I look at him and I mean it was like a waterfall, blood is coming out of his head." It was as gruesome a sight as anyone would want to bear. Crimson soaked the hallway floor, a backstage table, several towels, and Beach's socks and white boots. Graham had sliced his young opponent temple to temple, bone deep, with a razor blade, and Beach would bear that scar for the rest of his short, unfortunate life.

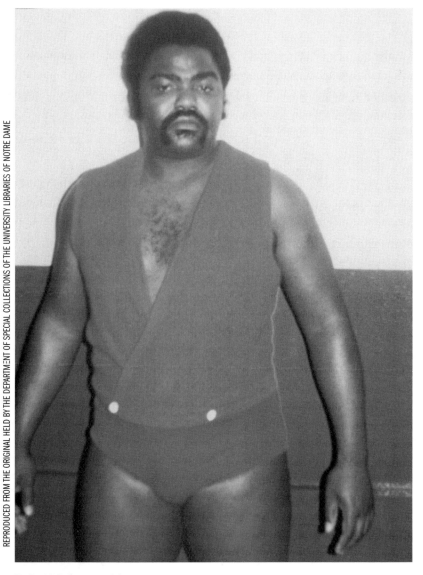

Dr. Beach before a match.

The cutting of Dr. Beach illustrates a larger point. For decades, promoters lined up "squash" matches to position name-brand wrestlers as beasts who tore through hapless opponents in seconds, laying the groundwork for bigger programs down the line. In many wrestling companies, squashees like Dr. Beach were bit players with no recourse if their opponents decided to take advantage of them. Their job was to take what the star dished out, even if it cost them seventy-six stitches across the forehead. "I always felt that we were a meat market," said Jim Lancaster, who trained around the same time as Beach at Lou Klein's gym in Allen Park, Michigan. "That was the idea that Klein put in our head too, which was, 'This is how you break in the business. Just go do what they tell you to do. If they want you to lose in thirty seconds, lose in thirty seconds.'"

The second youngest of twelve children, Emmanuel Beach grew up in Proctor, Arkansas, before moving with his family to Toledo, Ohio, as a teenager in the mid-1960s. Beach was working at a Jeep plant and a cleaning products manufacturer when he surprised his family by going into wrestling in 1972 at twenty-four. James Beach drove his brother an hour every day from Toledo to Klein's Gym in his quest for more income, fame, and some popularity among the fairer sex — Beach described himself as a "doctor of womens." At a stocky five-foot-ten, he worked the losing end of TV matches in places like Detroit, Pittsburgh, and Cleveland, and openers on arena shows.

If Beach was struggling to climb the wrestling mountain, Dr. Jerry Graham was tumbling down the other side, and fast. Once a red-hot heel with make-believe brother Eddie Graham, his penchant for boozing and troublemaking got him bounced from territory after territory. By October 1972, he was a 300-pound has-been when The Sheik, who owned the Detroit promotion, gave him another shot. It wasn't as though the good doctor exhibited newfound gratitude in return. On a trip from Columbus, Ohio, to Detroit, Graham was a passenger with Burzynski and Tony Marino in Killer Tim Brooks' new Cadillac. "The next thing you know we're getting attacked by this motorcycle gang, whipping Brooks' car with chains and stuff, and kicking it, trying to run us off the road," Burzynski said. "Come to find out Jerry Graham's throwing his beer cans out the window at these guys and swearing at them. So that's what caused that." The next day, Burzynski hooked up with Brooks for another trek, only to find his driver had spent a half-day trying to clean the car. "Jerry Graham had red pants on that day and he just pissed his pants and left a big red spot on his backseat. So Brooks was trying to rub it out and it never came out. It faded out but it never came out."

That, then, is the gentleman whom Beach entrusted to cut him with a blade before a sold-out crowd at Cobo Hall on April 7, 1973. It was unusual to spill blood in the second match of the night, but The Sheik apparently wanted to boost Graham's sagging career. "Beach was supposed to get color in a match at Cobo and since it was his first time he asked the good doctor to do it for him," said Ricky Brogdon, who as Rick O'Toole had wrestled in the opening match. Graham apparently relished the opportunity. In fact, he approached Burzynski backstage and asked him if he was shooting color film that night. "I said, 'No, I always shoot black and white for the magazine.'" "You should have color film," Graham replied.

The match was over almost as soon as it began. Long-time Detroit fan Eric Goldenberg was close to the action, watching as Graham grabbed his young rival in a front facelock and broke out his scalpel. "From the moment the bell rang, Graham was on Beach and was pounding his head. You could basically see Graham gigging Beach. He opened him up completely from one end of his forehead to the other. It was truly the proverbial crimson mask," Goldenberg said. "The match made no sense other than Graham trying to put himself over as some monster heel."

At that point, Graham's reputation mattered less than Beach's life. Pandemonium reigned. Wrestlers grabbed Beach by the arms and legs and carried him into the locker room. "Wild" Bull Curry, scheduled for the main event, pushed suitcases off a table and screamed at Beach to lie down. Brooks wrapped his towel around Beach's head and pressed with all his might. The Mighty Igor tore off a towel rack to keep feeding Brooks towels. Beach bled through them one by one. Lancaster was sitting two feet from the trembling wrestler: "I was kind of shocked in place. I just couldn't believe what I was looking at. I mean, the guy looked like he had been in a car wreck." Bobo Brazil and The Stomper (John Hill) worked to calm Beach as the flow of blood eventually subsided. During the interminable wait for an ambulance, wrestlers sponged off Beach and rinsed his blood-choked nostrils so he could breathe through his nose. Brogdon went to a hospital with Beach, still in ring apparel. It took seventy-six stitches to close the wound.

Back at Cobo, Graham was in heel mode. From the dressing room hallway, Burzynski listened to the racial epithets fly. "That's what it was, how you make a green nigger red . . . Taught that little fucker a lesson," Burzynski heard Graham rant from behind a closed door with The Sheik. The Stomper, with Curry right on his heels, banged the door open and headed for Graham, who was lucky to be in the company of his boss. "I thought Stomper was going to kill him if it wasn't for The Sheik being in there," Lancaster said. Brogdon grabbed a cab, took the freshly stitched Beach to Klein's Gym to get some clean clothes, then returned to Cobo while the show was still going on. The Sheik paid Beach $100 for the night's work. He did not pay Beach's hospital bill or reimburse Brogdon, who died in 2012, for cab fare back to the arena. He also aired the taped match on Detroit's weekly TV show. "Sheik may have been aghast by it, mad about it, but it didn't make him mad enough not to show it on television to the world," Lancaster said.

Brogdon said Graham later told him that Beach flinched at the moment of impact, but only two people know the truth of that. Beach wrestled Graham again, apparently without incident, on July 21, 1973, in an opener in Akron, Ohio. Beach also wrestled for regional promotions in Kansas City, Missouri, and Amarillo, Texas, as "Bad News" Beach and "Bad News" Jackson. In October 1974, he broke off from The Sheik's promotion and joined an opposition group headed by Marino and Brooks that ran shows as the Universal Wrestling Federation. "I was managing this tag team called the Destroyers and some other guys; we'd go against Beach and he was great to work with. For me, taking bumps and stuff, he protected me and he was light as a feather," Burzynski said. That UWF run was the first time Beach achieved notable success — as a good guy, he won the promotion's International championship in June 1975. "I might have went up in the ring that night. Pretty proud of him at that time," his brother James said. "You go a whole lot before you finally get up there to the top. They keep you at the bottom for a long time before you finally break through, and he was just about to break through, and that's when he had this bad accident."

In late summer 1975, Beach was a passenger in a rental car with Marino and Kay Casey when a tire blew out on a road in Canada. He took the brunt of the impact and was hospitalized for fourteen days, initially diagnosed with a dislocated hip, his brother said. After being transported to Mercy Hospital in Toledo, doctors determined that his hip was shattered. His wrestling career and his working days were over. Beach lived the rest of his life on disability; several operations to rebuild his hip were unsuccessful. He swelled to more than 300 pounds before dying of complications from pneumonia on September 10, 1994, at forty-six.

In wrestling, the lasting memory of his three year career is the night Graham carved his forehead in front of 12,000 fans. "To tell the truth, when I look back on it now, I couldn't even look at the floor, the hallway going back to the dressing room because it was just a river of blood," Burzynski said. "I've seen guys blade and stuff like that — Bobby Heenan, Jimmy Valiant, The Sheik — these guys just bled like hell but it was part of the card. So as a photographer, you look for that kind of stuff and you see it all the time. But the Beach one, it was a whole different game."

The Rise and Fall of the Territories

Introduction

From the 1930s to the 1980s, the territorial system was the dominant feature of professional wrestling. Wrestlers commonly spent a few months in a territory, then moved elsewhere. At its best, the system helped wrestlers perfect their crafts by working six or seven nights a week in front of live audiences against foes with contrasting styles. "When you got out in the territories, you'd learn how to work and tell a story because you could have a fifteen-minute, twenty-minute match," explained Tom Prichard, who came up through the territories. Each proving ground enabled wrestlers to add a little to their games — New York was a big man's enclave, Tennessee was a brawler's paradise, St. Louis emphasized competition without a lot of frills, and so on.

WWE CEO Vince McMahon put a stake in the heart of many territories by buying their TV time and subbing in a well-produced show that made local productions look third rate. To be sure, a lot of territories were already on the rocks. Some promotion owners like The Sheik in Detroit and Dick the Bruiser in Indianapolis kept themselves as main eventers long past their primes. They killed their own business, said wrestling wise man Frankie Cain, which gave McMahon an opportunity to change the direction of storytelling. "That's why when McMahon came in with the bodies, the youth and new faces, man, the people want to see new faces. And when

Wrestling's governing class: NWA President Sam Muchnick (c) goes over paperwork with (from left) promoters Morris Sigel, Cowboy Luttrall, and Dave Reynolds.

he came in, he cut the matches very short so the average fan who watched it couldn't tell if they could wrestle or not. You'd put thirty guys on the card and they've got their five or six minutes, which was smart on his part. Look at the money he made. Look at the pay-per-view. They made millions."

I. The Godfather of Wrestling

Take any major development in wrestling in the second half of the twentieth century and Jim Barnett's hand was in it. Building a national television promotion out of Chicago. Running the world heavyweight champion's schedule. Organizing the first WrestleManias. Arranging a sale to his friend Ted Turner to form World Championship Wrestling. Though he mainly stayed in the background, Barnett was a legendary operator, a starmaker with a knack for breathing life into dead territories by employing the power of TV better than just about anyone. In 1964, he and Johnny Doyle, his business partner and mentor, took on the challenge of putting wrestling in Australia back in the limelight. Emile Dupre was part of their small crew and remembered how a $50,000 investment in TV paid off. "We just went on doing television for six weeks. That's all we did was TV. When they opened up the arenas to this new show, they were four deep, almost a quarter of a mile long. All the arenas were sold out, unbelievable business," Dupre said.

Barnett was an unlikely godfather of wrestling. He wore over-sized glasses, spoke in the manner of a member of the British House of Lords, and was gay and Jewish in a tough guy's sport rife with prejudices. Yet he wielded uncommon influence for more than forty years. Kevin Sullivan called him "the smartest guy in the wrestling business, ever" and said Barnett's years of shrewd connections were instrumental when he helped Vince McMahon build a syndicated TV empire in the 1980s. "Program directors and station managers were wearing watches that Jim Barnett gave them. Without Jim's influence, Vince wouldn't have been able to get on all those stations because Barnett dealt with every one of them," Sullivan said. "There would be no WWE today if there wasn't a Jim Barnett."

Born in Oklahoma City on June 9, 1924, James Edward Barnett graduated from the University of Chicago, where he met Jim Oates, a lawyer who'd be his financial backer for life. After receiving his degree in December 1947, he bought a television set and got hooked on wrestling, one of the few programs on the air at the time. He wrote to Chicago promoter Fred Kohler about his newfound interest and landed an office gig with publicist Dick Axman in 1949. He helped Axman write and edit *Wrestling As You Like It*, the top publication of its day. By 1953, he was Kohler's road agent with stars like Verne Gagne, guaranteeing them $300 a week, splitting any surplus, and organizing the DuMont Network's national broadcasts from Chicago. With Kohler, he purchased the

The influential Jim Barnett (r) poses with Leroy McGuirk, promoter of the Oklahoma-based territory.

Indianapolis territory in 1956 for $15,000 and implemented his own ideas, the foremost of which was identifying a local station manager, bringing a gift or a cash-stuffed envelope, and getting wrestling on the air.

Barnett is sometimes incorrectly identified as the inventor of TV studio wrestling. That honor belongs to Ohio promoter Al Haft, who started it in 1950 in Dayton, finding that a small studio was an ideal setting for camera placement, controlled lighting, and fan reactions. Barnett took it a step further. Haft's promotion was established; Barnett was just cranking up. He would go into a wrestling-starved territory on the air for several weeks to whet the fans' appetite. In December 1958, he and Doyle moved into Cincinnati using WCPO-TV six weeks before their first monthly card. By March, they were drawing more than 15,000, the largest sports crowd in the city in years. "It was unbelievable. You had to be there to believe it," said Joe Smith of the Cincinnati *Enquirer*. In Detroit, Barnett and Doyle pumped $18,000 into half a dozen studio shows on CKLW-TV across the border in Windsor, Ontario. Their first show at Olympia Stadium drew 16,226 fans and a state gate record of more than $40,000. During the next four years, Barnett and Doyle would generate more than $1.8 million in gate receipts in Detroit and extend their reach to eighteen markets, including Denver, New Orleans, Atlanta, and Kansas City, Missouri. "Just like Lawrence Welk on his first tour after he hit television," Doyle told the Detroit *Free Press*. "We have tapped a new stratum."

COURTESY CHRIS SWISHER COLLECTION

Barnett was not about to see his TV model compromised. In fall 1959, a U.S. House of Representatives subcommittee investigated a series of quiz show scandals in which contestants received answers to jackpot questions ahead of time — rigged programming, not unlike professional wrestling. There were cries to investigate TV wrestling as well; the head of the Federal Trade Commission said it could conceivably be regulated as "deceptive entertainment." Barnett told several people during his lifetime that he went to Washington, D.C., with some cash and lobbied politicians to exclude wrestling from restrictions on fraudulent programming. The legislation, which Congress passed in 1960, banned fixed contests of "intellectual knowledge, skill or chance" — nothing physical. Whether Barnett had anything to do with the result was less important than the fact that his colleagues thought he did. "Nobody could prove it back then and certainly nobody is going to be able to prove it now," said Joe Hamilton, who worked with Barnett in Georgia and knew him for nearly fifty years. "Whether it happened or whether it didn't happen, whether he got to some senator and greased the palms, and greased the right palms or not, nobody really knows. But he got credit for it back then. And that skyrocketed him insofar as the power structure of wrestling was concerned and he became the almighty."

When business waned after nearly six years, Barnett and Doyle sold Detroit to The Sheik for $50,000, headed to Australia in late 1964, and turned it into the hottest property in the world with stars such as Killer Kowalski, Dominic DeNucci, King Curtis Iaukea, and Mark Lewin. "I truly believe that by the results you have proven the greatest manipulator in the business today," National Wrestling Alliance President Sam Muchnick wrote him. Doyle and Barnett alternated six-month duty shifts until Doyle died in 1969. Barnett drew on the same clamorous booking pattern he'd used in Detroit. "When Doyle was there, business was terrible, because he didn't want any heat. The business really jumped up when Barnett got there because he let all the guys do what they wanted. That's why he was so successful in Australia. He booked good talent in there with good ideas," said Killer Karl Kox. His payoffs were good, but he kept a strict grip on his wrestlers. "You had to dress up to get on the plane, wear a suit or coat, or wear a sportscoat or slacks with a tie," Rip Hawk said. "One day Tarzan Tyler, he thought he was going to go there in shorts and a T-shirt. Well, he did, but when he got off of the plane, James E. Barnett was there. And that was it for Tarzan Tyler."

Meanwhile, the legend of Jim Barnett, man of distinction and influence peddler *par excellence*, grew to mythic status. For a decade, he lived in a $20,000-a-year penthouse suite — $133,000 a year in today's dollars — at the Chevron Hilton in Sydney, usually with his partner, Lonnie Winters. He received the New York Times by airmail every day and became a serious art collector. He spoke in his own patrician language. Rip Hawk was "Rippola." Swede Hanson was "Sweedles." Just about everyone was "my boy." One time, Hawk and fellow wrestlers were bumped from a Trans Australia Airlines flight in Melbourne. "He called the head of the airline and said, 'I run people year after year through these airlines all over the country of Australia and you're shoving my people off?'" Hawk said. "Within two minutes, we were all aboard that plane, sitting where we should sit. That's a lot of strength to do something like that in another country. But that was James Barnett. Guarantee: he could do whatever he wanted in that country. Of course, he didn't do bad in this country either." Indeed, Barnett kept his finger in the domestic political pie even from afar. While in Australia, he rented his swank Louisville apartment to an old friend, U.S. Senator Marlow Cook of Kentucky, so the politician could maintain a voting address in his home state. The fee? A dollar a month.

Barnett returned stateside in late 1973; he had tired of being away from home, and a change in Australian laws made the business less profitable. While his finances were always sketchy, he told SLAM! Wrestling that he bought thirty-eight percent of the Georgia promotion for $268,000, cash on the barrel. Barnett's

Georgia Championship Wrestling won a head-to-head battle with the All-South Wrestling Alliance, a dueling promotion headed by Ann Gunkel, and became the dominant wrestling company in the country, thanks to exposure on Ted Turner's WTBS superstation. "He was more open-minded than most of the people that have the wrestling background," Hamilton said. "Barnett, he was all ears. Anybody that had any advice for him, that knew about the business, he respected them. He may not take your advice, but he always listened to you." Barnett was a good visual judge of talent, as well. One Saturday morning in Atlanta, he encountered Tommy Rich, who had come from Tennessee to be massacred on TV by Abdullah the Butcher. "He went and told Tom Renesto, who was the booker, 'Hey, do not, do not beat that kid on TV today. I don't want him to open his mouth. I just want him to sit there,'" said Bobby Simmons, who worked with Barnett for eight years as a referee and office assistant. Barnett quickly struck a deal with Tennessee promoter Nick Gulas to acquire Rich, who became the first babyface of the national cable TV era and briefly a world champion.

The scope of Barnett's political contacts was staggering; he could hang with kingmakers as readily as with preliminary wrestlers. When President Carter nominated him in 1980 to the board of the National Council on the Arts, those who vouched for Barnett included Georgia governor George Busbee, Atlanta mayor Maynard Jackson, Carter administration budget chief Bert Lance, and Bob Strauss, former head of the Democratic National Committee and one of Washington's most influential power brokers. "It would not be uncommon for me to get a phone call in the office from Governor George Busbee's secretary, leaving a message as to which door they would meet Jim at the Capitol, and I would regularly see cars pull up with government plates," said Gary Hart, who booked for Barnett in the 1970s. When Andrew Young ran for mayor of Atlanta in 1981, Barnett attended his functions and sent Simmons to events for Young's opponent, playing both sides of the aisle. "When Young won, at his inauguration, I went with Jim and sat in the front row,"

Simmons said. Just as importantly, Barnett took care of people who took care of him, even Ted Turner. Take 1980, the year *Urban Cowboy* was a smash movie hit. "We gave everybody Stetson cowboy hats for Christmas that year — program directors, TV station managers, general managers," Simmons recalled. "Jim gave Turner that year a Stetson hat and a briefcase that looked like the side of a cow."

After his membership had been put off for years, Barnett rose to power in the NWA as secretary-treasurer and booker for the world champion. As always, he understood the power of television; at the 1979 annual meeting of the NWA, Barnett presciently warned his colleagues that "cable cannot be stopped." He agreed to brand his champions as Georgia-based so their appearances on TV would not undermine champs in other territories, and he refrained from taking his company national because of his relationships with other promoters. When Georgia Championship Wrestling started running shows in Ohio and West Virginia in 1982, Barnett paid The Sheik to operate in his territory, even though the villainous wrestler was no longer doing regular business there. "He honored that agreement that he would not step on other guys. Our TV was so strong, we could have done anything we wanted to," Simmons said.

Barnett could also throw his share of elbows. In 1973, he agreed to buy into Eddie Graham's Championship Wrestling from Florida promotion. Veteran Frankie Cain said Graham, whose business was split among about ten investors, confided that he planned to keep running slightly in the red, so Barnett would sell back to him at a reduced price. "I told him, 'You can't mess with Barnett. When you'll be sleeping, he'll be lying awake thinking,'" Cain said. "Barnett was really, in spite of what they say, an intelligent man . . . he was a devious bastard, flamboyant. He was the first one to really succeed in wrestling where others failed. He's never given credit for what he did."

He also was the first, and likely the last, wrestling promoter to sit on the National Council on the Arts. "He's always talking about the arts," said Vincent J. McMahon, father of the current WWE owner, who called Barnett "an outstanding promoter — probably the best in the country." But Ole Anderson and other Georgia wrestling shareholders didn't think so. They pushed him out in late 1982, accusing him of lining his pockets and mishandling the company's finances to support his posh lifestyle. Barnett landed with the WWF, where he helped develop a syndicated TV network and put together the first three WrestleManias. Meanwhile, Anderson scrapped Barnett's incentive payments to TV executives and arena managers, only to see his Georgia operation quickly nosedive. In response, Barnett was all too happy to help the younger McMahon loot Georgia wrestling's coveted Saturday night time slot on WTBS.

McMahon cut Barnett loose amid suspicions that he was keeping a back channel to NWA promoter Jim Crockett. After surviving an apparent sleeping pill overdose, Barnett did join Crockett, who also had national ambitions. But Barnett quickly determined that company was "B.S.," in his words, and facilitated its sale to his friend Turner. World Championship Wrestling was born, and Barnett remained with WCW as a senior consultant until its demise in 2001. "By then Jim was more of an emeritus status," said promoter Gary Juster, who was close to him in later years and executor of an estate worth only about $15,000. "Jim made good money, but Jim was like Ric Flair. He would make a dollar, then spend three."

Barnett died on September 18, 2004, at eighty; living in Atlanta, he had overcome a battle with lymphoma, but was frail, took a bad fall, landed in the hospital, and contracted pneumonia. "I had a twelfth-grade education, he had a college education, and he never at any time made me feel insecure about my intelligence or my ideas," Gary Hart said. "He accepted me at face value and always listened to what I had to offer. The only other promoter in Jim's class was Vince McMahon. They were the two classiest guys in wrestling, and knew the business better than anyone, neither of them ever having had a match in their life."

II. You Can't Fight City Hall

Johnny Powers was pleading for his wrestling company's life, and the city fathers of Winston-Salem, North Carolina, were having none of it. In a three-month period, Powers had taken an ambitious wrestling league off its deathbed, nursed it back to health, and rebooted it on a smaller, more manageable scale. But unbeknownst to Powers, Winston-Salem had struck a deal with Charlotte-based wrestling promoter Jim Crockett Jr. For the sum of one dollar, Crockett agreed to take a destitute hockey team off the city's hands and in turn get sole rights to a publicly owned arena, locking Powers' International Wrestling Association out of its base of operations. "All that we would like to request is that we can stay in business as a wrestling organization and supply a different and unique and separate product from the Crockett organization," Powers told the city's Board of Aldermen on January 5, 1976. Request denied. "We have a binding contract," Mayor Franklin Shirley announced, and when Powers protested, Shirley threatened to sic the sergeant-at-arms on him.

Powers slumped in his seat. You couldn't fight city hall, the judicial system, or the wrestling establishment, as the case of the International Wrestling Association showed. The industry remained firmly in the grasp of a small network of promoters despite a federal decree aimed at preventing a cartel in wrestling, and it wasn't about to open its ranks to competitive storytellers. "Business is business and business is not always a fair deal," Powers sighed years later. "After the Winston-Salem Coliseum got taken from us, that basically took the wind out of our sails."

Powers was trying to make a go of it with the remnants of the IWA, which kicked off in January 1975 in a bid to become a coast-to-coast player in a world of tightly held regional wrestling territories. Eddie Einhorn was a wrestling fan whose TVS network televised college basketball on a syndicated basis in the pre-ESPN days. He pumped $1 million into the IWA, built a national chain of TV affiliates, and handed the wrestling end of things to Pedro Martinez, a promoter based in Buffalo, New York, who had a wheeler-dealer reputation. Einhorn and Martinez enlisted some of the biggest names in wrestling, including former world title-holders Ivan Koloff, Lou Thesz, and Ernie Ladd. Mexican high-flyer Mil Mascaras was the promotion's inaugural champion and, with Argentina Apollo and Luis Martinez, added a more international flavor than regional promotions of the day. "The IWA's philosophy is 'Select, don't settle,'" IWA president Robert F. Hatch told *Wrestling World*. "Why should people have to spend their hard-earned money to see inferior talent week after week?"

Under pressure from his business partners, Einhorn pulled the plug after nine months and a half-million dollars in losses. Two things did him in. Wrestlers started complaining that Martinez cheated them on payoffs. "I was going to shoot Martinez one night in South Carolina," Rip Hawk said. "He shorted me on my payday and he sent the money with one of his stooges . . . I got my gun out of my bag and I guess he warned Pedro and he took off. I was just going to shoot him in the leg." From a business standpoint, the IWA was locked out of top venues because many arenas granted exclusive performance rights to sports and entertainment promoters. "There was ego there," noted Lars Anderson, an IWA recruit who said Einhorn wanted to promote in Madison Square Garden because he was from the area. "But Vince, the McMahon family, had the Garden locked for up sixty years. So he couldn't get into the Garden."

Powers had been Martinez's business partner and a top draw for nearly six years in the National Wrestling Federation, which stretched across parts of New York, Pennsylvania, and Ohio. He joined the IWA in mid-1975 to help with booking and suddenly found himself on an emergency phone call with Martinez. Not only was Einhorn pulling out of the IWA, he had called TV station managers to cancel the weekly wrestling show. Without TV visibility, the IWA was doomed. Powers raced to TV station managers in Virginia and the Carolinas, asking them to keep time slots open.

He found some matches that already had been taped, mixed in a few interviews, and created a slimmed-down product solely for the Mid-Atlantic market.

Crisis averted, but only for a while. In North Carolina, the Greensboro Coliseum was a stronghold of Jim Crockett Promotions,

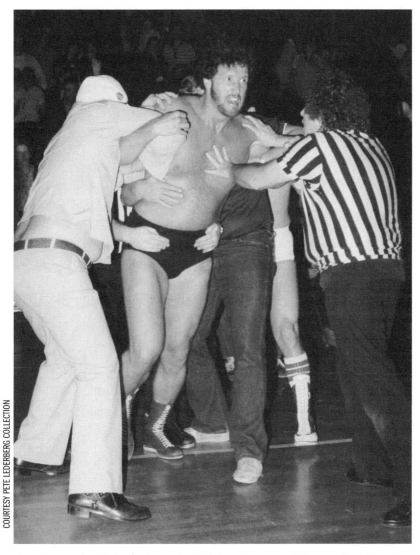

Given his struggles, it's hard to know whether Johnny Powers was being restrained from other wrestlers or other promoters.

so the IWA set up shop thirty miles west in Winston-Salem. At the time, Crockett had minimal interest in Winston-Salem. In 1975, the year the IWA geared up, his company ran five shows in the city coliseum, and only one after April, averaging 2,902 fans and receipts of $12,157. The IWA entered Winston-Salem in October, after Einhorn left, and put on five shows averaging 3,640 and fans and receipts of $13,357. That convinced Powers to buy out Martinez and establish Winston-Salem as the hub of a three-state promotion, similar to the one he'd handled around the Great Lakes. "It had some promise," he said. "Winston-Salem and the peripheral area was a big draw."

Then the hammer came down. The Winston-Salem Polar Twins of the Southern Hockey League played their home games at the city's 8,500-seat coliseum. In November 1975, the team's owners told city officials that they were on the verge of closing shop, which would cost Winston-Salem revenue from rental fees, concessions, and parking. On December 8, with the city manager as the mediator, Crockett agreed to take over the team and beer concessions for one dollar, and run monthly wrestling shows with a fourteen-day non-compete period before and after.

Powers was planning to up Winston-Salem to two cards a month when he learned about the deal. He begged the Board of Aldermen to rethink the protective clause and give the IWA a fighting chance. "Winston-Salem is sort of critical for us because we have been very well received here. This is sort of critical for our survival. This was one of the few bases that we were utilizing to get a foothold in the marketplace," Powers said. But the council silenced Powers for the night after hearing Jim Oshust, manager of the Greensboro Coliseum, opine that Winston-Salem wasn't big enough for both promotions.

Two days later, Powers was back at work, writing managers at arenas in Virginia and the Carolinas for possible IWA dates. Their responses smacked of collusion. From Charlotte, NC, Park Center: "There is not sufficient public interest in professional wrestling in Charlotte to justify professional wrestling events more often than weekly." From Dorton Arena in Raleigh, NC: "There is no chance of using the building for another wrestling event as long as the present contract is in effect." From Cumberland County, NC Memorial Auditorium: "It is not felt there is a need to add or detract anything from the program of professional wrestling being presented at this time."

On January 28, 1976, Powers and the IWA sued Jim Crockett Promotions, Crockett promoter Joe Murnick, and the city of Winston-Salem for $1.5 million in U.S. District Court in Charlotte, alleging Crockett's company had worked with officials in seven cities to create a business monopoly. On the surface, it seemed like the plaintiffs had a case. In 1956, three dozen National Wrestling Alliance promoters, including Crockett's father James Sr., signed a consent decree with the U.S. Justice Department pledging to refrain from restrictive contracts and monopolistic practices. In announcing the order, the department said NWA members had "prevented independent promoters from obtaining adequate bookings and denied to professional wrestlers their right to freely obtain engagements." In return, the government dropped an antitrust lawsuit against the NWA. "We took it to court, me a little naïve thinking that there was such a thing as restraint of trade," Powers said. "I wasn't looking for the money. I was just looking to go back into business on an even keel."

It turned out the consent decree was useless. Based on case law, Crockett's legal team, brought in from Chicago, successfully argued that only the government could enforce antitrust consent decrees, not outside parties like the IWA. Instead, the lawyers cited a 1973 federal court decision that upheld the validity of an exclusive lease between the city of Jacksonville and Eddie Graham's Florida wrestling company. It was the way the arena business had operated for decades, the lawyers said.

Ironically, Winston-Salem was big enough for Powers and Crockett. In January and February 1976, before the new contract kicked in, each promotion ran three shows at the coliseum. Crockett drew 11,783 fans and receipts of $46,751. The IWA did slightly better with 12,766 fans and $49,857. But as soon as the IWA lost the arena, it started bleeding money and talent. The Mongols, the IWA tag team champions, jumped to Crockett. Mascaras, Koloff, and Ladd gave way to Mike Boyette, Butcher Brannigan, and Phil Watson. Three shows at Ernie Shore Field, an outdoor baseball park in Winston-Salem, lured just 2,061 fans combined. Overall, the company lost $70,000 in a year, according to court documents.

The legal battle raged for nearly two and a half years. Crockett's lawyers won an order keeping its promotion's federal tax returns out of the public eye. An economist from Florida State University calculated the alleged monopoly cost the IWA more than $314,500 in Winston-Salem alone. The hockey team folded after Crockett owned it for just a year. The IWA, with Powers as its lead star, continued to run shows, mostly in small towns, through mid-1977, when it ran out of gas. The decision came down on May 17, 1978, as a twelve-member jury unanimously found for Crockett and Winston-Salem. "It wasn't in my nature to be a gypsy promoter or a promoter without substantial business, so we decided to call it a day," Powers said, "We were not a second-tier organization and we were not second tier when I took over. We became second tier because of the attack."

Powers dabbled a little more in wrestling before pursuing other business ventures. The big winner, though, was not Crockett. It was Vince McMahon, who bought his dad's World Wrestling Federation in 1982. He drew on the IWA's stratagems in wooing big-name stars and buying coveted TV time slots to forge the most all-encompassing promotion in wrestling history. So while the IWA means little to fans of the twenty-first century, Powers thinks it can claim some credit for paving the way for the modern business. "There's no question we shook them up and we shook up their format and their thinking. If you don't think someone is of some serious consequence, you don't go in and buy a losing hockey franchise to get a lock on a building," he reflected. "You can be too early or too late and this was a case of being too early."

III. Let Them Eat Cake

When Paul "Butcher" Vachon married Ophelia on December 18, 1984, little did he realize that he'd be crossing more than one threshold. That's because the bogus matrimony and ensuing fracas became a signature moment in the evolution of professional wrestling into the live-action cartoon world of the 1980s. There'd been plenty of wrestling weddings before — Gorgeous George married Betty Wagner in the ring way back in 1939 — but nothing rivaled the high jinks associated with the betrothal of Butcher. A sampling: little people, a fake fish, the Rev. Meyer Lipschitz, beer on TV years before Steve Austin, and the mother of all food fights. The pageant was part of *Tuesday Night Titans*, a cheesy precursor to *Monday Night Raw* on USA Network. The brainchild of budding showman Vince McMahon, it marked the first in-ring wrestling wedding on cable TV, and every bit of the inanity made it to TNT. How could some regional wrestling promotion compete with that?

"Butcher Vachon's wedding was the first total cartoon. I called Vince aside and asked him if he was going to use that tape on the USA show. I told him if he did that he might kill wrestling," said George "The Animal" Steele, who mutely escorted the bride down the aisle and then ate the wedding decorations. "The wedding showed three weeks in a row. That is when wrestling went to the top of the charts. I knew right then that wrestling had changed, so I changed."

There were loads of outrageous moments when McMahon bought the World Wrestling Federation from his father and moved wrestling from the realm of a guilty pleasure to mainstream culture. The old guard was dead — vanilla Bob Backlund was out as the world champion, the red and yellow of Hulkamania was in. Singer Cyndi Lauper grabbed Captain Lou Albano in a hammerlock during a music video and kicked off the Rock 'n' Wrestling Connection. Mr. T of *The A-Team* fame jumped out of a crowd in Madison Square Garden to defend Lauper's honor and set up the main event for WrestleMania I.

To get to that point, though, McMahon needed TV. From the 1950s through the 1970s, promoter Jim Barnett used TV to build robust territories around the globe. With Barnett now advising him, McMahon turned to TV in the early 1980s to annex multiple territories and nationalize wrestling in his own vision. "When McMahon came after everybody, what he went after was their TV shows first — the talent and the TV shows," said Greg Gagne, son of American Wrestling Association owner Verne Gagne. "He tried to buy the time slots because we had ratings in Minneapolis and a lot of the AWA area, a 24 rating with a 64 share of the audience. I mean those are Super Bowl numbers." Same with Calgary, Alberta, and its Stampede Wrestling promotion, according to Bruce Hart, son of promoter and owner Stu Hart. "For a while there, Vince was half working with us," he said. "Vince was going to give Stu a million dollars down and ten percent of the gross gates forever in Calgary and basically he didn't live up to any of that at all. Stu gave him his TV spot. He took the TV time, all the talent." When McMahon set his sights on Los Angeles, he doled out $2,400 a week to KHJ-TV, the sister to the New York City station that ran his shows. "Up until that time, all the promoters were getting paid by the TV station for wrestling," said Jeff Walton, publicity director for the Los Angeles promotion. "All you had to do was pay the station, which is what Vince did with everybody. That was Vince's key. He knew how to get his foot in the door." In the 2003 book Unscripted, McMahon said he concealed his plans from his father, who'd run the Northeast promotion for nearly thirty years. "Had he known we were gonna expand, he wouldn't have sold the business, because we were going into territories that belonged to his friends."

Lord Alfred Hayes, who worked as announcer and conduit to stations around the country, said McMahon set a target of 200 stations for his syndicated shows. "He said when he got 200 stations, then he could go to the big-time people who wanted to promote their merchandise, like Safeway or other big companies. He could get the big contracts, which he did within a short time. But he went way over that and in time he had way over 200 stations," Hayes told historian Scott Teal. In late 1983, McMahon picked up Southwest Championship Wrestling's time slot on USA, which had been costing SCW some $7,000 a week. A few months later, in May 1984, *Tuesday Night Titans* was born with McMahon and Hayes hosting a talk show against a city skyline backdrop, a sports entertainment version of Johnny Carson or David Letterman. Taped just outside of Baltimore, it became a smash hit, drawing 1.5 million to 2 million viewers a week as USA's top-rated program and one of the top ten in cable land. Piper's Pit was a staple of the show, where Roddy Piper insulted and mocked guests in ways that would have made Don Rickles cringe. George Scott, McMahon's chief strategist, was uncomfortable with much of what he called "the cartoony stuff . . . They did a lot of stuff they didn't tell me they were doing," he said. But TNT was part of McMahon's grand design to reach beyond a traditional wrestling audience. "There's another whole tier of folks who get into the craziness of the show — the zaniness, to use an old-time TV word," TNT producer Nelson Sweglar told the *Baltimore Sun*.

Vachon had none of that in mind when he revealed his marital plans to McMahon. Best known in the AWA for his tag team with brother "Mad Dog" Maurice, Vachon had been working on WWF undercards since June 1983. "I told Vince when I was working for him, 'I'm going to get married.' I lived in Connecticut," Vachon said. McMahon's response: let's have the ceremony in Madison Square Garden. Butcher's bride-to-be initially assented to the unusual venue but got cold feet about three weeks before the big day. She didn't want to get married in Madison Square Garden or anywhere else, for that matter. Vachon called McMahon to explain his predicament and didn't get the answer he was expecting. "He said, 'That's all right. We'll have it some other place,'" Vachon recalled. "I said, 'What do you mean we're going have it?' He said, 'We'll hire somebody.' And that's what they did."

That somebody was Diane Page, who played Ophelia, the love of Vachon's life and, in the storyline, his sixth wife. The wedding scenario played out on *TNT* over several weeks. During one episode, McMahon and Hayes visited Baltimore businesses that would have a hand in the ceremony, including the jeweler, the bridal shop, the florist, the cake bakery, and the travel agency that arranged for the couple's honeymoon in Hawaii. The ceremony was a hoot and a holler, and unlike anything with which pro wrestling had been associated. Staged in a ring in front of an all-heel audience, it took up the lion's share of *TNT's* two-hour show. Among the lowlights: Jesse Ventura ripping up the bouquet brought to the ring

Vachon (r) with manager Lou Albano, who was wary of his man's marriage to Ophelia.

by flower girl Diamond Lil, and Freddie Blassie tripping ring bearer Sky Low Low, then snatching the ring to check for imperfections. When Lipschitz asked if anyone objected to the marriage, Albano jumped into the ring to inform Vachon, adorned in his own top hat and tails, that his chosen one was far too chaste for his liking. "You're my friend; what are you doing this for?" Vachon asked. "Because she's a virgin, lily-white virgin," Albano insisted. Vachon waved off his friend's unease. "Don't worry about it, Lou. She's not a virgin." The exchange was impromptu, Vachon recalled years later. "That was all ad-libbed," he said. However, a post-vow body slam that "Dr. D" David Schultz administered to Vachon was a planned part of the package. "Vince asked me, he says, 'What can we do that's never been done before? How about a body slam?'" Vachon was quick to agree with the man who signed his paycheck. "I said, 'I work here. Let's do it.'"

The reception in an adjacent room had a predictable outcome — wrestlers plus a large cake historically equals a mess. First, Steele delivered a toast consisting solely of the word "pumpernickel." Albano gifted the Vachons a box of rubber bands. The slapstick started when Schultz jumped into the scene, insisting that Ophelia's spousal duties included changing her hubby's truck tires and fetching firewood for him. She unenthusiastically agreed, but when she balked at eating cake, Schultz slammed a coconut cream pie in her face. In seconds, the segment turned into a skit worthy of The Three Stooges, aided by cream pies conveniently planted on reception area tables. "Fuck, you can't rehearse something like that. I was surprised, I was really out of it. I wasn't drinking or anything, but I just let them do what they wanted to do. They never asked me, 'Can we do this? Can we do that?'" said Vachon, who can be seen chuckling during the fracas. "It turned into a wild party. We had a lot of fun doing it." The free-for-all met with critical approval, meriting a write-up in Sports Illustrated under the headline "The Groom Wore Black and Blue." TV critic Howard Rosenberg of the Los Angeles Times called it the "most bizarre" event among TNT's many over-the-top events. "It matters only that Wrestling TNT, like all of professional wrestling these days, is a grand howl, a great, great show that's getting greater. Forget about Olivier and De Niro. This is acting."

The campiness was part of a test run for what came next. Three months after the faux wedding, McMahon delivered the Colossal Tussle at Madison Square Garden. At least that was his chosen name for WrestleMania before Scott, the chief WWF booker, started mocking it by making voices with the name. Scott suggested WrestleMania as an alternative, recalling in 2003 that McMahon agreed to the name after realizing Colossal Tussle was easy to make fun of. Given how WrestleMania has become the Super Bowl of the sport, it's hard to remember that McMahon was rolling the dice with his TV purchases and celebrity-packed escapades. "Vince told George, 'If this thing doesn't work, we're bankrupt. We're going to have to close the company,'" said Scott's wife, Jean. McMahon needn't have worried; by 1985, the company was making $3 million to $4 million on weekends, George Scott said, adding, "Things just started popping." And WWF pastries kept popping as well. Two months after the first WrestleMania, Lauper dumped The Fabulous Moolah into a cake on NBC's *Saturday Night's Main Event*.

The Vachon wedding helped to usher in the cartoon era and launched a WWE infatuation with televised nuptials — at least sixteen of them, by one count. In October 1985, Uncle Elmer (Plowboy Frazier) legitimately married his long-time girlfriend Joyce Stazko in the ring on *Saturday Night's Main Event* despite Roddy Piper's heated objection. At the reception, conducted amid bales of hay and barnyard animals, an obnoxious Jesse Ventura was the one to plummet into a towering cake. Randy Savage and Miss Elizabeth professed their eternal love in the ring, while Triple H and Stephanie McMahon ended up together in real life in 1999 after he kidnapped and drugged her while she was engaged to Andrew "Test" Martin. But as an old-school wrestler emphasizing realism, Vachon, who worked with WWF through 1985, wasn't terribly happy with the direction that the company took. "I don't know how it could be turned around," he said in 2018. "None of us guys are very pleased, but what can you do about it?" Not much, but you can sit back occasionally and remember the night TNT lent its particular style of goofiness to Vachon's sacred-though-sham vows. Hayes' comments as the credits rolled on the episode would stand as a sort of short-hand for the Rock 'n' Wrestling era: "Never before have I ever been hit with a pie. Never before have I been subject to so much humilia-tion, yet with hilarity, and yet for some ridiculous reason, I liked it."

Newsstand

Introduction

How can you get in trouble as a wrestling magazine editor? Easy. Just insinuate that Jackie Robinson, who broke baseball's color barrier in baseball, was bigoted. That's not quite what Norman Kietzer, editor of *Wrestling Monthly*, intended in a 1971 editorial when he questioned whether the New York State Athletic Commission was a bunch of bigots for refusing to license women wrestlers. But since the former baseball great was a member of the commission, the implication was obvious. "I got a lot of negative heat for using the word bigot with him," said Kietzer, who spent more than thirty years publishing wrestling magazines, newspapers, and programs. Fortunately, he knew Mad Dog and Butcher Vachon from his days as a promoter in Minnesota, and convinced their wrestling daughter Vivian to join him on a New York talk show with sports personalities Bill Mazur and Lee Leonard. "We had quite a talk about how women could wrestle in most states and New York wouldn't allow them in the same way Jackie Robinson came into baseball at a time when Black people were not allowed to play professional baseball. So they didn't really cut me down," Kietzer said. The commission did give the nod to women grapplers the following year.

The dustup served to prove that some people took wrestling magazines seriously, maybe more so than the magazines themselves, which entertained newsstand browsers not even remotely interested in the sport. After all, no one could pass up a cover story entitled, "The Truth Behind This Bizarre Craving: Women Do Wrestle Bears." In time, serious journalism, led by the entrepreneurial Dave Meltzer, sprung up as an antidote to industry hype. But as long as the internet exists, the fluff and foolishness will never truly go away.

Dick "Bulldog" Brower reads about his favorite subject – himself.

I. Fake News

It was a risky but potentially rewarding scheme. Wrestling promoters Jack and Lou Daro would slip money under the table to southern California sportswriters. In exchange, they'd win coverage of a sport that newspapers looked upon with only slightly more favor than bandits and bootleggers. The Daros got their coverage all right, though it wasn't the kind they bargained for when they spent $128,000 to spread the word about the virtues of their wrestling outfit. Instead, a state legislative committee exposed the payola in 1938, some twenty sportswriters were fired, and the Daros lost their profitable Los Angeles–based promotion. "For now the newspapers could no longer contribute its support to the sinful business," mourned Art Cohn of the Oakland *Tribune*. "There would be no more phoney publicity."

Actually, there would be more fake news, but the wrestling trade would henceforth be in charge of it. Not long after the California scandal and a series of explosive exposés in the New York press, the industry came up with *Wrestling As You Like It* (*WAYLI*), a national magazine that took storytelling in a blemish-free and sometimes-fabricated direction. In one issue, for example, Chicago promoter Fred Kohler reassured readers that any fishiness they detected in the ring was actually quite intentional: "This is because the fan lacks the knowledge that clever wrestlers . . . will fake certain holds and maneuvers similar to the way basketball, hockey, football, or even soccer players will fake passes, blocks, and kicks to maneuver their opponents off balance."

WAYLI and its successor publications were the outgrowths of decades of bad ink. In the early 1900s, newspapers regularly celebrated wrestlers such as Frank Gotch of Iowa, the top heavyweight of his day, as paragons of virtue, but cast a skeptical eye toward the business as a whole. In 1908, the New York *Sun* shredded the sport with the help of an anonymous referee who explained how promoters bamboozled a gullible public. "There have been very few wrestling matches that have been pulled off strictly on the level," the *Sun*'s insider revealed. "Here in New York, the wrestling game is practically dead for some of the rawest fakes have been pulled off in Madison Square Garden and other big halls."

Lou Daro was determined not to repeat that folly. An Austrian immigrant, "Carnation Lou" started promoting in Los Angeles in 1921 after a career as a strongman in a circus. With the help of younger brother Jack, he built Los Angeles into a wrestling mecca, drawing a reported $2 million in five years of shows at the Olympic Auditorium. A boost from the world of journalism didn't hurt, either. In 1931, the *Los Angeles Times* ran what today is called an advertorial, heralding Daro for enhancing the local economy through jobs and tax receipts. "Daro, himself, is the answer to his own success," it proclaimed. At the same time, the Daros were ensuring favorable publicity by slipping money under the table to sportswriters. The payments were hush-hush for years until a California investigative committee uncovered them in April 1939 during a probe of the boxing and wrestling business. After the panel subpoenaed the Daro brothers' financial records, Jack acknowledged that they doled out about $128,000 over five years for public relations, mostly to reporters and editors. He contended that the money was a legitimate expense, saying he was simply soliciting tips about out-of-town wrestlers and not purchasing puff pieces. The committee didn't buy that and neither did dailies that dismissed some of their top bylines overnight. According to the committee, major recipients were Mark Kelly of the Los Angeles *Examiner*, with more than $11,200 in 1935, and Sid Ziff of the Los Angeles *Herald and Express* at $6,537. Editors Gene Coughlin of the Los Angeles *Post-Record* and John Connolly of the *Examiner* were also among about twenty journalists kicked to the curb for accepting payoffs. Kelly subsequently sued the Daros in a $775,000 libel case, but a court tossed out his complaint, saying the transactions surfaced during a legitimate government investigation. Even if Kelly had won, there would have been no money to collect. The flurry of bad news sent business reeling, and Jack Daro gave up his promoter's license about a year later after reporting a $70,000 loss.

If wrestling's name was being dragged through the mud on the West Coast, things were no better in the East. Starting in December 1933, crusading sports editor Dan Parker of the *New York Daily Mirror* lifted wrestling's veil of secrecy thanks to inside dope from disgruntled promoter Jack Pfefer. Parker started with Pfefer's allegation that the fix had been in when the revered Jim Londos beat Dick Shikat for the world championship in 1930. For the next two decades, Parker kept up a steady drumbeat of criticism, adding that while his chief source Pfefer was a knave, at least he was "honest about his skullduggery." Parker routinely foiled carefully crafted marquee matches by announcing winners ahead of time. "Louie Thesz will, through the intercession of a miracle, pin Ali Baba," Parker correctly foresaw on one St. Louis card. If there was dirt to be dished, Parker was ready with his ladle. In July 1937, he took the wind out of Bronko Nagurski's world championship victory over Dean Detton. Parker disclosed that Nagurski threatened to walk out on

Los Angeles promoter Lou Daro takes the witness stand in a 1935 court case.

the business' agreed-upon title switch four hours before the match unless a promoter forked over $15,000 on the spot. "That's how ludicrous the Burping Business has become," Parker said. Wrestlers were frantic about the damage Parker was doing by portraying them as charlatans and frauds. "Say, Jack, can't you put the damper on this bastard Dan Parker?" ex–world champ Dave Levin pleaded to Pfefer, his former manager, in a 1936 letter. "He's got my mother scared stiff. Because of his column, she's received threats against me." There were other reasons for wrestling's decline in popularity in the mid to late 1930s — double-crosses in the ring, crooked promoters, competition from other sports — but the wave of negative publicity from Parker and his ilk was among the most crippling. After reviewing Parker's work, St. Louis columnist Bill Wray concluded from afar: "Whether wrestling and wrestlers deserve the epithets applied to them in New York, it is certain that the campaign against the sport has caused serious lack of interest in the greatest city in this country."

It took a dyed-in-the-wool spin doctor to figure out how to counter wrestling's sorry image in the press. Richard T. "Dick" Axman started his literary career with letters to the editor of the *Chicago Tribune* that detailed the percentage of women he found "beautiful" while he lingered on a Windy City street corner. (Either selective or chauvinistic, Axman decided not more than one in 100 fit the bill). From there, it was a short jump for the Michigan native to a newspaper boxing column and press work for an amusement park. Axman started with Chicago wrestling magnate Fred Kohler in 1936, eventually handling all the boxing and wrestling marketing for Marigold Gardens, Chicago Stadium, and the International Amphitheatre.

In January 1946, with Kohler's blessing, Axman launched *WAYLI*, a slick, sixteen-page weekly that took fake news in a new direction. Wrestling had received nominal attention in publications like *Ring* magazine for years. Now, the industry had its own house organ to provide fans with sanitized stories and personality profiles that they couldn't get elsewhere. Armed with that new source of information, nasty aspersions tossed out by newspaper columnists didn't matter as much anymore. When TV wrestling took off in the late 1940s, *WAYLI* was the perfect companion to learn more about the stars of the boob tube. The magazine might have been wrestling as fans liked it, but it was publicity as promoters liked it.

Running fifteen cents a copy, *WAYLI* served multiple purposes. At its heart, it was a program for Chicago wrestling with results and upcoming cards. It represented a publicity vehicle for Kohler, the most important promoter of the 1950s, and his legitimate civic contributions were a standing feature. "Recently Fred presented the Heart Fund with a check for $2,000 from the gate receipts of one of his Amphitheatre shows. This was done with no fanfare nor did he ask for publicity on the donation," Axman wrote. Enthusiastic profiles brought young wrestlers to the public's attention; reading between the lines, they could identify Kohler's next hyped hopes.

"We believe that Red Bastien, of Minneapolis, who now campaigns around Chicago, will be a serious heavyweight challenger within a short period," Axman said in one self-fulfilling prophecy. Axman also gave a break to Bob Luce and Jim Barnett, a pair of twenty-somethings who helped with stories and pictures before taking the lessons they learned into long careers as promoters.

Importantly, *WAYLI* connected fans from around the world for the first time. It was the first national publication to give editorial space to a network of far-flung correspondents who submitted reports on feuds and shows from California to India. Its letters to the editor page touted fan clubs across the country that united admirers of everyone from Gorgeous George to Killer Kowalski. An attempt at running a "most beautiful fan" contest in 1953 didn't come off as intended, though. The honor went to Ramona Durand of Carmel, New York, who, as it turned out, was an exotic dancer arrested that same year for indecent exposure at a girlie show at a New York City lodge.

The magazine ran through March 1955, when it morphed into *Wrestling Life*. By the end of the decade, it had diminished in importance as publishers took advantage of a growing market with larger, more exciting, and sensationalized magazines. Stanley Weston's *Wrestling Revue* in 1959 heralded a new generation of publications that gave promoters multiple outlets to plug their wrestlers or build feuds and storylines. For his part, Axman worked through the mid-1960s for Kohler and former editorial assistant Luce, who became the promoter in Chicago. The publicity genius who took wrestling journalism down a new path died in 1969 at seventy-two. "Axman was the Boswell of wrestling," said *Chicago Tribune* columnist Dave Condon with a tongue-in-cheek throwback to one of history's great diarists. "Each week he delivered thousands of stories about wrestling to the sports desk of Chicago newspapers. One of 'em finally was printed for one edition. We should honor the late Dick Axman for that achievement."

II. Puppetry

Oogie must have been scared to death. He was alone in the studio of *The Uncle Floyd Show*, a wacky daily production out of New Jersey that was equal parts adult slapstick and kiddie fare when Larry Zbyszko came storming in. A top bad guy in the Northeast, Zbyszko had been on the show before and for some reason had a bone to pick with it. Words were exchanged and an irate Zbyszko tore up the studio in front of a cowering Oogie. Later, Oogie told a writer about the ill-tempered Zbyszko and the damage he inflicted on the TV workplace.

Which was interesting, considering Oogie was an orange-haired hand puppet. But in Craig Peters' "On the Road" column in publisher Stanley Weston's *Inside Wrestling* magazine, Oogie came to life in 1981 as a wisecracking dummy recounting a harrowing albeit fictitious tale. "Patently absurd, but what the heck?" laughed Peters, a wrestling magazine writer and editor for fifteen years. "There was a time when we were very fast and loose with the facts and reality."

Actually, Oogie was a perfectly logical part of the world of pro wrestling magazines, which for three decades put words in mouths that didn't move and assigned characters traits they didn't really have. Paul Diamond (Paul Lehman), a handsome grappler from Toronto, was a casualty of that literary neofiction in November 1969. Writer/photographer Roger Baker featured Diamond and his wife, Serena, in a photo essay for Weston's *The Wrestler*. Baker delivered a tasteful set of pictures, including Serena giving Paul a bubble bath, and wrote the story as straightforward as could be.

The Diamonds and Baker cringed when they saw the result. The cover displayed Diamond wielding a mace over his prone bride. "Weston sensationalized whatever I sent him and made out Paul Diamond like he's a caveman type and women should be submissive," said Baker, adding that Serena called to curse him up one side and down the other. "I tried to tell her, 'I didn't even write that story. My words were different.'" Of course, a bad cover story was better than no cover story, Diamond said later. "In those days, how do you get over? How do you make a buck? Publicity's publicity."

The common denominator between Oogie and the Diamonds was Stanley Weston, who was to boxing and wrestling what Henry Luce was to traditional journalism. Only Luce, founder of *Time*, *Life*, *Fortune*, and *Sports Illustrated*, didn't develop film in his own basement then run upstairs to type a story and lay out a magazine like Weston did. "He was an amazing storyteller, whether he was talking about a cruise he took or writing in a publication," said his daughter Toby Weston Cone. "He loved to tell stories and he annotated them however he wanted, whether it was true or not. What I remember he said to me my whole life was, 'Give the people what they want, not what you want them to have.'"

Born September 25, 1919, Weston was smitten with boxing growing up on Long Island, where a neighbor was Nat Fleischer, founder of *Ring* magazine and author of a landmark pro wrestling history book called *From Milo to Londos*. Weston started by mowing Fleischer's lawn and worked his way up to office boy, writer, photographer, and artist, eventually painting fifty-seven covers for *Ring*. He launched his own boxing magazines in the 1950s, with wrestling news often included in the back of the book. But the sport got top billing in fall 1959 when Weston debuted *Wrestling Revue*, which fast became the world's best-selling mat mag. "He loved the history about boxing and everything about boxing, the characters, but boxing didn't make the money that wrestling did," his daughter said. "He was very attracted to Ringling Brothers and P.T. Barnum

COURTESY WRESTLING REVUE ARCHIVES

A symbiotic relationship evolved between wrestling and the folks who covered it. Brian Bukantis (l) looks over a mag with Jimmy Valiant.

and the whole freak show aspect of it. He was fascinated by all that. And that ties into wrestling because of the freaks like Andre the Giant. They were sideshows."

By no means did Weston hold exclusive title to the Land of Make Believe. The mantra in the wrestling magazine industry was "Write now, fact check later, if at all." After Weston left *Wrestling Revue* in 1966 to start *TheWrestler*, new publisher Lew Eskin decided he needed a piece on Haystack Muldoon for the October 1967 issue. He tasked correspondent Earle F. Yetter with a forty-eight-hour dead-line, which prevented Yetter from consulting traditional sources such as Muldoon's manager Jack Pfefer. So he spun a yarn. A few days later, Yetter wrote Pfefer, explaining his predicament. "I am working you into the story, how you went to the farm and made a wrestler out of him, etc. and because I did not have the time to get some of the facts from you regarding him, I went ahead and used my own imagination and worked on the story to the best of my ability," Yetter said. "I wanted to help Muldoon because he claims no magazine ever gave him a story before and he was tickled that I was going to do one on him."

What was kept out of the magazines was often more scan-dalous than what went in. Gary J. Rowell started writing and taking pictures for *Wrestling Revue*, *Wrestling World*, and their ilk in the late 1960s. While stationed with the U.S. Air Force in San Bernardino, California, Rowell and his girlfriend chatted with Dr. Jerry Graham, a cover boy on Weston's first *Wrestling Revue*. The good doctor was such a fascinating conversationalist that Rowell envisioned a unique story for *WrestlingWorld* — a Sunday dinner with Jerry Graham, to be hosted by the parents of his girlfriend. The story ran in *WrestlingWorld* all right, but not the way it happened. "We went to L.A., picked up Jerry Graham, and brought him back to the house," Rowell said. "After dinner, he had got all liquored up and wanted to go to Palm Springs, California. I said, 'Well, okay, I'll drive you.' We got just outside the city of Palm Springs and he was so obnoxious and so rude and crude to my girlfriend that I kicked him out of the car. So the last I saw of Dr. Jerry Graham that night, he was walking down the Desert Highway."

Over time, *Wrestling Revue*, *Wrestling Monthly*, and *Ring Wrestling* became more correspondent-based. "We always seemed to have people willing to submit stories. We didn't pay for it. We had a lot of stories we did ourselves," said Norman Kietzer, who edited the magazines for years. That left the tabloid field wide open to Weston, whose portfolio would grow to more than half a dozen wrestling magazines, as well as non-wrestling titles. "Early on, particularly in the 1960s and early 1970s, Stanley was all about creating controversial storylines and covers that he felt would scream out to our readers," said Stu Saks, publisher of the Weston-founded *Pro Wrestling Illustrated*, who started working for him in 1979. "Bloody covers, outlandish angles, girl apartment wrestling — he left an indelible mark on readers, but also upset a lot of people in the business. And you know what? He really didn't care. He sold magazines."

Mythmakers and mythbusters: Stanley Weston (seated) with his *Pro Wrestling Illustrated* staff (from left) Craig Peters, Stu Saks, Bill Apter, Steve Farhood, and Charlie Foster.

Weston also professionalized wrestling magazine publishing in a way it hadn't seen. He hired the indefatigable Bill Apter as an assistant in 1970, moved operations from his cramped home into a five-story building in Rockville Centre, New York, and built a full-time editorial staff — no wrestling know-how needed. Peters said he had been to "maybe" one card before he joined the team in mid-1981. "We'd all come out of collegiate English and journalism programs; we worked on our college newspapers. It wasn't wrestling fans putting out wrestling magazines; it was editorial professionals putting out wrestling magazines." Still, the process at Weston's magazines in the 1980s was exactly the opposite of what professors taught at Columbia Journalism School. Photos dictated the headlines, which dictated the teaser, which dictated a 1,000-word piece that followed storylines pushed by promoters. Apter was pondering an artsy photo of Tommy Rich with fellow writers after the do-good hero turned heel. "I called Tommy Rich when we came up with the headline. I said, 'Is this okay with you?' He said, 'Damn, they're going to want to kill me. Go ahead and do it, Bill.' So we came up with the headline, 'Tommy Rich: The Fans Can Go to Hell.' That blew away everybody. The fans were furious. There were fans who burned the magazine. There were fans that ripped up the magazine in front of him. We got a lot of a letters, but we got tons of hate mail for him. It just went along with what they were doing with him, making him a bad guy."

When Weston stepped back from day-to-day management, his charges knew his tastes and preferences, especially when it came to the cover. In July 1987, the front of his *Sports Review Wrestling* displayed Ugandan giant Kamala (actually a Mississippian) in face paint holding a stick with the dismembered head of Hulk Hogan. "Bring Me the Head of Hulk Hogan," the headline screamed in a display of political incorrectness. Weston had plenty to say about that one, Saks recalled. "It was by far the highest-selling issue of *Sports Review Wrestling*, which he of course liked. But it also was right out of Stanley's old playbook, which had to be very gratifying for him."

When the World Wrestling Federation introduced its own magazine in 1983 — Apter declined an offer to be editor —Weston's publications reached deep into their creative tool kit. The WWF barred competing magazines from photographing ringside at its events. Fine. They'd shoot from the stands. Making up quotes was verboten since WWF wrestlers were under strict contracts. Fine. The *Pro Wrestling Illustrated* family fabricated a WWF source named Thomas Pilliard, who was less real than Oogie, to provide insights and analysis. Apter and Peters appeared in press conference settings for the competing Jim Crockett Promotions on Ted Turner's WTBS superstation. "It really raised the profile of the magazines and me at that point," Apter said. "We were the internet before the internet — months behind, though."

Weston sold his publications in 1993 to a Pennsylvania company that still publishes *Pro Wrestling Illustrated* in print and online. He died of pancreatic cancer in April 2002. "There was, in fact, very little about Stanley Weston that could be considered traditional," Saks wrote in memoriam. "He was a writer who never read a book. He was a millionaire who drove a Ford Tempo. He was a former military officer, yet rarely barked orders. He was at the same time a man who watched every penny and the most generous soul I have ever met."

A lot of the craziness is gone, and *Pro Wrestling Illustrated* reads and feels more like *Sports Illustrated* than the wacky days of yore. "We never try to duplicate the story WWE is telling. We'll use that as a base point and try to expand it in areas that WWE will not," Saks said. "Sometimes that means being analytical or critical. WWE's attempts to expand to the mainstream have only served as a positive for us. New fans discovering wrestling expands our potential audience." But the tale of Oogie, the hand puppet who ridiculously came to life, remains one for the ages. After his story hit the newsstand, Peters had just gotten out of the shower at home when his mom said a strange caller was on the line for him. It was Uncle Floyd, the brains (and hand) behind Oogie. "He ran me down and thanked me for that column, which was great."

III. Dirt Sheets

There was a point when Gary Hart hated, absolutely hated Dave Meltzer, publisher of the *Wrestling Observer* newsletter. "I have no time for him. He's a lying, conniving, fucking asshole," Hart vented in 2006. "He writes gossip and tells lies. He's a revisionist historian and has no insight to wrestling. He rips about 2,000 to 3,000 fans a week off for his newsletter." Hart had honed his opinion over twenty years from the time he booked World Class Championship Wrestling in the 1980s just as Meltzer's insider pub — a "dirt sheet" in wrestling lingo — gained steam. He couldn't believe that Houston promoter Paul Boesch not only subscribed but even talked to Meltzer. Hart's mentality was strictly old-school — protect the fiction of the business at all costs, a carny practice known as kayfabe that he drilled into his colleagues and the talent under his thumb.

But Hart came around. Court Bauer, who launched Major League Wrestling while still in his twenties, was a disciple who turned to Hart for advice and life lessons. As a thank-you, Bauer got Hart a subscription to the *Observer*. "He was so offended by that gesture," Bauer chuckled. Then "The Spoiler" Don Jardine died in December 2006; he was probably Hart's closest friend in an industry where true friends were few and far apart. Naturally, Meltzer wanted to talk to Hart, and an interview was set up. "His whole perspective changed on Dave Meltzer and his thought on what his presence is in wrestling," recalled Bauer, a subscriber since a teenager to Meltzer's densely packed, text-only, single-spaced weekly. "He wasn't exposing the business; in fact, he was kind of critical to connecting yesteryear with today and curating what wrestling has been, is, and will be."

Hart's sudden death in March 2008 from a heart attack meant another lengthy obituary for Meltzer, whose *Observer* and Wade Keller's *Pro Wrestling Torch* are the industry's primary trade journals. While Meltzer doesn't recall any vitriol from Hart, whom he talked to regularly, he knows it has existed through the almost fifty years

Wrestling journalists Wade Keller (l) and Dave Meltzer at a Hall of Fame award ceremony in Waterloo, Iowa.

he has written about pro wrestling. "Even now there's plenty of people who don't want to accept it, because wrestling's so behind the times," said Meltzer. "Wrestling has this weird world — you're not supposed to tell the truth and you're not supposed to give information, and somehow this having information will kill the whole business. Granted, that has changed somewhat, but the vestiges of it still remain."

No one has written more words about wrestling than Meltzer — in 2013, the *New York Times* estimated it at thirty-three million. Like most fans, Meltzer fell for wrestling when he was growing up in California. "You're trying to get more information on wrestling in that era and the first place you go is the newsstand magazine," he said of his early 1970s interest. "When I started reading them, they weren't what I wanted." Intrigued by listings for newsletters and fan clubs in the back of *Wrestling Monthly* and *Wrestling Revue*, Meltzer sent away for a select few and began down a new road. "I admired the people who were doing the newsletters. I thought they were very good."

It seems quaint now, but correspondents across the country would clip wrestling-related goodies from the local paper and send them to be shared on a wider basis with the likes of Tom Burke's *Global Wrestling News Service*, begun in 1975, and Terrance Machalek's *Canadian Championship Wrestling* publication. The king of fan-produced titles was Terry Justice of Rochester, New York. He encouraged contributions, and you only got one of his issues if you sent in a clipping. At one point, he was sending out *Championship Wrestling* weekly, and had another half-dozen titles, annual yearbooks, and a newsletter called *T-N-T Power* devoted solely to the wrestling Gilbert family. "Terry visited Nashville one time and I had the honor of having him stay with me," said Scott Teal of Crowbar Press, a newsletter veteran and compilator of the essential *Whatever Happened To . . . ?* series. "I introduced him to everyone at the fairgrounds the night he was there. To say he was 'living a dream' was an understatement. Terry loved wrestling and getting to meet the guys he had read about put him on top of the world." At thirty-two, Justice died when a drunk driver hit his car head-on in Sodus, New York.

As Meltzer studied journalism at San Jose State, he pursued his venture amid a community of fellow students who wanted a more adult approach than the make-believe tales found in wrestling mags: "They didn't want to read the magazines, which really weren't written for them, but they were interested in solid information. 'Why is this happening? Where did this guy come from?'" *Sports Illustrated* put Hulk Hogan on its cover for the April 29, 1985, issue with an eighteen-page profile by writer Bruce Newman, and Meltzer found himself reaching a higher level of acceptance. "They quoted me a lot and the reporter told me that he's never covered anything like wrestling, and that he's never been lied to by so many people in his life, and he said, 'You're the only one who tells the truth in the entire business.' I thought that was something because I was twenty-five years old, and I thought, 'I'm in *Sports Illustrated!*'"

Around 1986, Meltzer determined that the level of newsletter interest was worth ditching his day gig as a sportswriter in Texas.

"I said, 'Wow, I'm making more money doing this than I am at my sports writing job. Let's give up the sports writing job because it's killing me doing both." Bruce Mitchell, a long-time columnist for Keller's *Pro Wrestling Torch*, discovered an ad for Meltzer's publication about that time in the back of a magazine. "Once I got the *Observer*, I stopped buying wrestling magazines because you were getting the news within four or five days instead of six or seven weeks."

Meltzer gained even more exposure with a column in famed journalist Frank Deford's short-lived *National Sports Daily*. "You could cover the Vatican or State Department and not do as good a job as Dave Meltzer does on wrestling," Deford said in 2013. He became the go-to guy for radio, TV, and newspapers swooping in to cover wrestling stories like the 1992 conviction of Dr. George T. Zahorian on steroid distribution charges and WWE owner Vince McMahon's acquittal on a similar charge two years later. "Who do we go to talk to besides Vince McMahon and Hulk Hogan, and these guys that are clearly kind of full of crap? Where can we go to find a talking head on television that's not connected with the industry?" Mitchell said of the thought process. The Chris Benoit double murder–suicide in 2007 and a horrific number of premature deaths from steroids and recreational drugs only heightened the role of impartial voices like Meltzer and Keller.

For his part, Keller went from a high schooler doing a newsletter in Minneapolis, convincing notoriously closed-lipped promoter Verne Gagne to talk to him about the American Wrestling Association, to a college journalism grad who could pay the bills with the *Torch*. He's seen a lot of change in the way the media treats wrestling. Today's decision-makers at ESPN, SI.com and RollingStone.com came of age in the 1990s, when wrestling had the top-rated shows on cable television. As a result, the sport's stigma is gone. The protectiveness of Gary Hart gave way to wrestler Buddy Wayne using one of Mike Rodgers' *Ring Around the Northwest* newsletters as a weapon in a match, and the Young Bucks tag team naming a move the Meltzer Driver. "The [mainstream] editors don't have any kind of hang-up about looking like they're . . . covering something that's fake," Keller said. "They see it as something cool in the late '90s that spawned Dwayne 'The Rock' Johnson, 'Stone Cold' Steve Austin, John Cena, and Brock Lesnar."

Meltzer and Keller have had a huge influence on the business; they have each received the James C. Melby Award from the George Tragos/Lou Thesz Professional Wrestling Hall of Fame for their contributions to pro wrestling journalism. They make an interesting contrast, said Conrad Thompson, podcasting partner to Ric Flair and announcer Tony Schiavone. "Dave is just the news," Thompson said. "But if you really just want to know opinion and in-depth analysis about the rights and wrongs, and shoulda, woulda, coulda, that, to me, is what you turn to the Torch for. The Torch is more of the moral compass of wrestling, as silly as that sounds, in that they're going to tell you what's good and what's not, and what's working and what's not, and why it's not."

Meltzer didn't invent the five-star system of rating matches — you can find scattered instances in old news reports and newsletters — but he popularized it to the point that online sites have collections of his five-star showstoppers. Ask wrestlers on the record and they will deny that it matters. "I feel like match ratings are subjective. I mean, how can you say one match is a five-star and this match is a two-star?" asked Moose Ojinnaka of Impact Wrestling. Austin Aries argued the usual point: "I don't know how guys who have never actually put boots, have actually ever had to go out there and perform a match, compete in a match, I don't know how they have the expertise to sit there then, and break it down and critique it."

Meltzer is familiar with the objections, though he's also seen wrestlers wearing their match rating "like it's a badge of honor." After all, up-arrow ratings can lead to attention and a higher-profile job. Getting people to talk, as Ricochet and Will Ospreay did at New Japan's Best of the Super Juniors in May 2016, made them into bigger names. Therefore, Meltzer said, having the "reputation for having consistent good matches is more important now than it's ever been historically. So I guess in that sense, people use star ratings; they took on a life of their own. To me, it's the least important thing I do, but it gets the most attention, both good and bad."

Like Meltzer and Keller, Mike Johnson of PWInsider.com is a key player, armed with a wealth of sources and the ability to publish a story as it happens. He takes issue with a lot of the coverage by ESPN, *Sports Illustrated*, and *Rolling Stone*, primarily with their websites treating wrestling as clickbait. "Instead of enjoying it, I worry that it encroaches on what we do and hurts us," Johnson said. "Not everything is terrible, but I think a lot of it, especially a lot of the ESPN stuff, has been very shallow . . . I think they're happy to have it for the traffic." WWE clearly prefers the rub from large media organizations to an insider website. Johnson shared an example: WWE set up an interview for him with Triple H, WWE's executive vice president, to talk about a just-launched website on recruitment. Johnson spoke to Triple H first and posted the story first. But it was a later *Sports Illustrated* piece that WWE retweeted as an "exclusive," ignoring Johnson's piece altogether.

Mitchell agreed that much of the big-name media coverage runs toward the superficial — in July 2018, ESPN.com and its companion magazine featured a visual presentation showcasing the nude body of Charlotte Flair, Ric's wrestling daughter. That's all the more reason for the *Observer* and *Torch* to keep doing what they've been doing, Mitchell said. "There's definitely still a dirt sheet pushback against the people who are applying the regular rules of journalism to professional wrestling," he said. "I do think there's something to be said for independent, knowledgeable people where if something goes wrong, like the Chris Benoit thing ten years ago, they can go to besides WWE and get a better sense of what is really happening."

We're Hardcore

Introduction

Tully Blanchard and Magnum T.A. were hardcore before hardcore became popular. That's the conclusion from their "I Quit" steel cage match at Starrcade '85 in Greensboro, North Carolina. There were no rules, no holds were barred. The only way the match could end was if a combatant cried, "I quit." Blanchard called it "the most brutal brutality I've ever been part of . . . Frankly, there were people who thought they'd see somebody go out on a stretcher or somebody go out and never come back in their career." The contest was hard-hitting and gory; it easily rivaled Extreme Championship Wrestling's most violent events of the 1990s. About thirteen minutes in, Blanchard, caked in blood, caught a wooden chair thrown into the ring by his valet, Baby Doll, and smashed it into the mat. A wooden spike broke off. Prone on the canvas, Magnum couldn't believe the good fortune. "That was just a fickle finger of fate, that a chair could produce the most god-awful looking instrument of destruction. We couldn't have scripted that," he said. "It produced the nastiest-looking device in the ring and I think everyone there was aghast thinking about what happened if that went through one of our heads." Magnum emerged victorious when Blanchard, the weapon hovering above his eye, conceded, though he never actually said, "I quit." No matter. Hardcore wrestling soon soared in popularity and regularity with weapons much more frightening

Magnum TA (l) and Tully Blanchard recount the story of their "I Quit" match that was hardcore before hardcore was fashionable.

than a broken chair leg. But the "I Quit" match showed that hardcore is at its best when used as part of an intense program rather than violence for violence's sake. Body slamming an opponent onto a bed of thumbtacks still can't equal the threat of driving a wooden spike through your opponent's skull.

I. Rung by Rung

Dan Kroffat knew he had to let the creative juices flow. The product of Vancouver, British Columbia, he was never the biggest, strongest, or fastest wrestler in the business, so he was always on the lookout for something that might raise his profile and benefit fellow grapplers at the same time. Like putting a stepladder in the ring. Kroffat invented the ladder match in western Canada in fall 1972, clamping bad guy Tor Kamata's head between the supports like a vise and taking hardcore wrestling in an entirely new direction, free of blood but hardly free of excitement.

"I knew immediately we had a winner," Kroffat said, remembering the ladder match with Kamata before 3,000 screaming fans at Victoria Pavilion in Calgary, Alberta. "The place was almost deafening, every move, every high spot. People had never seen anything like this before. I knew immediately, 'Now what I have to do is to strategically plan this over a long period of time because this is a winner.'"

The ladder match has become as much of an institution in wrestling as entrance music and fully articulated action figures. Shawn Michaels and Razor Ramon stole the show at WrestleMania X in 1994 with their match, which is regarded as among the annual extravaganza's greatest bouts. Nowadays, you can go to almost

PHOTO BY BOB LEONARD

Tor Kamata works over Dan Kroffat during one of their groundbreaking ladder matches.

any independent wrestling show on any weekend and see where someone had to make a run to the hardware store to buy a ladder. But in Kroffat's vision, the ladder was no more than that. It was just a prop to abet a well-thought-out feud, rather than a single-shot deal to determine who could take the most electrifying bump. "The ladder match to me was all about storytelling. Really, the ladder was just the book. What we put inside the book was the story," he said.

In this case, Kroffat handpicked Kamata (McRonald Kamaka), a former U.S. Air Force airman from Hawaii who started wrestling under his real name in 1965 and segued into a classic Japanese heel. At 270 pounds, Kamata was hardly a high-flyer. But Kroffat felt he was nimble for his size and a perfect foil for the program that he outlined to Stampede Wrestling promoter Stu Hart and his prospective opponent. "I said, 'I would like to have a match where we could hang a bag of money or eventually the belt from the ring light . . . We will set up suspense with a ladder. We'd set it up outside and then the first guy to bring it in could set it, climb it, and get the money,'" Kroffat said. "Stu Hart, he started drooling. I could see he liked it."

A ladder unfolds; so does a wrestling story. In an unusual step, Hart gave Kroffat control over the program outside the purview of booker Dave Ruhl. (Kroffat is often incorrectly cited as Stampede's booker, but he'd been in the business for less than four years at that point.) First up: three weeks of tag team matches against Kamata in September 1972. In each encounter, Kamata gleefully joined in if — and only if — Kroffat was down and out, prone on the mat. The moment Kroffat showed signs of life, Kamata tagged out to partner Sugi Sito like he was late for an important appointment. The message to the audience was unmistakable — Kamata wanted no part of the guy. That's when Kroffat induced him during a TV interview with the lure of green. "What I finally did was say to him, 'Listen, I'll give you $5,000 to stay in the ring with me.' He said in his Japanese accent, 'No-o-o chance. Five thousand dollars? Maybe,'" Kroffat recalled. "So here's what we're going to do. We're going to hang a bag of money above the light. I'm going to put a ladder outside and then that way you're not going to run anymore because you're going to stay in the ring and fight me because you want the money." The importance of that backstory can't be overstated. Kroffat said fan reaction was "over the moon" in large part because he hadn't been able to keep Kamata in the ring during the tag encounters.

Hart got Kroffat a ten-foot stepladder, and he and Kamata went to work before they went public. In one move, Kroffat turned the ladder into a pair of scissors, put Kamata's head at one end, and slammed the ladder shut. "Then I'd walk him around the ring and we practiced that before we went into the ring," Kroffat said. In another move, Kroffat put the ladder across Kamata's head and dropped a flying elbow on him. One of the signature spots: the two climbed opposite sides of the ladder, tipped it over, and crashed outside the ring. "He was agile but he also was a good follower," Kroffat said of Kamata, who died in 2007. "He loved the idea and he said, 'Whatever you want to do with the finishes, it's your show.'"

Kroffat and Kamata took their ladder to Calgary, Red Deer, Regina, Lethbridge, Saskatoon, and other stops on the Stampede Wrestling circuit in October 1972. In the first round, Kroffat claimed victory, snatching the $5,000 money sack from the ring light. Even though the two had worked through some in-ring scenarios, new opportunities arose, Kroffat said. "One of the highlights was trying to get the ladder in the ring. We'd go outside and have a tug of war on the ladder so we could get the ladder halfway in the ring, then it was out of the ring, halfway back in, so it took a while for one of us finally to get it in." And just as Kamata reached for the stash of cash, Kroffat, battered and lying on the mat, shook off the cobwebs, dropkicked the side of the ladder, and sent his foe tumbling. "The crowd . . . it was deafening, the sound in the place as he went over with the ladder. So you were kind of learning on your feet too."

Round one went to Kroffat, but the program was just getting started. "My vision of storytelling was not to do it in one chapter. If

you were good with an idea, you could turn it into several chapters...
You know how to bring it back and utilize it again and again, almost
like *Survivor* or *Dallas* or *Dynasty*," he said. Kamata returned on TV and
said he wanted another crack at Kroffat, only this time, he'd put up
the $5,000. At first, Kroffat balked at a rematch, but then decided it
might be sweet to flatten Kamata a second time, grab the bag, and
toss his opponent's riches to the crowd. To be sure, promoter Hart
wasn't about to put $5,000 in the sack. "Not a chance. None of
us ever saw a check that big from him," Kroffat chuckled. But the
purse contained about $300 in ones, two, and fives that fluttered
like leaves from the ceiling to the floor when the victorious Kroffat
ripped it open. From that point, the stakes grew. Ten thousand
dollars. Twenty thousand dollars. The North American heavyweight
title belt. It was, as Kroffat envisioned, just like *Survivor*, except on a
stepladder at the Regina Exhibition Auditorium instead of a South
Seas island. "Here we are four weeks later and we're selling out
every arena in western Canada because the fans think I am going to
throw the money to them. So the crowd shared in the psychology,"
Kroffat said.

The ladder match also put a different spin on hardcore wrestling,
which had been marked for decades by brass knuckles and bloodlet-
tings. Abdullah the Butcher's first big runs were in Calgary, where he
gouged everyone including himself; his forehead eventually turned
into a graphic relief map of the Rockies. That's not psychology, said
Kroffat, who refused to let Abdullah draw blood when they met face
to face. "It's almost like the Roman gladiators when the lion comes
out and kills the gladiator. That's great to the viewers but the bottom
line was I saw psychology was a better weapon than violence. I could
tell a story with the ladder, whether it was by throwing money to
the crowd or hanging the belt up there."

Kroffat took the concept south in January and February 1974 for
promoters Leroy McGuirk and Grizzly Smith. "Bruiser" Bob Sweetan
assumed the role of Kamata, and the playbook was similar to the one
in Canada, though less bountiful. Sweetan refused to fight Kroffat

man to man until Kroffat proposed hanging a bag with $500 from the ring light in Shreveport, Louisiana. First man up the ladder got the dough. Kroffat won, so Sweetan insisted on a return affair, putting up $1,000 of his own money. Kroffat took the second fight too, and hurled greenbacks into the crowd in Shreveport and other arenas in the Louisiana-Mississippi territory. A year later, Kroffat was back in Stampede Wrestling, reprising a series of ladder matches with 300-pound King Curtis Iaukea. "These ideas weren't for me alone to be successful," he said. "They were to help them be successful. I used to tell them, 'I could care less if I win or lose. This is about filling the house. We're storytellers and this is about entertainment.'"

As ladder matches evolved, the story often became secondary to the device. In May 1975, the Mighty Yankees beat Rip Tyler and Big Bad John in Mobile, Alabama, in a $500 "Asian ladder match" despite the fact that none of the participants were Asian. J.C. Dykes, manager of the Yankees, set up the ladder, which was outside the ring, and grabbed the cash from a pole. In 1986, Verne Gagne's American Wrestling Association touted several $10,000 ladder matches in Wisconsin and Minnesota between Colonel DeBeers (Ed Wiskoski) and an out-of-shape Jerry "Crusher" Blackwell, whose diet consisted of quantities of hard rock candy. Looking back thirty years later, DeBeers didn't see the point. "It was just a card filler because there was no angle leading up to it. I think they just threw it in," he said. "I didn't think there was anything leading up to it . . . I did the best I could but Jerry wasn't exactly at that point in his life the worker he once was." Back in Canada, however, the ladder match continued to be a staple of Stampede Wrestling. Bret Hart called his 1981 ladder match with the Dynamite Kid in Regina one of the greatest of his career, even though he got bloody and bruised for a mere fifty-dollar paycheck. Slowly, the money got better as ladder matches were introduced to national audiences. Hart took the model with him to the World Wrestling Federation, and Kroffat said WWF owner Vince McMahon called to inquire about the particulars as well. In July 1992, Hart and Shawn Michaels wrestled the first ladder match in the company's history.

Two years later, Michaels and Razor Ramon (Scott Hall) climbed the ladder to history. They'd been going around the WWF circuit with "pretty good matches," Hall said, when he saw the nightly lineup posted on the wall at one show in January 1994: Shawn Michaels vs. Razor Ramon — Ladder Match. "Whoa! What's this?" Hall recalled thinking. He'd never been in a ladder match. In the next two months, he'd fight more than a dozen on both coasts, often on unimposing six-rung ladders. The most challenging? One night in New Jersey with a ceiling so low they had to duck when they reached the top of the ladder. "It was like a VFW hall. We still did all the moves but there was no room up there," he laughed. On March 20, 1994, Hall and Michaels fought their WrestleMania X classic and sent the ladder match into stratospheric popularity. "It paid for my first house," Hall said. Ladder matches soon became a mainstay of WWE booking on more than twenty TV or pay-per-view shows in the ensuing decade. Thanks to bump-taking teams like the Dudley Boyz and Hardy Boyz, tables and chairs were added to the mix in 2000, culminating in annual shows such as Money in the Bank and TLC: Tables, Ladders & Chairs. In short, WWE took the ladder from hardcore to mainstream.

A retired businessman in Cochrane, Alberta, Kroffat keeps up with the execution of his creation and is fine with it, as long as wrestlers, bookers, and writers understand that the ladder is not the star of the show: "It's almost like they're doing stunts off the ladder. And that's not the key. The key is telling a story and how do you bring the fans back, week after week, whereas they use the ladder match now as one dramatic match. They might use it at WrestleMania or a pay-per-view and it might be for the belt or something, but that's where they end it. It's a one-time-only thing. I believe strongly in telling stories. I believe to this day it's a great formula for wrestling if you can tell a story."

II. Jawbreaker

As a teenager, Rob Van Dam trained with Sabu under the watchful eye of The Sheik, Sabu's uncle, in a half-sized ring that the master wrestling heel had wedged into a garage in Michigan. One winter day, feeling a little frisky while The Sheik was absent, Van Dam thought he might want to experiment with a back kick off the second rope, but was afraid he would break his friend's jaw. Just do it, Sabu insisted; try not to break my jaw and if you do, screw it, we'll try it again next time. So Van Dam springboarded out of the corner, whirled for a kick, and wham! Sabu was sucking protein shakes out of a straw for a couple of weeks. "He had some wires putting his teeth together and stuff. It's so crazy," Van Dam recalled. "But as soon as he got better, he said, 'Okay, try it again, but this time try to pull back some.' And that's how I learned."

Van Dam learned so well that within a few years, he'd be at the top of his profession with a hybrid style that mixed violence, risk-taking, and blood-and-guts wrestling — call it athletic hardcore. "The cockier and more arrogant Rob Van Dam got, even doing anti-ECW tirades, the more popular he got because his character was so cool," said Extreme Championship Wrestling owner Paul Heyman. "He became an anti-hero in the sense that he was a heel that just became so popular, he just became a babyface."

That conversion happened to a lot of wrestlers during ECW's run from 1992 to 2001. The company's in-the-know fans appreciated and cheered the emphasis on anything-goes action more than they cared for the traditional distinction between good guys and bad guys. In turn, they set a standard that wrestlers felt they had to meet lest they be on the wrong end of an ECW crowd's infamous "You fucked up!" chant. "Oh my God, I hated hearing, 'You fucked up! You fucked up!'" Van Dam said. "Being the self-perfectionist that I was, that put so much pressure on me to never mess up . . . That really made me step my game up and I'm glad that I learned to really put it together in front of that crowd."

ECW was made to order for Van Dam. The promotion started as Joel Goodhart's Tri-State Wrestling Alliance in 1989 in Philadelphia. Goodhart wanted all of his fans to enjoy front-row seats, so he was fine with wrestlers like Eddie Gilbert and Cactus Jack (Mick Foley) taking the action into the stands even if it ramped up the level of brutality. "The kicker was, when these guys were out there, they were beating the shit out of each other because you cannot be standing in front of somebody who's fifteen feet back and do a whiff," he said. Goodhart's vision was bigger than his checkbook, though; he sold out to Tod Gordon in January 1992, who sold ECW to Heyman, his head booker, in 1995. Make no mistake — ECW had all kinds of wrestling; Eddie Guerrero and Dean Malenko were among the most talented performers in the game. But violence, the sense that somebody could get . . . killed . . . tonight, was one of the company's calling cards. Fans handed Pitbull Gary Wolf their prosthetic limbs so he could batter his opponents. "I took legs off of guys and beat the shit out of guys," he said.

While ECW was in its emergent phase, Rob Szatkowski was pulling together the lessons he learned as a daring youth in Battle Creek, Michigan. His high school gym teacher remembered how one of Szatkowski's classmates missed a backflip off the gym bleachers, then dared his friend to attempt the stunt. "Rob took it one step further and said he could do a backflip off the top of the school, and he did," Dave Hudson said. "That's the kind of kid he was, he just wasn't scared." Born December 8, 1970, Szatkowski wanted to be a wrestler from the time he was young and signed up for a kickboxing class solely because it enabled him to get some time in a ring. He started with The Sheik when he was eighteen, learning a stiff style from a man best known for pulling a fork from his trunks to engrave hundreds of foreheads. "He never taught us the secrets that the outsiders would expect to learn in a wrestling school," Van Dam said. "He trained us to be really rough with each other. Like I said, never once did he ever say anything remotely close to teaching us to not hurt each other.

He would always say that we're not being rough enough. That would be the only thing."

The Hardcore Revolution of the 1990s was actually more of an evolution, combining bloody matches associated with The Sheik and Abdullah the Butcher, brawling familiar to fans in Tennessee and Puerto Rico, and accoutrements like tables, a particular specialty of Sabu. When Wolf started in Japan in 1990, he wouldn't go down for a single clothesline by his opponent. "You're going to have to hit me with two or three," he said. "You've got to lay it in. When I'm in Japan, I'll hit the rope, but I won't sell. They love that shit over there." Van Dam headed to Japan in 1993 after a stint as a standard-issue ponytailed, pretty boy babyface in World Championship Wrestling in Georgia. At that point, he was still what insiders call a "spot monkey," a wrestler who can do a lot of tricks but can't tell a story in the ring. "Stan Hansen gave me hell all the time since my first Japan tour in '93," said Van Dam, christened by a promoter who thought he looked and moved like actor Jean-Claude Van Damme. "Like he would say we had a tag match and we would be talking before the match — he called me Quad — he said, 'Why don't you tag me back in and I'll try and make it believable again?' And he was just saying little things like that, but it was always there."

The turning point came in June 1995 at Budokan Hall in Tokyo when Van Dam challenged Danny Kroffat (Phil Lafon, not the '70s Kroffat) for the junior heavyweight championship. Before the match, Kroffat patiently worked with Van Dam to show him how to use his skills to tell a coherent story. "He wanted me to come up with every spot that I do, like all the moves that I want to do, and he had me write them down and give them to him, which I don't think I've done since. He ended up placing them accordingly to get sets of reaction out of the crowd," Van Dam said. He lost the match, but won the day. "It enlightened me to a whole new world that I didn't even notice before. Before I just knew how to make them go oooo! I didn't know how to build them up," he said. "Every little thing matters. You lock up, you back a guy in the corner, and do a break.

You're telling a story. It means something and you're causing a reaction in the emotional investment from everybody that's watching. You have to be connected to that to understand it."

ECW came calling next. The homicidal, genocidal, suicidal Sabu was already there; Van Dam's contemporary and teacher would bust tables by hand if they didn't break in the course of his matches. After pinning Axl Rotten with a split-legged moonsault in his January 6, 1996, Van Dam decided he needed to add to his arsenal if he was to tell the kinds of stories that ECW fans craved. The Van Daminator was born. "I sat there and I was writing on a paper, 'What if I throw a chair up and then jump up and do a spinning back kick and kick that into someone's face?' Okay. I'll write that one down. I had no idea that was going to be my finishing move that was going to be winning championships and replicated on video games," he said. "I wanted to connect with this hardcore crowd and I was coming from Georgia southern style, walking around the ring as a babyface,

PHOTO BY GEORGE TAHINOS

Rob Van Dam hits the Van Daminator.

showing my dimples, and clapping." More than a moonsault, a back kick, or a trademark five-star frog splash, though, ECW alums believe the company was about an attitude. It might not have been storytelling in the conventional WWE or WCW sense, but there was clearly a market for it that helped to inspire wrestling's Attitude Era in the late 1990s. What other promotion would allow Van Dam to bill himself as "The Whole F'n Show"? "ECW was a group of guys that got together. They banded together. They were oddballs, crazies, absurd misfits, whatever they were. But one thing that they did have in common was that they loved the world of professional wrestling and they wanted to perform, and they needed a stage to perform," said hardcore legend Terry Funk.

Van Dam's biggest moment, the night he became a superstar, occurred on April 8, 1998, in Buffalo, New York, against Bam Bam Bigelow, the ECW TV champion. He was supposed to soften up Bigelow for his buddy Sabu. During the match, Van Dam hurled himself on Bigelow from the top turnbuckle, over the guardrail, and three rows deep into fans chanting, "ECW! ECW!" He followed it up with another top-rope somersault plancha into the crowd. Van Dam won the title with Sabu's help but didn't realize what he'd accomplished until a card in Queens, New York, soon thereafter. He was trying to think up new moves and told Heyman he'd invented a double guardrail springboard to use on Mikey Whipwreck. "Paul just looks at me with this big smile and he says, 'Rob, I don't think it matters what you do tonight, anything you do, these people are gonna love you,'" Van Dam said. "I didn't understand it until I came out and felt that love and that energy. It was on such a different level that it was obviously a point of elevation for me that, you know, thank God I never went back below."

With championship gold around his waist, RVD said he told stories differently; no longer the plucky underdog, he was at the top of the promotion. "Sabu had been blowing my head up. I thought like, 'I am the best wrestler in this company and who knows, maybe I'm one of the best in the world. That's what fans are telling me,'" he said. "During my best years, I had to be in such a competitive mindset and I think you have to be in order to really be at your best." But the competition proved too fierce for the low-budget promotion. ECW folded in 2001, around the time that WWE bought what was left of WCW. Van Dam's only option was a federation that had strict prohibitions on the kind of freeform creativity that ECW wrestlers enjoyed. The WWE's Jim Ross told him he'd have to adapt his style because there was no place for chairs, floor crashes, and crazy bumps six and seven nights a week. "The first time I was in there, I saw a list," Van Dam recalled. "Don't anybody use your middle finger because Stone Cold [Steve Austin] is going to use it in the seventh match. Don't anybody take a bump into the guardrail because Kane's going to do that in his match. That was when I first got there; there was literally a list in a dressing room [and] I was like, 'Oh, my God.'"

Despite the limitations, Van Dam's stock soared; he's the only man to hold the ECW, WWE, and TNA world titles, and Ross became a big fan. RVD was as responsible as anyone for WWE's 2005 One Night Stand pay-per-view reuniting ECW wrestlers, which led to the brand's revival on TV. He also loosened Vince McMahon's teeth with the same spinning kick that he tried on Sabu during his apprenticeship. Always thinking about his personal growth, Van Dam picked and chose his spots after leaving WWE in 2007, mixing stand-up comedy performances with appearances in TNA, the independent circuit, and Japan. And he came to earn the respect of Stan Hansen, his disbelieving tag team partner of the early 1990s. Wrestling the big cowboy in Japan several years after they teamed, Van Dam jumped, did a backflip, and ran at him with a striking attack. Afterward, Hansen told Van Dam he had thought all his fancy moves were "bull crap" that had no place in wrestling. "He goes, 'I gotta tell you, you were there one second and then you like disappeared. I didn't know where you went,'" Van Dam recalled. "That was full circle for me. And I said, 'Yeah, you used to tell me that I didn't belong in the business.' And he said, 'Well, you didn't. But now you do.'"

III. Don't Try This at Home

Michelle Cooper counts numbers, but Jewells Malone counts stitches. When the two sides of the same person meet, things come to a head. Blood seeps through Cooper's white dress during her day job after surviving a night of death match wrestling as her alter ego, Malone. An accountant by trade, there is no way to hide her Mrs. Hyde–like side gig as she sports a black eye and limps at work. "My bosses know; they watch my wrestling. I'm very open about it. Usually, I book the next day off," Cooper said.

Just about any death match wrestler will tell you there's more to the business than swinging a barbed-wire baseball bat at an opponent, crashing into a pile of fluorescent light tubes, or using a staple gun in the ring — and then dealing with the aftermath of the mayhem. "There is an art form to death match wrestling. There are techniques, there are ways to do things. You don't just go out there and smash a light tube on somebody's head; it doesn't work that way. It's not supposed to. A lot of people do that, but that's not what it is," said DJ Hyde, owner of Combat Zone Wrestling and its King of the Death Match competitions.

Cooper prefers to discuss unique arts and crafts. At her home, she has crates with a variety of implements she will need when it's time to prepare for chaos. Thumbtacks, check. Nails, check. Broken glass, check. She can't do it all herself. For one thing, airlines generally frown upon weapons of mass destruction, so she will ask a promoter to have her supplies handy and enlist a brave colleague to aid with the more challenging constructs. "When I'm working with barbed wire, it's good to have a second hand because that stuff can be pretty tricky," Cooper said. On one occasion, her trainer, Rob Fuego, was setting up barbed wire around the ring for her bout when the spikes sprung into his face, badly bloodying him for a crowd that eagerly anticipated more bloodshed.

This was not the training that the Toronto-based Fuego had initially instilled in Cooper. She started out as a valet and dreamed of being a high-flyer, the kind of female athlete she and her father loved to watch. He died when she was ten, and Cooper often wonders what he would have thought of her violent turn; her mother hates it, though she approves of the accounting. After Cooper started the hardcore spots and matches, Fuego warned her: "Be careful out there. The more you do this stuff, the more people are going to see it, and the more people are going to expect you to do it and book you specifically to do this kind of stuff. It can only escalate." Before Cooper's nephew was old enough to understand, he went to see his aunt wrestle at a cosplay-themed show, where he witnessed four Mortal Kombat characters beating Princess Peach senseless until Elmo made the save. Her brother has only recently started bringing her nephew back to the matches.

There's a practical side to Cooper that is not evident when she is "Hardcore Princess." Her ideal ratio is seventy-five percent "normal" wrestling and twenty-five percent death matches. She keeps her first aid training up to date, gets her blood tested regularly, and visits her doctor after shows. Her travel bag contains rubbing alcohol, antibiotic ointment, and alcohol wipes. "For cosmetic reasons, I always have a lot of proper skin care stuff. I like to clean things up, but at the same time, I'm a germophobe after. I'm like, 'Okay, no infections please,'" she said. A strong stomach is a must.

At one CZW show, hardcore pro Tommy Dreamer helped Cooper pull "giant pieces" of light tube out of her arm. "He was going get sick because there was a big flap of skin hanging," she said. Dreamer encouraged her to go to a doctor, which she did after the five-hour trip home to Ontario. It was unusual to seek help, said Cooper. "I'm usually the person that sticks people back together, and I clean up the blood."

Looking back, Dreamer regrets the broken fluorescent tube light bulbs, their insides spewing small amounts of mercury, and the chair shots to the head, given the sporting world's greater understanding of the long-lasting effects of concussions. "A chair shot on a back makes just as much noise as it does to your head," said

Dreamer, who gave and took many of them during his time in Extreme Championship Wrestling. "But there's also on the other end, there's people who can hit you, can hit you in the head with a chair, and be safe as can be. They are few and far in between. But fans want to see people that were like Balls Mahoney, who would just destroy your brain cells with a chair."

Ah, the fans. "I truly believe that wrestling is subjective," said Hyde, who gained notoriety through a Vice.com documentary that followed him during the fifteenth annual Tournament of Death, held outdoors in his parents' backyard in Delaware. "Look at it like we're looking at women. You have your taste, I have mine. There's obviously a very large percentage of the population out there of professional wrestling fans that really love what some other fans will say is garbage wrestling."

The term "garbage wrestling" is generally attributed to Shohei "Giant" Baba, the promoter of All Japan Pro Wrestling. He spit it out as an epithet to dismiss Japanese promotions Frontier Martial-Arts Wrestling and W*ING, and garbage's greatest proponent, Atsushi Onita, king of the no-rope barbed wire death match. Onita's bout with Terry Funk on May 5, 1993, at Kawasaki Baseball Stadium in Kanagawa is legendary for its barbarity. "Take one crazy person. Put him in the ring with his mentor, the person who taught him most of what he's learned about being crazy. Surround the ring with barbed wire laced with explosives. And 15:00 into the match, blow the entire ring up," wrote Dave Meltzer in the *Wrestling Observer*. "The end results? Two men drenched in blood hugging each other. One going to the hospital needing 72 stitches in his back and upper stomach. The other had his nose nearly shredded from the barbed wire. And a packed house of 41,000 fans (approximately 32,000 paid) paying $1.8 million gate made it the biggest and most successful financially over-the-edge wrestling show in history."

Mike Kirchner, an ex-paratrooper with the 82nd Airborne Division, was one of the Americans who succeeded in the FMW promotion. He had a short run in World Wrestling Federation

Jewells Malone with one of her tools of the trade, and the barbed wire is real.

as Corporal Kirchner. But his real stardom came as Super Leather during more than sixty tours of Japan. Inspired by the movie *The Texas Chainsaw Massacre* and its flesh-eating antagonist, Kirchner entered the ring with a mask made to resemble human flesh, wearing a blood-covered butcher's apron, and wielding a chainsaw. "Working on that character with the chainsaw was a shock appeal in itself. You're like a circus freak, but a dangerous circus freak. So anybody who got in the ring with you, it's like, 'Wow, he's got to fight Super Leather. I hope he doesn't get hurt too bad,'" Kirchner said. "It was sadistic. It's what was expected of you. You're never going to be a fan favorite. They wanted you to do horrible things. I could go out there and hit them with every spectacular wrestling move and they wouldn't care. I bring out a nail brush and brutalize somebody with it and they'd just be in awe. 'Did you see what he did? He's a monster.' So I became, I don't know, more of a horror figure than a wrestler."

IWA Mid-South was the first North American promotion to promote the death match style on a regular basis. Others, like CZW, which started under John Zandig before Hyde took over, gained even greater traction. WCW and WWE both tried to get into the action with hardcore divisions, though they ended up being as much comedic as violent. But don't dismiss all garbage wrestlers in one condescending sweep, Hyde said, pointing to brand-name stars who cut their teeth and other body parts in death matches. "Dean Ambrose has done death matches; heck, he's wrestled me in count-less of them," Hyde said. "Kevin Owens, Sami Zayn, Cesaro, they've done hardcore in CZW, they've done it. The list goes on and on and on." The women too — WWE's Sarah Logan used to be Crazy Mary Dobson, and was trained by Mad Man Pondo (Kevin Canady) and Mickie Knuckles. Dylan Summers, who wrestled as Necro Butcher, might be the most mainstream death matcher thanks to his appearance in the 2009 Oscar-winning movie *The Wrestler*, where he employed a staple gun on Mickey Rourke's chest and then attached a dollar bill to his own forehead the same way.

Unlike some of the death match wrestlers, Pondo never went mainstream, but he's content with his thirty years in the ring and released an autobiography in 2018. Based just west of Chicago, he has turned promoter with Girl Fight; sometimes it's more traditional women's wrestling, sometimes it's a death match tournament. Finding participants isn't hard, he said. "Just going different places and doing different things, you pick up on who's the craziest and who will get bloody and who's the bravest," he said.

For Knuckles, who debuted in 2003 after training with Chris Hero, bloody and brave was the only answer. "I knew that when I started wrestling that I needed to make myself a commodity. I knew I was never going to be the pretty and thin type," she said. Looking around, she saw an opportunity to put her mark on the death match scene. "I thought to myself, 'Hey, I have a high pain tolerance and I have the ability to do it. I think this could be my niche.'" It was. Other than a pit stop as Moose Knuckles in Total Nonstop Action, she's stayed on the hardcore side of things ever since. To Knuckles, there's not that much difference between a traditional wrestling match and one that features bats, barbed wire, and lemon juice (it makes open wounds really sting). "Each match has the same goal . . . to win. The psychology is much like a great roller coaster ride where the buildup leads to the ultimate thrill," she said. "In death matches, this thrill includes the utilization of the stipulated item and the end result is still very much the same — one winner, one loser, and a crowd that shows no signs of indifference to the spectacle they witnessed."

Knuckles briefly retired in April 2015 when she was pregnant with her second child, but returned to the ring at the behest of her first child. "She said, 'Mommy, when do you wrestle next?' I told her I didn't know and that I was done with wrestling. She got sad. When I asked her why, she said, 'Because I like it when you wrestle. You're like a superhero . . . like my superhero.' That day I realized the reason why I wanted to wrestle to begin with. Because people come in all different shapes, sizes, and colors. None of us are the same but we all have hopes and dreams. Who am I to take that away from anyone, including and especially my little girl?"

Wrestling with an Attitude

Introduction

TV announcer Eric Bischoff was shocked. Or at least he said he was shocked. Right in his presence on *WCW Monday Nitro*, Madusa appeared out of nowhere and dumped the World Wrestling Federation women's championship she'd earned as Alundra Blaze into a pop-up trash can. "This is where the big boys play and now this is where the big girls play," she declared. Actually Bischoff, in his role as head of *Nitro*, had engineered the whole thing. He got in touch with Madusa (Debra Miceli) right after WWE cut her loose in late 1995. As Madusa recalled in a 2017 interview with WWE, Bischoff's first question was whether she still had the belt. "Can you throw it in the trash?" he asked. "Are you kidding me?" Madusa replied. "Just so I get it back, Eric."

The Monday Night Wars between WWE and WCW brought more viewers to wrestling than ever before. In that competition, when quarter-hour ratings first became crucial, both companies pulled out all the stops. Mick Foley brought his puppet sock to entertain a hospitalized Vince McMahon. "Stone Cold" Steve Austin crashed the Pepsi Arena in Albany, New York, with a beer truck. It made for compelling television. But was it wrestling? And did it hurt the sport in the long run? "That's when it started going over the top a little," said James Beard, a long-time referee and former director of operations for the National Wrestling Alliance. "You

PHOTO BY STEVEN JOHNSON

Nothing says attitude like "Stone Cold" Steve Austin knocking back a brewski on the ropes.

had the personal issues going on with Steve and Vince but it was more about kicking somebody's ass. You started to see them book things just to get a reaction. It used to be that you booked things to create an emotional investment."

I. Fool Me Once …

Here we go, Jim Cornette thought. The manager was standing on the apron of the ring in the Richmond Coliseum, an early '70s construct with the interior décor of a UPS warehouse. Cornette draped his left arm around Owen Hart's neck, trusty tennis racket in hand in case he needed to swat a few overexuberant fans. Across the ring, Shawn Michaels was lying face down, left arm shielding his face. A minute before, Hart had nailed Michaels with a kick to the side of the head. The Heartbreak Kid responded spectacularly by sending his foe to the arena floor with a clothesline, then flipping himself over the ropes to get back in the ring. He preened for a few seconds, put his right hand to his right temple, and collapsed as though he'd been flattened by some GIs.

Which he had been, five weeks earlier. Michaels got the snot kicked out of him outside Club 37 in Syracuse, New York, in the early morning hours of October 14, 1995. While WWE claimed ten vicious thugs attacked Michaels without provocation, most accounts say he was in a less-than-coherent state and had been hitting on the wrong woman. Michaels staggered outside to a car and passed out in the front seat when the tough guys — five is a commonly accepted number — dragged him to the ground, stomped on his face, and shoved his head into the bumper. The assailants nearly ripped off his right eyelid; Michaels said he didn't recall the assault and declined to press charges. Unable to wrestle in the aftermath of the beatdown, Michaels forfeited his intercontinental championship to Dean (Shane) Douglas a week later. But the fallout from the Syracuse incident was just starting. Maybe Michaels could fool the fans and build a little intrigue buzz in the pre-internet days by fainting dead away in the middle of a match. "It was my idea and the reason for it was we had played up so much about Shawn's concussion and there was a lot about this post-concussive syndrome," WWE producer-turned-podcaster Bruce Prichard said in 2018.

In wrestling jargon, it is called a "worked shoot," an angle that has some basis in real life but is engineered to trick an audience. It is a script that seeks to come off as unscripted by preying on fans' knowledge of events like the one-sided skirmish in Syracuse. To be sure, Michaels' collapse was hardly the first fictional wrestling blackout. Just a few months after Mike Von Erich committed suicide and brother Kevin Von Erich legitimately passed out in the ring, their father and promoter Fritz collapsed on Christmas night 1987 in Dallas and was "critically hospitalized," according to the promotion, which tried to pass off the flop as another Von Erich family tragedy.

The Michaels faint — call it the Richmond Swoon — had more going for it, though. Unlike Von Erich's caper, it occurred in primetime on *Monday Night Raw* in front of about two million viewers. It was the first worked shoot angle of the three-month-old Monday Night Wars, competing directly against the marquee matchup of Hulk Hogan versus Sting on *WCW Monday Nitro*. And it opened the doors to a flood of worked shoots that continued for years as creative personnel spent considerable time trying to outsmart their smartest fans. "It became, 'We've got this television show and we've got to outthink the guys who are doing the analysis,'" said Bruce Mitchell, a columnist for the *Pro Wrestling Torch*. "They got farther and farther off the track of what they were doing, which was to draw people to watch television."

Owen Hart stands over a collapsed Shawn Michaels during their controversial angle on *Monday Night Raw.*

In his autobiography *Heartbreak & Triumph: The Shawn Michaels Story,* Michaels said plotting for the Richmond Swoon was closely held, with only WWE owner Vince McMahon, announcers Jim Ross and Jerry Lawler, and Hart in on the secret. "This was one of the first times we ever used a real-life incident and integrated it into an angle," he wrote. In fact, Cornette was a major part of it as a manager and strategist. "I structured half of it because they were sitting around wringing their hands," he said years later. "If somebody had done that and they hadn't told me, that'd be the last time you'd see me in the WWF." The Richmond Swoon was planned for November 20, 1995, during the live portion of a *Raw* taping. The upstart Nitro had scored three ratings wins against *Raw* since their head-to-head started in September and was gunning for a fourth with Hogan-Sting, a free TV match that easily could have headlined a pay-per-view.

During the pre-swoon deliberations, Cornette said he was puzzled about how the collapse would advance the storyline surrounding Michaels, who'd wrestled without mishap several times during the previous week. "They said, 'Well, we just want to get people thinking because it's live.' They just wanted to get people talking," Cornette explained. Prichard and Michaels both pressed a reluctant McMahon to go to dead air with the collapse instead of continuing to call the inaction with Lawler. "What if everybody goes silent?" Prichard recalled asking. "If we say nothing, 'Now, oh my God, that's real' . . . This is no longer a show. We're giving you a glimpse into real life."

Michaels wilted a few minutes before *Raw* signed off at 10 p.m. ET. "Owen and I go, 'What the fuck?' and we're on the floor and you see me kind of concerned looking at the referee," Cornette said. Outside the ring, Cornette waved his tennis racket like a fan in Hart's face, vamping. Ten seconds went by, then twenty, then thirty as referee Earl Hebner stood over Michaels, not counting him out. After seventy seconds, McMahon climbed into the ring, followed by WWF officials J.J. Dillon, Gorilla Monsoon, and Rene Goulet. Lawler got up from his broadcast perch, approached the ring, and spread his arms as if he was asking for guidance. A paramedic provided oxygen to Michaels, who nodded a couple of times in response to questions. A camera locked in on Michaels' face and the oxygen tank as the closing credits rolled. Off the air, two EMTs helped Michaels to the back, with one flashing a forefinger-up sign. Michaels went to a nearby hospital, his concerned friend Triple H in tow, to add legitimacy to the angle.

The reaction among the 4,500 fans in the arena was short of panic but beyond puzzlement. "I remember the conversation around us. A lot of people were going, 'What's going on? Is this for real? Is he really hurt?' So there was definitely a lot of doubt in the building that I recall," said long-time wrestling photographer Dave Layne, who was sitting a few rows back. "We didn't know what was going on TV and what wasn't. So it made it more semi-believable because we didn't know if they cut to something else. Is anybody else seeing this?" It didn't fool the wrestlers. Tom Prichard, Bruce's brother, had just rejoined the WWE as one of the Bodydonnas. He was watching backstage and got the impression that the architects of the angle were trying to dupe his brethren. Like most wrestlers, he had a finely tuned B.S. detector and quickly deduced that no one was panicking or rushing for medical assistance. "I'm always on the lookout for that. I don't believe anything until it is verified and for me, it rang as a work," he said. "It was kind of like, 'Eh, here we go.' I don't even remember any real reaction like 'Holy shit!' There wasn't any of that."

In some ways, the Richmond Swoon produced as intended. "I think a lot of people just thought he kicked him too hard," Layne said of the live crowd. "That type of thing had not really happened that much before and it seemed like it was better done than a lot of stuff that came after it." Dave Meltzer of the *Wrestling Observer* reported an uptick in calls to his hotline as fans dialed up to get the inside scoop on whether the collapse was real or fake. Michaels took time off, teased a retirement, then won the Royal Rumble match in January 1996 to earn a shot at the WWF championship at WrestleMania. "It wasn't overdone. They did not come out and have an ambulance driver ride in within thirteen seconds," Cornette said. "So it worked in that respect." But the critical acceptance was brutal. Unwittingly, WWF opened itself to scorching condemnation by running the Richmond Swoon just hours after two-time Olympic champion figure skater Sergei Grinkov of Russia collapsed and died of a heart attack at practice. He was twenty-eight, two years younger than Michaels. Syndicated columnist Alex Marvez said the WWF "reached a new low — even for pro wrestling . . . The WWF did such a good job pretending Michaels' injury was real (and milking it on television) that Abe Lincoln would have been proud." Marvez was among many who saw the stunt as a counter to Nitro's big event. "The Michaels injury was designed to shock fans into staying tuned," he said. Over on Nitro, announcer and head honcho Eric Bischoff said years later he didn't know and didn't care what was happening in Richmond, and dismissed speculation he wanted Michaels for his own. "The last thing I wanted to do was bring in Shawn Michaels to add fuel to that fire . . . He could have said to me, 'Eric, I'll come and work for you for free,' and I probably would not have hired him." The angle did nothing to jolt ratings. *Raw* ran on the heels of the Survivor Series pay-per-view the day before, which ordinarily boosted Monday night viewership. But it lost the November 20 ratings battle to Hogan and Sting 2.6 to 2.3 and dropped three of the next four weeks as well.

Following the Richmond Swoon, worked shoots popped up like flowers in the desert. In February 1996, Brian Pillman uttered the phrase "I respect you, booker man" to Kevin Sullivan as part of his ploy to get a new contract; acknowledging Sullivan was WCW booker had been strictly taboo. That September, Ross criticized McMahon for the well-known indignities he inflicted on the broadcaster, then brought out a fake Razor Ramon and a fake Diesel to mimic wrestlers who had jumped to WCW. At the 2000 Bash at the Beach, WCW writer Vince Russo employed a worked shoot angle to switch the world title from Jeff Jarrett to Hulk Hogan to Booker T in one night; Hogan — for real — sued Russo for insulting him during a rambling speech. On it went to the point that WWE put forth a complicated love quadrangle among Matt Hardy, Lita, Kane, and Edge in 2005 based on a real-life affair between Edge and Lita. Some of the worked shoots succeeded and some didn't, but they were all symptomatic of what Tom Prichard calls the "wrestling bubble," the tendency of front office personnel to communicate only with themselves. "You don't understand how much that bubble really exists when you're inside it and you hear from people who are not inside that bubble," he said. "You don't get a true outside feeling; you don't get an outside opinion. You get in that bubble and you start thinking, 'Well, we shocked them last time; that's what they want.'"

A repeat of the Richmond Swoon is unlikely; fans have become wise to worked shoots thanks to the internet and social media. Imagine the uproar today if a wrestler pretending to be injured or concussed took up valuable time and resources in a hospital emergency room. But there's no doubt that Michaels' collapse represented a departure point in the development of worked shoot angles. "To this day people ask me if he really passed out," Cornette said. "There are some things that people still question and I almost hate to pop their bubble. It was a work."

II. The Magic Makers

David Sahadi's first day with the World Wrestling Federation came on October 13, 1992, at a TV taping in Regina, Saskatchewan. Feeling stifled at NBC Sports, where he was the head of sports promotion, he needed a new challenge, so why not wrestling? His father, Lou Sahadi, had been one of the best-known chroniclers of the mat game as editor of *Wrestling World* magazine, so he felt he knew the business. But one word from his new boss resonated with the younger Sahadi that day in Canada.

"Vince McMahon pulled me into his office and said, 'David, everything we do here is all about one thing: emotion.' That really stuck with me," said Sahadi. "Every image campaign I wrote and directed, every video feature I produced, that was my mantra. I tried to evoke some sort of emotion with the viewer, whether it be joy, anger, or laughter in everything I did. I wanted the viewer to feel something, to be moved."

Eleven years later, Sahadi left WWE, burned out. When TNA Wrestling approached him in 2006, after a year and a half break, he was ready to get back at it and directed virtually every episode of the company's Impact show until Anthem Sports & Entertainment bought it in December 2017. For those twenty-five years, Sahadi affected the visual side of professional wrestling storytelling more than just about anyone, dragging it kicking and screaming from the pastel-and-cartoon feel of the early 1990s into the Attitude Era and beyond. He did the "Legends" spots where the stars of the past

Visual storyteller David Sahadi (l) locks up with Kurt Angle.

provided a symbolic laying on of hands to current superstars. He crafted the WWE Super Bowl spot in 1999 with mayhem breaking out behind McMahon as he strolled through the company's headquarters. He created the "RAW" logo burning on the top of the WWE Titan Towers complex.

"I initially went a little outside the box with my writing/ shooting/editing style. And they liked it. So I kept on pushing the envelope further, doing things that had never been done in wrestling before," Sahadi said. "We went behind the curtains; we tore the old walls down. That creative freedom was invigorating. It energized and inspired me. It literally was a new era we were creating and it made WWE such a fun place to work at the time."

The buck might stop with Vince McMahon in WWE, but he can't do everything. All facets of the business of TV have to combine to tell a story, just like Sahadi working NFL broadcasts or creating promos for the 1992 Summer Olympic Games in Barcelona. In a sporting event, the "script" is the game clock or the event itself, and thinking on the fly is necessary to tell the story. In pro wrestling, there is a framework as creative strategists settle on a storyline and wrestlers and backstage producers execute it. After all, a Swanton bomb off a twenty-foot ladder means nothing if the cameras don't catch it. The soldiers behind the scenes run the gamut from the cameramen, audio crew, and lighting specialists to pyrotechnic geniuses, ring crew, costume makers, and makeup artists. The wrestlers might think they know it all, but their performance in the ring is like seeing only the tip of an iceberg floating past the shores of Newfoundland.

Domenic Cotter is one of the most sought-after music production men in the world. His Sounds Off company has filmed everyone from Mötley Crüe to Jennifer Lopez in concert. NBC hired Cotter to be a part of the broadcast team for the initial season of the XFL in 2001. A lifelong wrestling fan, that got him curious about WWE, and he joined the company as a backstage producer, overseeing and executing the vignettes. Cotter only spent half a year with WWE, but came away with a greater appreciation for it all. "I have compassion and empathy for the workers, for the performers, the wrestlers. That would be my biggest takeaway from my six months there. Growing up, is wrestling fake or real? It is beyond real."

Given his own successes in music production, he can look back and know why he didn't fit in. "I produce large music festivals that are broadcast worldwide. So it wasn't the stress, it was more the environment. It just wasn't the right fit for me," Cotter said. "They have a certain way of doing things there and if you don't conform to that, it's certainly not going to be a place that's going to work for you."

Even something as straightforward as setting up the ring has changed through the years. Former WWE referee Jim Korderas used to do double duty as the third man in the ring and one of two guys in a ring truck that drove around and set everything up for house shows. While there is still a ring to set up, it's not a two-hour job anymore. Ring crews get in the night before a house show so they can set up the ring, the lighting, and the stage with accompanying screens. Korderas' WWE days also spanned the transition from timekeeper to earpiece. Today, a timekeeper basically rings the bell, but the job used to be key, alerting the combatants as to how much of their allotted time remained. A flipped-up tie could mean stall for time, or a pencil in the mouth could mean to wrap up the match, pronto. The earpieces referees wear also evolved from timing for TV to today when production workers will ask the ref to pass on information — call a spot — mid-match. "The referee needs to be invisible until he needs to be visible. At the same time, you're part of the storytelling process," said Korderas, still active on Ontario's independent scene and sharing his wrestling knowledge with viewers on Sportsnet's *Aftermath TV*.

Sometimes wrestlers chafe at the storytelling restraints that agents, usually ex-wrestlers, place on them. Tony Garea, a championship wrestler in WWWF, spent more time as an agent — twenty-five years — than he did as an active competitor. "You might say that we were babysitters on the road," he said. Two agents usually worked each road trip, one dealing with wrestlers and managers, and the other dealing with the building itself, including collecting the gate. "I enjoyed talking to the talent and helping them," Garea said.

The setup is similar today with two road agents who generally show up mid-afternoon the day of a TV show. One agent huddles with wrestlers, who are expected to arrive roughly two hours before bell time. Unlike in the past, WWE usually does not announce house show matches ahead of time, so rearranging a card is easier to account for travel issues or wrestler illness. Agents tell the wrestlers what they expect and the finish to the match. Meanwhile, a second agent oversees arena issues, which means security and policing, fire codes, emergency procedures, merchandise areas, the national anthem, and WWE's promotional videos that play on the big screens in the arena.

A talent producer at WWE TV sits in on afternoon meetings to hear what the creative side has planned and then goes back to the wrestlers to present the story they need to tell. Producers also share the game plan with the team in the TV truck so that the camera crew knows what to shoot. When the assigned match is in the ring, the producer is at the "gorilla" position, just outside the entrance curtains. That way, the producer can communicate with the video production team or the referee in the ring. If Vince McMahon decides on the spur of the moment to change something, the message is frantically passed on. It's high pressure in the ring and behind the scenes.

Cody Rhodes' career didn't overlap with Garea's role backstage, but his sentiments are revealing. Many of the WWE agents are people he has known all his life. "How the hell are you going to tell me what to do out there? You don't. And that was my biggest mistake with WWE, ever listening," Rhodes told Brent Brookhouse of CageSideSeats.com. "There's a difference between collaboration or advice and being told to do this. Because that's not how it works. You go out there and you're the one on TV. You take the heat if it sucks and you reap the rewards if it's a grand slam."

The baseball reference is appropriate because wrestling is a team game. During his 2014 WWE Hall of Fame induction speech, The Ultimate Warrior used some of his time to "thank the superstars that you never see . . . The ring guys, who back in the day would get to the building, set up the ring, tear it down, drive all night, get to the next town, get a couple hours' sleep, grab a cheeseburger, couple Coca-Colas, go back to another arena, set the ring up again, right before the matches take a shower, and then come and ask me or the other guys, 'Can I get you anything? Is there anything I can get you, man?' I'll never forget those guys."

In the end, you're only telling a story on TV if someone shoots it. "For me, when it comes to directing a live wrestling match, I always love to shoot tight, close-up shots of faces of the wrestlers during the critical parts of capturing the story the wrestlers are trying to tell," said Sahadi. "Faces, visuals, capture and tell the story just as well as announcers could, if not better. TV is a visual medium after all."

III. SARSA

Eric Bischoff's epiphany came in the form of a newspaper clipping. In summer 1996, Bischoff came across a USA Today story in which NBC Sports President Dick Ebersol explained how he planned to combat declining ratings for the Olympic Games. In just a few years, Bischoff had climbed the ladder from a TV announcer in the dying days of Verne Gagne's American Wrestling Association to the head of World Championship Wrestling. But he was ever on the lookout for a paradigm that could help him evaluate which wrestling stories would work and which ones would flop. "When I got to WCW, it was kind of like a cluster, a collage of things just thrown up against the wall," he said. "I knew that there had to be a formula that you could go to and use and predictably have a reasonably good outcome, fairly consistently. But I didn't know what it was."

Ebersol held the answer. To him, TV coverage of the Olympics was all about telling stories, not just reporting results, and to accomplish that, NBC needed to concentrate on storylines, action, and anticipation. That's the formula I've been searching for, Bischoff thought. He clipped the article, thought about Ebersol's comments, adapted them to wrestling, and SARSA was born.

SARSA — Story, Anticipation, Reality, Surprise, and Action — was Bischoff's contribution to the world of acronyms, a five-pronged

From left, Eric Bischoff with Steve Austin and Greg Gagne.

way of looking at wrestling plots, programs, and angles. Bischoff has legions of admirers and detractors since his *WCW Monday Nitro* show trumped *Monday Night Raw* for eighty-three straight weeks, yet an adrift WCW closed up shop three years later. While critics credit Bischoff as a TV whiz, some also contend his methodology under-valued wrestlers' actual work in favor of special on-screen moments that turned out not to be so special. Regardless of the successes and failures, Bischoff's approach represented an unusually systematic way of thinking about stories in a business known for booking by the seat of its pants. "Any time anybody comes to me and says, 'Eric, I've got this great idea for a wrestling angle. What if this guy does this and this guy does this and then next week they do this?'" he recounted. "Okay, great. Let's break that down into the little pieces."

The first element in Bischoff's construct was the story. Just like a movie, the story had to be set up so the audience could understand it. "You just don't throw shit up against the wall," he said. "If he's going to hit me over the head with a chair on a Monday, well, what did I do to him on a Friday to make him want to do that? What's the backstory? What's the reason?" Properly executed, the story would create enough interest that people would want to tune in the following week to see what happens, creating anticipation.

The reality aspect of SARSA was probably the trickiest. Bischoff said he learned the significance of believability and reality from Gagne, an old-school wrestler and promoter to whom the words "sports entertainment" were anathema. "If you don't have those moments where the audience goes, 'Oh, yeah, that could be true,' the rest of it doesn't matter," he said. "That's what made *Nitro* work. It wasn't always believable. We had Glacier, for God's sakes. My bad. But there were throughout that two-hour episode, in some cases three-hour episodes, there were moments where 'Holy shit, Kevin Nash powerbombed Rey Mysterio!' 'Oh my God, the cops showed up!' You didn't know if it was true or not."

From his experience in the industry, Bischoff knew wrestling audiences loved surprises, the fourth element in his typology. "It's kind of inherent in our television culture, especially on a live show, you want to see something where you go, 'I didn't see that coming.'" That could be something as simple as a camera operator tripping over a cable, he said. But the possibility of an expected surprise keeps up the spontaneity and reality. Action, the final part of the equation is closely tied to wrestlers' in-ring skills. "The action has to be exciting enough and dynamic enough that we're not doing thumb wrestling, right? It's got to be fun to watch," Bischoff said. As a result, SARSA became the standard by which Bischoff judged ideas that wrestlers, writers, and bookers presented to him. "Anybody can come up with an angle. Anybody can come up with a finish that's really exciting. But what I always did was when [writer] Vince Russo or anybody else who came to me with an idea, I would say, 'Great. Where does it go?' Ninety-nine times out of a hundred, they'd go, 'I don't know.' 'Next.'"

The Monday Night Wars between *Raw* and *Nitro* had been underway for less than a year when Bischoff formulated his creed. It found its fullest incarnation in the New World Order, when

Scott Hall and Kevin Nash, fresh out of WWE, appeared on *Nitro* intimating they were planning a hostile takeover of WCW. Some wrestling journalists suspected Bischoff borrowed the invasion angle from one in New Japan Pro Wrestling. He said that was not the case; he had long been mulling over a "turf war" type of story to incorporate into WCW. In any event, it scored big-time on all five SARSA measures. The story began with the sudden appearance of Hall, known in WWE as Razor Ramon, accosting Bischoff on camera on May 27, 1996, asking if WCW was ready for a war. The anticipation built each week as to which WWE talent would join Hall; Kevin Nash, the former Diesel, came on board the next week. Reality? Hall and Nash used their own names, a practice uncommon in wrestling. The great surprise came on July 7, when Hulk Hogan, an idol to a generation, turned heel and announced the formation of the nWo during the annual Bash at the Beach card. Veteran Kevin Sullivan, booking for WCW, called it the hottest program he ever saw. "We had taken all the work that Vince did to get those guys over. I didn't have to wait five months or three months to get these guys over. They were over when they walked in. If we had done that with guys nobody knew, it would have been a popcorn fart," he said. "It worked because we took Vince's guys and they were over when they got there and people believed it was WWE versus WCW."

From September 9, 1996, through April 6, 1998, *Nitro* beat *Raw* non-stop in the Monday Night Wars. Not everything was a SARSA five-star program, nor did Bischoff expect it to be. "It's impossible to get all five every single time. But if you go through a storyline and you lay it out on a calendar, you really break it down like a story, if you can get four out of five, awesome. That story could last for a year or two. If you hit three out of five, that's a short-term story. Two months, three months. If you hit two out of five, you're toast," he said. But cracks in the logic started to appear. In September 1997, Hogan, the man who body slammed Andre the Giant at WrestleMania III, picked on 55-year-old J.J. Dillon, the pretend head of WCW, in a disagreement about a match. Hogan threw an airball of a punch at Dillon, who nonetheless fell like he'd been rocked by a brick. Hogan delivered two leg drops to Dillon, and Bischoff spray painted "Bite Me" on the victim's shirt. In theory, the incident showed the nWo had no time for authority figures, but the elements of action, suspense, and believability seemed absent. "That was something they wanted to do. If somebody is paying me and they think it is important, for whatever reason, unless it's totally out of bounds, I'm going to go with it even though it might not be something I'd be excited about," Dillon explained more than twenty years later. "To me, I'm old school in that believability is important and continuity is extremely important. I had the sense that it wasn't as much of a priority with [Bischoff] as much as it as with me."

Dusty Wolfe was on the WCW roster during part of the Monday Night Wars and thought the Bischoff storytelling consisted of too many attempts at creating a water cooler buzz. "He used to call it a 'Nitro moment.' I sat in on a couple of meetings and heard him call it that. He tried to get that 'wow' right there, right now," Wolfe said. "Bischoff never followed it up. Someone would come through the curtain and then that was it. You've got the 'wow' moment, now what do we do? . . . He did that well at times. But he had no clue how to follow it up. None."

As time progressed, the nWo became the least exclusive club in wrestling. What started with Hogan, Nash, and Hall cycled through more than sixty members by the time WWE acquired WCW's assets in 2001. There was nWo Hollywood, nWo Wolfpac, nWo Elite, nWo Black & White, and nWo 2000. There was regular Sting, a WCW icon, and nWo Sting (Jeff Farmer), who enjoyed a good run in Japan before he debuted on Nitro in 1996. "When I came back to the States and did a little bit of the nWo Sting, it was a little more confusing and the fans weren't sure if it was Sting, nWo Sting. Again, part of this is promoters," said Farmer, who became the sixth member of the nWo. "I made it very clear to promoters, I said, 'Look, do not book me as Sting. I'm the nWo Sting. I was the one that came out [with the nWo]; that was my character, I'm a bad version, I was with Hogan and all that. Don't make it out to be Sting.'" Sullivan said diluting the nWo beyond Hogan, Nash, Hall, and possibly Randy Savage took the storytelling in the wrong direction. "If it had stayed just the four of them, we'd probably still be talking about it today in a different way," he said.

Disappointed with WCW's slide, the Turner Sports brass sent Bischoff home for a few months in 1999, but he returned in April 2000 with another storyline built on his model — to admit past mistakes openly, strip all champions of their belts, and put them up for grabs among all wrestlers. "WCW was getting hammered in the press; the audience was tired of things that we did. We knew by the time I came back, we knew we had to fix this. How do we do it? The idea was to wipe the slate clean and try to make the belts mean something by everybody competing for them," he said. "What we were trying to do was create stakes and a journey that everybody was trying to fight for to help tell our story." Bischoff was one of the heads of the New Blood, a faction of younger wrestlers, but he left WCW for good in July when writer Russo reversed a storyline without his knowledge.

Bischoff later worked in WWE and TNA, though without the power to implement SARSA that he enjoyed as president of WCW. Always the big-picture thinker, one of his few regrets is that he couldn't pull off the show of the millennium to play on Y2K fears about clocks, computers, and the fate of civilization. His pay-per-view would have run on New Year's Eve 1999 in an outdoor stadium in Tucson, Arizona. Wrestling would be at one end of the stadium with KISS at the other. The final bout would conclude with a referee's count of three at the stroke of midnight. "It was going to be a combination KISS concert/WCW End of the World event," he said. "A bunch of [AOL/Time Warner] employees complained to human resources that they had to work over Christmas and New Year's and they didn't want to do it. So ask me how pissed off I was. I wanted to kill about 100 people."

When Wrestling Became Content

Introduction

At one time, here's what wrestling scriptwriting consisted of: Danny Miller, a wrestler who pitched in to help with front office duties, strewed booking sheets across his living room floor in the 1970s to make sure the right Mid-Atlantic wrestling interview and pitch went into the right market. "Each TV market had to have a promo for that particular area. That is an art form," said Miller, who learned the skill from tag team partner Les Thatcher. "It was handwritten with a magic marker on yellow papers."

Those days are gone, and not just because Microsoft Excel has replaced marked-up spreadsheets. There are more stories to tell in more ways than ever. Since the turn of the century, WWE has maintained a stash of writers to keep the content ball rolling. Some of them have wrestling backgrounds, some don't, which is an endless source of frustration for veterans like Jim Cornette. "It'd be like me writing *Family Guy*," he quipped. "I've got a boxed set of all twelve seasons, but I can't write the thing." Still, the writers are here to stay and, if anything, their responsibilities are increasing. "There's a little group of folks that write NXT, there's a team that writes *Raw*, a team that writes *SmackDown*," said Triple H, an executive vice president under CEO Vince McMahon, his father-in-law. "When I say write, it's more than just the creative, when they do this, then they do that. It's formatting the shows and everything, timing, all the stuff that

252

Ronda Rousey (l) and Stephanie McMahon square off at the press conference announcing WrestleMania 35.

goes into creating a television show — I shouldn't even say television, creating a show, because distribution is so varied now. There's a lot of components that go into it."

I. The Write Stuff

Oh, the boundless joys and endless frustrations of being a WWE writer. Dan Madigan experienced both. During the company's Ruthless Aggression Era, he penned material for JBL (John Layfield) during his anti-immigrant crusade, which was directed mostly at Eddie Guerrero. As Madigan coached from the sidelines, JBL ranted during a filming in Texas that the Guerrero family snuck into the United States under the bellies of burros crossing the Rio Grande. "We just went off and destroyed the Guerrero legacy. John was just brutal," Madigan said. "And there's the Guerrero family watching me do this and after it was done, Eddie comes up to me and goes,

'That was fucking awesome. That was great! Please write for me. Please, Dan, write for me.'"

At the other extreme, Madigan invented Mordecai (Kevin Fertig) as a white-clad, hypocritical religious zealot and a dream evil-versus-good foil for the Undertaker. WWE CEO Vince McMahon bought into Mordecai, who beat Bob Holly at the 2004 Great American Bash. Then the company abruptly deep-sixed the gimmick. "Wait a second," Madigan recalled thinking. "Yesterday, they thought this was the greatest angle ever." Fertig didn't help his cause by getting in a real-life bar fight, but Madigan, known for his edgy storytelling, said the unexplained about-face underscored a lesson he learned at WWE. "It's like writing on an Etch A Sketch because nothing is going to stay."

As a WWE writer, you worked alongside world-class talent, making good money by putting your creative juices to purpose in an industry you probably loved as a kid. In fact, Madigan once considered training to be a pro wrestler with Killer Kowalski, though he instead landed in Hollywood as a scriptwriter. But your life was not your own. Eighty-hour work weeks piled up regardless of holidays or weekends. Your best and brightest ideas were changed on the fly or, even worse, shot down inexplicably. Wrestlers were insulted by the notion that someone who's never taken a bump should be able to tell them what to say. "It's some of the worst shit that you can do is to discourage somebody's professional ways to express their feelings, express their character, who they are," said Scott Steiner. "For the idiots that script interviews, it's a travesty doing that. You're basically cookie-cutter having characters. It's one of the worst things you can do." No wonder former WWE head writer David Lagana, who previously worked in Hollywood as a part of the Friends writing team, could say it's not a life for everyone. "There is this stigma about WWE writers that they're this faceless, nameless, odorless, tasteless Borg that writes really bad television," he explained. "There's no credit, there's never credit. You do something well, it's on the talent . . . do something poorly, it's your fault."

The emergence of professional writers scripting WWE shows and pay-per-views is a relatively recent phenomenon. Throughout most of wrestling history, storylines were hammered out by bookers and wrestlers with little more than a few talking points provided for interviews and promos. Despite no previous training, Tom Prichard was part of the WWE writing team in the late 1990s; it was a small group of McMahon and a handful of others. "I just started showing up. I had no frigging idea how to do it, how to make this TV flow," he said. When he rejoined the company in 2007, he was taken aback at the fully staffed writers' division. "There were like twenty-five writers, each one with a laptop, each one taking a match. I felt like, 'Wait a minute. This is really overproduced.'"

In part, the business was changing; WWE needed scriptwriters to generate ideas and fill increasingly available amounts of time on the air and online. But the shift of power from wrestler to writer that Prichard and others saw was quite intentional. "We weren't even allowed to say the word 'wrestling.' Vince didn't look at it as old-school wrestling. It was entertainment. It was a TV show," said Kevin Eck, a writer for WWE from 2011 to 2014. "So he appreciated having someone from soap opera or episodic TV, that background, who could approach it and not have the bias, so to speak, of, 'Well, I grew up watching wrestling in the 1970s and this is how it's done.'"

Court Bauer had a foot in both camps. Growing up north of New York City, he had designs on getting into the more adult-oriented Extreme Championship Wrestling rather than WWE. But ECW went under when he was in college, and Bauer wound up running Major League Wrestling for a couple of years before going into film and TV work. That hybrid background in wrestling and entertainment plus the support of Wild Samoan Afa Anoa'i, to whom he'd turned for advice as a budding collegiate scriptwriter, helped him win a position with WWE in 2005.

One storyline remains close to his heart. Because of his ties to the Anoa'i family, Bauer was tasked with what to do with Afa's nephew Edward Fatu. In his first run with WWE, the company cut Fatu loose after an altercation with police in Pensacola, Florida. But he rose overseas to the top of All Japan Pro Wrestling. WWE brought him back, unable to resist an agile six-foot-three 300-pounder. "That connected me right back to where I started in the business," Bauer said. He came up with Umaga, The Samoan Bulldozer, a face-painted beast with a mysterious past and a vicious streak. Beginning in April 2006, WWE strapped a rocket to Umaga with big wins over John Cena, Triple H, Shawn Michaels, Kane, and Ric Flair. Umaga, who died in 2009, was McMahon's weapon of choice in the Battle of the Billionaires with Donald Trump at WrestleMania 23, which drew 1.25 million buys, the largest 'Mania to that point. "To see him have that kind of opportunity and to live up to the expectations was phenomenal. It was very rewarding," Bauer said.

Done right, then, a collaboration between writer and wrestler can pay enormous dividends. Nick Dinsmore worked for a decade as a skilled technical wrestler who couldn't break through until he developed a Rain Man–like character who was also a wrestling savant. With input from trainer Rip Rogers, fan favorite Eugene was born and gave head writer Brian Gewirtz and Madigan plenty to work with. "For every Lou Costello, you need a Bud Abbott. That guy has to play off that or it's not going to work. I said, 'We need someone who's completely polar opposite than Dinsmore,'" Madigan said. That was William Regal, who became part of an odd couple and championship tag team with Eugene until he, as a born heel, betrayed the naïve wrestler. "The crew really got attached to that piece because even though it's a goofy wrestling angle, we've gotten to know these characters and the guys playing the characters, and we see the characters coming together and you know what's going to happen," Madigan said. For his part, Dinsmore said script-writers are a way of life, and wrestlers need to give them something to work with, like Eugene. "It's essential now. They're the ones that are going to put your character on TV and give it direction. Guys refuse to do a finish in the ring; they just don't get written for. If I've got an idea, as opposed to all the writers kicking around rocks saying, 'What can we do with this guy?' 'I don't know,' it's that ability to have a character writers want to write for."

Still, success stories have been mixed with disappointment. "Unless you were a headliner or one of Triple H's allies, wrestlers had very little input on creative back then," said Ranjan Chhibber, a WWE writer from 2004 to 2005. "Stephanie McMahon would reprimand new guys like me if she saw us talking to wrestlers since she felt we were 'acting like marks.'" Chhibber wrote a chapter in his doctoral dissertation on Sabu's days in ECW. When he taught film studies at George Washington University, the professor entertained his students with wrestling stories, clips, and impressions. After running into wrestlers Jimmy Yang and Ryan Sakoda at a restaurant, he sent in a note to WWE on a whim and got hired. But the scoldings took their toll, and Chhibber got in hot water for talking to Eric Bischoff, then the acting general manager for *Raw*. "This was like being in a cult," said Chhibber, now at Florida State College at Jacksonville. "If you were seen speaking to the wrong person or allying with the wrong creative faction, you were punished. A few wrestlers were banished to [lower-tier TV show] *Velocity* if they pitched creative ideas back then. Other wrestlers got the message."

Andrew Goldstein's experiences were similar to Madigan's — one minute a high, one minute a low. He was twenty-six when he hooked on with WWE in 2006. A lot of his work focused on the little-remembered launch of MVP (Montel Parker) and a brief program between Undertaker and Mr. Kennedy (Ken Anderson). "There's a great promo that Mr. Kennedy cut in front of just a black screen and he talks about Undertaker's parlor tricks not working on him, and he's not afraid of the Undertaker," Goldstein said. "At the time, Vince called it the best promo that Kennedy had ever cut and I wrote that thing word for word. So I was proud of that."

The flip side: the aborted character switch of popular Tatanka at a time when WWE was short on high-level heels. Tatanka had his plan mapped out and told Goldstein, who pitched it to a room of writers. "We did the Tatanka heel turn, though it only lasted one promo. Vince saw it and was like, 'Nope, pull the plug. We're not doing this.'" Ultimately, the efforts of the writers live and die with McMahon, Goldstein said. "We would have full-on, plotted-out, months-long storylines gridded out. 'This week this is going to happen, then next week this happens,' the whole thing. Pitch it to him, he signs off. Then we get to TV and he changes his mind, and then that whole thing goes away and you have to scramble." Jimmy Jacobs, "The Zombie Princess," said he had a great experience writing in WWE from April 2015 until October 2017, but thought some writers tried too hard to curry favor with the boss. "People stop worrying about or thinking of things in terms of what will be the best product. What will put on the best show? What will draw the most money? What will get this guy over?" Jacobs said. "People stop thinking in those terms and they start just thinking, 'What will Vince want? What will make Vince mad?' And when you're just catering to one guy, I see that as a big problem."

There was a definite pecking order among wrestlers at WWE. "You don't proceed without taking the temperature of The

John Gaburick sits at the head of a TNA Impact Wrestling writers meeting in 2016.

Undertaker," Bauer said. Still, plans and directions changed so regularly that Eck, who worked as a journalist for the *Baltimore Sun*, a writer for WWE, and a magazine editor at World Championship Wrestling, felt uncomfortable conveying too much information to wrestlers he worked with. "The end game can change. If the plan was, 'Hey, in three weeks, you win the title,' you didn't want to say that because that could change, and then in three weeks when they don't win the title, they're 'What the hell? I thought I was winning,'" he said. The pressures and uncertainties of the writing game led to burnout, said Bauer, who revived his Major League Wrestling promotion in 2017. "There were guys that basically quit. They just were so emotionally connected to ideas and devastated when Vince would reject it. Sometimes Vince would give the courtesy of explaining the logic behind his concerns with the idea or his rejection of it. Other times, it was a 'Goddamn no!' And that was it. And God, I saw guys crushed by it."

Which doesn't mean writers ignore wrestling once they're no longer an active part of the industry. "I do love the business. I won't deny it," Madigan said. "Wrestling is Bible 101. It's biblical. If you broke down the New Testament, it's all the Bible. Like God is the greatest promoter in the world, right? He's got this hot young kid babyface named Jesus in the territory. We've got to get this guy over! This kid's hot. Who's he call? Satan . . . I mean, the apocalypse is like the biggest WrestleMania event of all time. It all comes down to promoting, instruction, and building the babyface. That's what it comes down to for me."

II. Takeover Bid

In March 2014, irate fans banded together under the #HijackRaw hashtag to attempt a hostile takeover of WWE's flagship show by spreading instructions to bark "same old shit" should Batista, Randy Orton, Triple H, or Stephanie McMahon wrestle that night.

And they planned a "CM Punk" chant in honor of their hero at the show's opening. WWE foiled the plot by acknowledging Punk at the top of the broadcast and turning to popular Daniel Bryan to suggest, "Let's hijack *Raw*."

In February 2015, infuriated that a women's tag team match on *Raw* lasted all of twenty-nine seconds, fans mounted a social media protest with #GiveDivasAChance, which trended worldwide for three days. In response, WWE, infamous for its bra-and-panties matches in the 2000s, ditched the term "divas" and elevated its rebranded women's division. "I like to give the credit to our audience," chief brand officer Stephanie McMahon told a British interviewer. "We heard them and we responded."

Two scenarios, two results, one common denominator — like other wrestling enterprises, WWE must account for a new style of fan engagement that can dramatically affect the process of story-telling in and out of the ring. "Our audience tells us what they love, what they don't like, and worse, what they don't care about. And you have to be listening, and in WWE, yes, we do, we pivot on the fly," McMahon said.

For most of pro wrestling's history, the communications avenue between promotions and fans ran one way. Promoters and wrest-lers controlled the direction of the action, and if fans didn't like it, they could stay home or change the channel. But Twitter, Instagram, Facebook, YouTube, and other social media tools have changed the dynamic as wrestling organizations and fans test their respec-tive roles in the evolving digital universe. "We're all connected as a human race much more so now than we were even five years ago," said WWE Hall of Famer Jeff Jarrett. "If you put your head in the sand and act like social media doesn't exist, that's basically like coaching basketball and pretending the three-point line doesn't exist. It's just not reality."

To be sure, WWE is still in charge since it puts on the show for the bulk of wrestling fans. The company's social media numbers are staggering. In 2018, WWE had 1.1 billion fan engagements on

Facebook, Twitter, YouTube, Instagram, and Tumblr. Its YouTube channel is the most-viewed sports channel in the world with 20 billion total views and 40 million subscribers as of early 2019. The federation has developed social media strategies for each of its wrestlers. Social media producers follow them from show to show to post action in real time; Kevin Owens even grabbed a phone from one in May 2018 to become his own live producer. John Cena has regularly been the most liked full-time U.S. athlete, not just wrestler, in the world of social media with 45 million followers. And accompanying ads have helped WWE generate $34.5 million, or about four percent of its total revenues, from digital media alone, a number that's certain to grow. Want a point of comparison? WWE bought the entire rights to defunct World Championship Wrestling and its video archive for just $4.2 million.

The returns can be overwhelming, said former WWE champion Roman Reigns. When announcer Michael Cole started referring to him as "The Big Dog," Reigns' social media reacted, and not in a good way. "People tweet me this all the time; they despise the way he says this. I don't know. I'm going to have to sit Cole down and have a talk. 'There's ten more people that hate me because of you,'" Reigns said sarcastically before acknowledging Cole was just doing his job. "That's all a part of our process and that's why we have a commentary team to help explain the story that we're telling." Rosa Mendes, who wrestled in WWE during its "diva" phase, said she reaped huge bonuses from Twitter and its companions. "I actually love social media. I love the WWE Universe. Even people who contact me that are not wrestling fans and they start to watch, people who like my pictures, and stuff like that. I think social media has welcomed new fans for us," she said. "It's opened a lot of doors for us, and now we have a lot more fans than we ever had before."

At the same time, encouraged by WWE and emboldened by social media, fans have assumed a new and potentially more powerful part in the production of wrestling. In its immersive experience, WWE writers incorporate fan involvement as an active

In 1938, fans watch wrestling matches in Sikeston, Missouri.

part of their stories, a far cry from the days when paying customers sat in the seats and clapped without prompts. "In the contemporary wrestling industry, fans feel more empowered than ever before to shape, tweak, resist, or even protest the narrative direction of the creative team of companies like WWE," said media analyst Sam Ford, who writes and teaches about wrestling and popular culture. "It's not just as a recipient, a spectator, or as a participant, but they have actually been scripted a role." By and large, fans are willing participants in that process. As wrestler, trainer, and announcer Les Thatcher put it: "You and I sit down and watch *Raw* together every Monday and have a couple beers or whatever and we know they're coming to our town in three months. We've got our tickets, and by the time we get to the arena three months down the road, we know what to chant when this person comes out, we know what to do when this guy comes out, and we want to be part of the show."

Ohio Valley Wrestling owner Al Snow calls that the "psychology of the anonymity." A mass of revved-up fans in a half-darkened 20,000-seat arena is more willing to play "follow the leader" than

In 2017, fans are part of the matches with Bayley in the ring.

fans in a small wrestling venue who can see their neighbor across the ring. "The vocal minority starts these chants and hijacks the show and the rest of the crowd joins in not because they know what's going on or because they genuinely care, but because there's a large group of people chanting for this," Snow said. And it doesn't take long for a chant or protest to go viral, whether it's in an arena or on a smartphone. Witness the March 2018 uproar on Twitter that led WWE, with prodding from prime sponsor Snickers, to ditch the controversial Fabulous Moolah as the honoree of its inaugural WrestleMania women's battle royal. "Now you've got the audience talking to one another and colluding again," said Ford, who has studied fan behavior and also worked as a heel manager in a Kentucky promotion. "We've seen this happen a lot. If we don't like the battle royal being named after Moolah, we'll reach out to the advertiser."

Fans also are exerting more control over who wrestles as a hero and who wrestles as a heel, said DJ Hyde, owner of Combat Zone Wrestling. "In the new age of social media and in the new age of the way the world functions, who determines who's a babyface and a heel? People do. Fans do. Now with social media, they have a voice," he said. "Is the Joker a good guy or a bad guy in *Batman*? It depends on how the person viewing him feels about him. The same thing with a character like Roman Reigns on *Raw*. People are booing him, but he's booked and presented as a babyface." In fact, the big story coming out of the June 2018 Reigns–Jinder Mahal Money in the Bank match in Chicago was not the outcome, but the incessant squawking by the boo birds. "This is awful," "Johnny Wrestling," and "Let's go, beach ball," were among the loudest chants. WWE referee Charles Robinson called the response "disrespectful," saying Mahal and Reigns were giving fans a "great match."

The quality of the contest might have been disputed, but wrestlers and trainers believe it will take more than a critical tweet to keep the fans in their place. Ford noted that WWE has had some success co-opting fan reaction by acknowledging it and turning it into a positive. "If you look at what they've done with John Cena, for instance, it was to take the constant negative reaction or mixed reaction he would get in some arenas and further build it into the idea that he's never going to give up, even if half the audience hates him. That's actually a further sign of his perseverance," Ford said.

Remember whatever you say on social media is out there forever and can be used against you, and as fuel for fan reaction. On May 8, 2013, Ring of Honor grappler Jay Briscoe tweeted out in anger after the Delaware State Senate passed a bill allowing gay marriage. He posted, "The Delaware Senate passed a bill yesterday that allows same sex couples to get married. If that makes you happy, then congratulations!!!!!! . . . try and teach my kids that there's nothing wrong with that and I'll f*cking shoot you." His Twitter account disappeared the next day. Ring of Honor distanced the promotion from his comments and forced him to make a public apology online and at the next ROH live show. Two days of pay went to the Partners Against Hate charity. Jay and tag team brother Mark now maintain a minimal presence on Twitter. "There's some people, I believe, they can handle it and they can keep their social media posts and whatnot within the realm of their character," Mark said. "But then people can get offended by what people are saying, people can just take something completely off topic."

Sometimes, fans aren't sure how to react. "Fantastic" Bobby Fulton, an independent promoter in Ohio, attended a WWE card in Columbus and was impressed by the level of inactivity during what should have been the meatiest part of the evening. "Fans get up when guys come to ring and when they leave. They sat through the moves. That's not what it's about. It's about that five, ten, fifteen minutes of wrestling match where you get the people connected," he said. Thatcher believes fans can be re-educated to the point that they tweet about the match they see, instead of the match they plan to disrupt. "It's not going to happen overnight. Getting them to where they are now didn't happen overnight. You don't have to take everything away from them," he said. "Give them two or three matches where they are deadly serious, where there are nice take-downs, where they're not asking the fans what to do."

Ultimately, fans will never totally take over WWE or any other promotion. But they're certain to make their voices louder as technology enables them to participate in pro wrestling, and not just observe it. "The fans get what they want when they see wrestlers not doing ten-minute pre-choreographed, pre-ordained matches," said Joel Goodhart, promoter of the Tri-State Wrestling Alliance, the forerunner to Extreme Championship Wrestling. "If you give them what they want, they don't take over. They take over when they start booing."

III. Digital Storytelling

The internet was not ready for Ring Warriors. The idea, hatched by wrestling star Hiro Matsuda and brought to fruition with the help of promoters Howard Brody and Sheldon Goldberg, was to repackage the hot New Japan Pro Wrestling product that was syndicated throughout Europe, Africa, and Asia, and repurpose it for the North American market through streaming video.

But it was 1995. "It was actually a failure because most people did not have high-speed access," Goldberg acknowledged. The promoters were on to something, though. Goldberg viewed the budding internet as a new avenue of distribution, providing the opportunity to reach people "in a totally different way and just go directly to the people, rather than go through a TV station or a network."

Today, New Japan Pro Wrestling is available worldwide on streaming video through its own in-house production. So are a myriad of wrestling companies, from monsters like the WWE Network with 1.5 million subscribers at the end of 2018 to small, independent promotions that rely on loyal fans for extra revenue. Others like Tommy Dreamer's House of Hardcore and Impact Wrestling have teamed with Twitch to stream video of individual matches and entire cards. A wrestler seeking a job no longer has to send in a VHS tape, but can instead point the promoter to his or her YouTube channel.

"Twitch is, I feel, the future of how we watch television," said Dreamer, first known for his work in Extreme Championship Wrestling. His HOH promotion has a weekly show on Wednesdays, mostly promos with a few matches, and streams live shows. He went down the road with i-pay-per-view and FloSlam, which were pay models. Twitch is free with an Amazon Prime membership; Dreamer sees it as a response to YouTube. "I was putting on these events, spending a lot of money, and then I'd see 100,000 views the next morning of that same event. People would be putting it up illegally on YouTube. I was just like, 'If I had a million views at ten dollars a view, my life changes. The wrestling business changes. And because somebody put that up there, that kills me.' But with Twitch at least, it is free. You still get people putting it up on YouTube."

To give Goldberg credit for internet-based wrestling is a reach, to be sure, but not a long one. The roots of his web-based stab at New England Championship Wrestling were laid in the early 1960s when the World Wide Wrestling Federation captivated him at the Boston Garden. Live was the only way to see it since the WWWF did not

Sheldon Goldberg was the man behind New England Championship Wrestling.

have a local TV outlet. Coming of age, Goldberg learned broadcasting through a high school program. But no full-time work came from the experience, so he jumped when he got a chance to work in public relations for a theater company. "Before I knew it, I was doing publicity for Broadway shows on tour that would come through Boston," he said. Goldberg followed that up by creating and producing a musical revue called *Dancing in the Street*, a forerunner of shows like *Jersey Boys*.

The wrestling bug was still there, though, to the point that Goldberg hung out in wrestling promoter Abe Ford's office, conveniently located where he worked in Boston's theater district. On a lark, Goldberg started the *Mat Marketplace* newsletter in 1989, helping wrestling fans connect so they could buy and sell goodies from their collections. That brought him further into the wrestling world through Tony Rumble. Goldberg went from selling his newsletter at Rumble's Century Wrestling Alliance shows around New England to running his website in the early days of the internet.

And then Rumble died. In part wanting to honor his friend's legacy, Goldberg began New England Championship Wrestling.

With experience in wrestling, running live theater events, and broadcasting, Goldberg was able to push a regional independent operation to international status by offering NECW TV, the first pro wrestling television series created and distributed exclusively via the internet. Running from November 17, 2004, to December 24, 2009, with 195 episodes hosted on its website, NECW TV was a success that attracted tens of thousands of viewers worldwide every week. "What NECW started doing in 2004 was actually to produce content specifically for online distribution. That had not been done since Ring Warriors," Goldberg said. "So we were really the first in that space to do that. And it was a primitive attempt, but it was effective, it was valuable."

Today, with mobile devices connecting to the internet everywhere, allowing for wrestling on the go, NECW seems quaint. But it wasn't. Goldberg likened the website to a store window that just got bigger and bigger, showing off more of the merchandise. "At the time it was really unique because nobody was doing it," he said. "It was like, 'Oh, wow, I can watch this stuff and see what they're doing.' Some of the stuff, really early on, was really primitive and really not great, but as time went on and we started to improve the production, and as technology improved, we were able to improve what we were doing to the point that we were doing some pretty effective stuff and it really did help drive our business."

Proof that the relationship between new and traditional media had flipped came in 2009 when Comcast SportsNet New England approached NECW about creating a show. After the free-flowing internet run, NECW had to restructure for its spot on Comcast On Demand. An internet show could run twenty-two minutes or forty-four minutes; it really didn't matter. In conventional TV, Goldberg was locked into thirty- or sixty-minute shows with specific carve-outs for commercials. It's a long way from 2009 to 2019, though, and Goldberg recognizes that the clips promotions use today are generally shorter than the ones NECW TV delivered. It's long-form storytelling versus short form. He sees value in both. "It certainly expands the number of options on your palette, if you were a painter, it just adds a whole lot more colors to your palette that you can use to paint the picture. In media terms, it just gives you a whole lot more options of what to produce and how to produce it."

Besides the cutting-edge internet show, Goldberg is equally proud of some of the talent that came through, drawn by the NECW TV platform. Eddie Edwards, Bobby Fish, British star Doug Williams, Frankie Kazarian, and Kofi Kingston were among the alums. When The Prototype (John Cena) wrestled in NECW in 2001 for the first time, his father, John Cena Sr., bought eighty tickets for friends and family. Goldberg knows he is not responsible for anybody's career, but it still is nice to be thanked. "I'll see Finn Balor and he'll say, 'You believed in me when nobody else did.' And that means a lot."

Where does storytelling go from here? Goldberg sees two sides of it. One is similar to the return of vinyl records to the music industry, with television needing content more than ever. Dave Marquez's syndicated *Championship Wrestling from Hollywood* is on more than 100 TV stations in the United States, creating a loose affiliation with promoters on a local basis. "I'm a believer now in terms of the backward technology of broadcast television," said Goldberg. "I think that's a space that we want to be in and that's a space that we want to occupy. We have occupied that space before and we got very good results."

Like Goldberg, Marquez has put many years into pro wrestling and has had his share of ups and downs. He was ahead of the curve with New Japan, running an affiliated dojo in the mid-2000s. He also worked on the groundbreaking but ultimately doomed *Wrestling Society X* for MTV and was the face of the National Wrestling Alliance for a time. Based in Los Angeles, he knows TV inside and out. "Network television is evolving and changing, at least in the U.S., and local television is staying the same, which is why I've stuck with syndication," he said. "You'll always have your local news and you'll always have a network schedule, but then the rest of the day is

PHOTO BY GREG OLIVER

From left, Dave Lagana, NWA World champion Nick Aldis, and David Marquez.

wide open and it's still the best way to get your message out as far as I'm concerned." Marquez said his show is "very much 1979, 1980. The way we sell it to our stations is, yes, it's a genre, there's a pro wrestling genre, there's a real popular wrestling show on cable, but over the air, there's only two, and the other one [Ring of Honor] is on proprietary stations. So we're the only independent, syndicated wrestling program on local television stations. We found that niche and we're owning it."

On the other end of the scale is the National Wrestling Alliance run by Smashing Pumpkins singer Billy Corgan. The alliance tells stories on the internet with vignettes that introduce, hype, and promote stars off the radar of the major companies. The company took an aging regional wrestler from Texas named Tim Storm and placed him as its world champion. That meant his successor, Nick Aldis (formerly Magnus in Impact Wrestling) had beaten a worthy opponent. "Tim is not a mustache-twirling bad guy," said Dave Lagana, the veteran behind the scenes of Corgan's videos. "He's never going to be the guy that goes around and goes in and robs a bank. Now if he's pushed to it, maybe. But his general, idling character is not that. So that's the story we told."

Lagana brings an impressive résumé to the NWA — writer in Hollywood, head writer for *WWE SmackDown*, producer of Ring of Honor's show on HDNet, and senior director of creative at TNA Impact Wrestling. For the short YouTube videos created for NWA or ROH, Lagana is self-taught from the technical side and the viewpoint of attracting eyeballs on YouTube and the internet via keywords, metadata, and other advanced metrics. He is decidedly proud of the growth of the NWA's YouTube channel, even though the promotion has not run a single show and only showcases its world title, which dates from 1948. "Stories are not new; stories go back to the fucking caveman, scratching on walls around fires. That's all any of these mediums are and if you look at what gets the best traction digitally, it's stories."

Where does it go from here? Goldberg, Marquez, Dreamer, Lagana, and the like have shown an ability to adap, thrive, and think outside the box. "You have to put the information or the story where people are watching it. For example, five years ago, six years ago, WWE would never have put their clips up on YouTube within, let alone twenty-four hours, let alone five minutes after it happened. Now they know," Lagana said. "The idea of search-based content is the way the audience wants it . . . You have to connect with the audience where they are."

Afterword —
Fifty Shades of Gray

Who is Roman Reigns? Good guy, bad guy, or something in between? It wasn't easy to tell on the March 18, 2018, edition of *Raw*, when the suspended Reigns staged an in-ring sit-in to force a match with Brock Lesnar. *Raw* general manager Kurt Angle sent three (pretend) U.S. marshals to the ring to arrest Reigns, who beat them up and dislocated one authority's jaw (not pretend). While law enforcement vamoosed, Lesnar attacked a handcuffed Reigns. "Where the hell did the marshals go?" asked celebrated trainer and wrestler Les Thatcher. "They're not filing charges. You've attacked a fucking federal officer. Three of them. And we supposed to be cheering a guy who beats up cops, for heaven's sake?"

Who is Dean Ambrose? Good guy, bad guy, or something in between? In 2014, *Raw* cameras filmed him as he left an arena in Brooklyn to get a hot dog at Coney Island. Eventually, he'd return with a hot dog stand to use as a weapon, but never mind that, said veteran booker and wrestler Kevin Sullivan. "I'm a kid from the streets. I used to take the subway. But I jumped over the rail and the cops chased us. Here the loose cannon takes the coin out and puts it in the turnstile! Wait a minute. Is that what a loose cannon would do?"

If there's one thing that old-school and new-school wrestlers, promoters, and analysts agree on, it's this: the division between hero and babyface, between good guy and bad guy, that sustained North American wrestling for most of its first 150 years is disappearing.

Black and white have become gray. "In my opinion, there's only one story and that's good versus evil. I don't know that the art is lost but WWE, I think, does not present that story on their programming," said former WWE trainer and star Nick Dinsmore, known to fans as Eugene. "I don't feel it's a heat-driven company anymore. It's a series of high spots, feel-good moments, a variety show that tours and sells merchandise."

Part of that is unavoidable. Technological innovations have brought wrestlers and their fans closer together than ever. In the old days, it would have wrecked Rip Hawk's cultivated image as heel in the Carolinas if word got out that he donated the first professional-style goalposts for the football team at Charlotte Catholic High School. Now, it'd be a picture on Instagram. "I don't blame the fans for wanting to read what goes on behind the scenes, and what's going on in real life, but I miss those days," lamented Gail Kim of Impact Wrestling. "I miss the days of what I fell in love with . . . I hated the heels and I loved the babyfaces, and I got drawn into every storyline emotionally in every way, and that's what I miss."

And make no mistake: WWE is not a wrestling company. You won't find the word "wrestler" anywhere in its annual report. Instead, it features "athletic performers who have the physical presence, acting ability, and charisma to portray characters." So remember John Cena, Reigns, Ambrose, and the whole lot of WWE's 215 contracted superstars are athletic performers, which brings a different and less intense feel to stories than the good/evil division. Bobby Fulton, one-half of the Fantastics, runs an independent promotion in Ohio and also senses fans' longing for the days of virtue and vice. "The people, as in a movie, they want a hero and they want someone to hate. When we take that element out of professional wrestling, the hero and someone to hate, then we take a very important element out of it," Fulton said. "Most of the independents see what Vince is doing and that's where they get their education."

On the other hand, why should WWE change a formula that has increased its stock value tenfold since 2003? WWE now has 915 employees, not counting athletic performers, with $930 million in total 2018 net revenues, $199 million from WWE Network, and 10 million monthly visitors to its website — and that was before it got $1 billion to move *SmackDown* to the Fox network in October 2019. The feeder system from NXT and 205 Live should keep the main roster healthy for years. "It takes time to build things from zero, and to learn this business from zero, but when you look at some of the talent that we have, with either no experience or minimal experience, coming in and handling things at a level, it's just amazing to see," Triple H told reporters in a 2018 conference call. But when some doors close, others open. Many wrestlers and other entities have quit trying to become extensions of WWE, in the process finding story-telling voices that didn't exist as recently as a decade ago.

Kenny Omega has his admirers and detractors, but there's no doubt he has been one of the hottest wrestlers in the world in the mid-2010s. To him, WWE got stale as week-old bread starting in the Attitude Era, when the sheer star power of The Rock, Steve

PHOTO BY MIKE MASTRANDREA

Kenny Omega is always shooting for the top.

Austin, and Mankind was enough to counter overwrought or weak storytelling. "I do believe that storytelling is probably the most . . . important part to a match, and I feel that, in general in North America, especially, people, new wrestlers, young wrestlers, are being told how it should be from people twenty, thirty, forty years ago," he said. "It comes across as lifeless, soulless, and not something that they actually understand, not something that the wrestlers themselves feel. That is actually why I feel that the stories I see a lot on television, unless they are told through dramatic TV drama–like scenes — I'm talking about the actual physical stories told through pro wrestling — those come across as not so interesting to me."

What to do about it? How about taking a new approach to storytelling, starting with a Twitter war? For weeks, Omega and Chris Jericho, two natives of Winnipeg, Manitoba, engaged in a social media spar leading up to their January 2018 match at New Japan Pro Wrestling's Wrestle Kingdom.

Jericho to Omega: *Your matches are incredible. Too bad nobody seems them . . . #minorleagues*

Omega to Jericho: *Nah, I'm just the guy having six star classics you keep hearing about. Surely Y2J's had plenty of those with "BIG LEAGUES", right?*

Jericho to Omega: *Best in the world? @KennyOmegamanX isn't even in the best in Winnipeg . . . #overrated*

It was old-fashioned trash talking in a digital age, a way of self-promotion that went beyond an over-the-top grappler screaming into "Mean" Gene Okerlund's microphone. With the New Japan World streaming service available to anyone willing to pay for it, enabling die-hards to watch live pro wrestling at strange hours, Jericho-Omega had appeal. In particular, Omega saw an opportunity to break new ground in the way wrestlers tell their stories.

"I'm using the tools that are available to me and I'm trying to innovate in a way that people haven't done yet. Maybe people have tried to do the same thing, I don't know, but the fact that I don't know means that they didn't do it successfully, or successfully enough to make waves," Omega said. "All I tried to do was take advantage of today's technological era and embrace a new type of storytelling that people hadn't really seen in the mainstream. Luckily, we succeeded. And if not, whatever, we would have failed in a blaze of glory, but at least we went out trying something new. I definitely don't mind that, and I don't mind failing. I'm never afraid to fail." In the end, Omega retaining his IWGP U.S. Heavyweight title, hitting a second One-Winged Angel, this time on a chair, to finish off Jericho was almost anticlimactic compared with the well-thought-out build.

Omega and the Young Bucks (Matt and Nick Jackson) have created videos to broaden their personal brands and hype sales, whether it's Bullet Club merchandise or tickets for the massive All-In show in Chicago in 2018. Is it traditional storytelling? No. Have the Bucks turned the superkick into a party favor instead of a deadly finisher? Yes. Does the whole package veer sharply from WWE style, where writers and bosses write for the characters they want, rather than the characters as they are? Absolutely. "I feel very fortunate that I was sort of forced into a situation where I have to tell the bulk of what I want to say through my actions in the ring," Omega said.

In February 2019, Omega signed with All Elite Wrestling, an upstart that debuted on YouTube and represented a backlash against the WWE way of micromanaged scripts. Cody Rhodes, a driving force with the Young Bucks behind the creation of AEW, portrayed the company as a younger, sports-based alternative to WWE. "We're the writers," he said. But like any company, you still go with what's worked in the past. Jericho — who else? — broke into Omega's celebrated signing, setting up another main event between the two.

Other entrepreneurs are taking the sport in different directions. The initial Gorgeous Ladies of Wrestling syndicated show, which ran from 1986 to 1989, used skits to de-emphasize the wrestling since, for the most part, its hokey, cheesy stars couldn't "tell a wristlock from a wristwatch," as smart-aleck manager Bobby Heenan often cracked. People scoffed when Netflix announced a new GLOW series, loosely based on the earlier one. Instead, it became a good reminder that storytelling still works; as long as you become invested in the characters, you can plop down on the couch (or stream while on the subway) and binge-watch.

GLOW founder David McLane, who started out helping Dick the Bruiser in his Indianapolis promotion at age thirteen, left the initial run after two seasons over creative differences and established Women of Wrestling. He loved the GLOW series. "I take my hat off to the writers of the Netflix GLOW series on how well executed their fictional and non-fictional writing has been blended to create a semi-true account of what took place in the creation of GLOW," he said. "Telling the sisterhood of GLOW and the story from the wrestlers' window of perspective is why the show is resonating with so many people, including those females who don't even like or watch professional wrestling. It's great storytelling. It's something everyone can relate to."

For all its ludicrous, over-the-top-ness, fantastical characters, and colorful action, Lucha Underground, airing on the El Rey Network, has latched on best to the changing tastes of society. Dark and challenging, it's a marriage between writers with a vision and a long-range storyline over many seasons, and pro wrestlers who assume a persona for a short period of time when the season is shot. The backing of Hollywood power players Robert Rodriguez and Mark Burnett has both helped and hindered; it opened doors, but perhaps set the bar too high initially as production values were forced to drop after the top-end first season for financial reasons. It's the crowd that is the throwback, though. A mixture of wrestling fans and the curious who want to sit in on a television show, they are both going in blind — no spoilers, no notes from the show the night before in another town. "They expect the supernatural," explained Martin Casaus, who is Marty the Moth. "They know that they're only getting part of the story when they're at the live shows. They have no idea what's actually happening in the background to set up these matches that they're seeing."

Being forced to be part-actors, part-wrestlers is a big part of the reason to work in *Lucha Underground*. Unlike a live *Raw*, there's a chance for retakes in the vignettes, but in the ring, it's business as usual. "I'm a very firm believer that no matter what narrative you give to an audience, if the work rate is there in the ring, people will suspend themselves in a state of belief to be entertained," said Killer Kross, likening it to watching *Alien* when the alien jumps out of John Hurt's chest. "Every single match means something in *Lucha Underground* because of the way they develop those episodes. Everyone is over. There are no sleeper matches, no piss-break matches, every match means something there and that's something very special that a lot of companies still even to this day haven't figured out."

Photographers

We have made a lot of friends along the way, and called in many favors for some great photos for this book. Plus, so many more libraries have digitized their photo collections or at least listed what's available in text format, that we struck gold on more than one occasion. Many of the photos came from the personal collections of the interview subject or the family, and we are thankful for those who shared. However, we did want to spotlight a few photographers and collections.

Roger Baker was a writer and photographer for magazines like *The Wrestler*, *Inside Wrestling*, *Wrestling Revue*, and *Boxing Illustrated* from 1958 to 1973.

Dave Burzynski was a regular photographer around the Detroit territory until getting to live out his dream as manager "Supermouth" Dave Drason.

Terry Dart is a long-time wrestling fan from London, Ontario.

Ricky Havlik (rickyhavlik.com) is a sports and portrait photographer based out of the Chicago.

Joe Hrycych (hrycychphotography.com) can be found on the field shooting for the Buffalo Bills and rinkside at Buffalo Sabres games, and plenty of places in between.

Photographer Roger Baker in action during a boxing show at Maple Leaf Gardens, circa 1967.

Pete Lederberg (facebook.com/PeteLederbergsWrestlingPhotos) lives in Fort Lauderdale, Florida; owns negatives from other photographers dating back to about 1970; and has been shooting wrestling himself since 1987.

Bob Leonard shot images of Calgary's Stampede Wrestling from 1963 to 1989. He died in 2016.

Mike Mastrandrea (mikemastrandrea.com) is a Victoria, BC–based photographer and has been shooting wrestling for more than twenty-five years. His work has been seen in publications across North America, Europe, and Asia.

Brad McFarlin got into pro wrestling through "Nature Boy" Buddy Rogers and was soon shooting the matches. In the 1980s, he became "Handsome" Johnny Bradford wrestling near his homebase outside of Detroit.

Joyce Paustian of Davenport, Iowa, got into pro wrestling as a child and never stopped. Her photos were featured at the National Wrestling Hall of Fame Dan Gable Museum and she received the Red Bastien Friendship Award from the Cauliflower Alley Club in 2008.

George Tahinos, based in New Jersey, has been shooting since 1993, and was fortunate to be ringside for the glory days of ECW.

COLLECTIONS

Chris Swisher Collection (csclassicwrphotos.com) — Includes the Lil Al collection of negatives and photos, negatives from part of the Earle Yetter collection, the Detroit area from the '60s and '70s, negatives taken by Scott Teal from the '70s, the collection of photos and items from promoter Fred Ward of Columbus, GA, all encompassing the 1930s to the 1980s.

Courtesy Wrestling Revue Archives (wrestleprints.com) — Brian Bukantis is the publisher of *Wrestling Revue* and curator of the *Wrestling Revue* Archives.

Department of Special Collections, University Libraries of Notre Dame — The photos in this book come from The Jack Pfefer Wrestling Collection, housed at Notre Dame (nd.edu).

Scott Teal Collection (CrowbarPress.com) — A deserving recipient of the James C. Melby Award by *both* the Cauliflower Alley Club (in 2008) and the Tragos/Thesz Hall of Fame (in 2011) for his contributions to professional wrestling journalism, Scott Teal has published books and newsletters, put out DVDs, and hosted reunions of legends.

Acknowledgments

After we wrote *Heroes & Icons*, *The Heels*, *The Tag Teams*, and *The Canadians*, we looked at everything we had accumulated and said, "There's enough for another book here." So we started down the road on *The Storytellers*. The end product is much different than our initial vision, though. The book changed over time; it became more focused and more narrative as we interviewed more people. Drawing on our years of research, it's fair to say we've incorporated more than 200 personal interviews in this volume. So there's no way that every single person we talked to could be contained in one book, or even three. If you didn't make the cut, thanks for the time; your insight into the professional wrestling business and storytelling in particular helped us shape the book even if you aren't quoted here. That knowledge might make its way to SLAM! Wrestling, to a blog post, or to a future project.

We owe a lot of thank-yous, starting at home with our families. From there, it's a combination of wrestling historians, fans, photographers, performers, promoters, and more: the late J Michael Kenyon, the late Fred Hornby, Tim Hornbaker, Dave Cameron, George Lentz, Matt Farmer, Scott Teal, Lib Ayoub, Dave Burzynski, Rob Bauer, Jian and Page Magen (but not Celine Jian), Don Luce, Mark Hewitt, Phil Lions, Mark T. Dunn, Greg Price, Steve Yohe, Tom Burke, Dan Murphy, George Schire, Michael Norris, Dan Anderson, Greg Mosorjak, Dan Westbrook, Bob Kapur, Kevin Canady, Kari Williams, Vance Nevada, Ken Raftery, Pat Laprade, Sebastian Suave,

David Chappell, Dick Bourne, Pam Morrison, Mark James, Tommy Fierro, Chad Barclay, John Pozarowski, and Gary Juster. As always, the SLAM! Wrestling squad were team players, slipping in a question that we needed here or there. Oddly, Greg's friends in the Society for International Hockey Research asked about the book more than wrestling colleagues; thanks especially to Todd Denault and Eric Zweig.

The publicists through the years at the various wrestling companies never get thanked enough, so we'll do it here: Adam Hopkins and Joe Villa at WWE; Marc Kruskol and Jeff Jones at Ring of Honor; Ross Forman at Impact Wrestling; and many others. To find actors and screenwriters, IMDbPro came in handy, leading to a number of other gatekeepers before the doors were opened. The good people behind the Cauliflower Alley Club, the National Wrestling Hall of Fame Dan Gable Museum, and the Pro Wrestling Hall of Fame in Texas were conduits to names we needed and are valued friends.

A few libraries and librarians went over and above with help: Virginia Commonwealth University, Richmond, Virginia; University of Virginia Library, Charlottesville, Virginia; Library of Congress, Washington, D.C.; Meriden, Connecticut Public Library; Sara Brewer, National Archives and Record Center, Atlanta, Georgia; George Rugg, Special Collections Curator, Hesburgh Libraries, University of Notre Dame, South Bend, Indiana; Toronto Public Library. Magen Howard, Michael W. Kahn, and Anne Youngblood read parts of the manuscript and offered suggestions that greatly improved the book. Finally, thanks to ECW Press for all the hard work in completing the Pro Wrestling Hall of Fame series. (We think.)